Incest In The Organizational Family

THE ECOLOGY OF BURNOUT IN CLOSED SYSTEMS

WILLIAM L. WHITE

Foreword by Russell Hagen

D1600154

A LIGHTHOUSE TRAINING INSTITUTE PUBLICATION

Additional copies of this publication may be obtained by sending $13.00 plus $2.00 shipping and handling to:

The Lighthouse Training Institute
702 West Chestnut
Bloomington, Illinois 61701
(309) 827-6026

Library of Congress Cataloging-in-Publication Data

White, William L., 1947-
    Incest in the organizational family.

    Bibliography: p.
    Includes index.
    1. Job Stress. 2. Burnout (Psychology)
3. Oganizational behavior. I. Title.
HF5548.85.W46 1986   158.7   86-80819
ISBN   0-938475-00-2

This book is dedicated to my parents, Alice and Billy, to my daughter Alisha, to my four sisters and to my twenty-two foster brothers and sisters who have all taught me the meaning of family.

Acknowledgments

The research and the training and consulting experience upon which this book is based and the writing of the book have spanned more than a decade of my life. The book would not have been possible without the encouragement and assistance of numerous friends and professional colleagues. I wish to express my particular gratitude to the following: Alan Walker, Ph.D. for encouraging me to write the first preliminary paper on organizational incest; Bruce Fisher and Roger Krohe for their assistance in applying family systems concepts to organizations; Gary Schoener for providing the first thorough critique of my early papers; Carl Akins, Ph.D. for his role as mentor, friend and reviewer of my early writing on organizational stress; Tom Russell Ed.D., Martha Russell and Barbara Bedford whose encouragement and recognition of my work led to the publication of the early monographs on burnout through HCS, Inc.; Jerry F.X. Carrol, Ph.D., for helping extend my model of organizational incest into his model of burnout as ecological dysfunction; and to Russell Hagen for his publication of this book through the Lighthouse Training Institute.

The following individuals provided invaluable service as a sounding board and source of support through the concept development and writing process: Randy Adams, Marie Boehlke, Paul Bucholtz, Bill Coats, Rita Chaney, Joe and Pat Difiore, Cindy Kunz, Charlene Ortiz, Sonia Rosorio, Bob Stachura, Carmen Townsend, Curtis White, and, all my friends at St. Mary's Hospital in Decatur, Illinois who suffered through my daily progress or lack of progress on the book.

Particular gratitude is expressed to Keith Corley who provided invaluable assistance in editing the various drafts, to Glenda Rawlings for coordinating the manuscript preparation, and to Pat Tipsword for typing the manuscript.

WILLIAM L. WHITE

Bloomington, Illinois
June, 1986

iv

Table of Contents

10. Predicting And Managing Individual Vulnerability

11. Systems Interventions: Boundary Management

- Avoiding the High Priest Role
- Adding New Members to the Organizational Family
- The Code of Professional Practice
- Exclusive Versus Inclusive Program Philosophies
- Planning Change
- Tearing Down Walls / Building Bridges
- Strokes for Boundary Transactions
- The implementation ofa Comprehensive Human Resource Development Strategy
- Termination: The Art of Letting People Go

- Role Modeling of Managers
- Orienting Staff to Problems in Social and Sexual Intimacy

- The Code of Professional Practice Revisited
- Changing the Conditions of Violating Personal Life Space
- Structuring the Social Needs of the Organizational Family
- Shaping the Sexual Culture of the Organization
- Sexuality and Supervision
- When to Confront Outside Social and Sexual Relationships

- Good Intentional Strategies that Create Casualties
- What to do with the High Priest
- Bringing Replenishment to a Depleted System
- Making Sense out of the Pain and Chaos
- Providing Structure and Safety
- Letting People Out / Bringing in New Blood
- Untangling Current Relationship Agendas
- Burying Old Ghosts
- Renegotiating Values and Beliefs
- The On-Going Process of Opening the System
- Interventions into Disengaged Organizational Families

12. Promoting Health and Productivity in the Microsystem

- The Recruitment, Screening, Selection and Role Placement Process
- Honesty Versus Salesmanship in Position Promotion

Table of Exhibits

Foreword

Incest In The Organizational Family is many books within a book.

It is first and foremost a book about how individuals experience stress and distress in the world of work. The personal concern over what is called the worker "casualty process" is evident throughout the book. This is not, however, just another book on stress and burnout. The definition of burnout as a breakdown in the relationship between the organization and an individual worker and the outline of system interventions offers a bold contrast to treatments of the subject that attribute causes of burnout within the individual and offer simplistic techniques and platitudes as remediation strategies.

At a technical level, this is also a book about organizational systems and the relationship between organizational health and employee health. William White has put flesh and blood on what have been extremely abstract principles of systems theory. The conceptualization of the organization as a family system provides new insights that are within the range of everyone's experience. The concept of "organizational incest" provides a radically new perspective on organizational health and organizational decay.

At an experiential level for the reader, this is a book about the organization as a soap opera. This book tears the protective veneer off the organization and reveals the internal secrets and problems that we often don't even talk about inside, let alone expose to the outside world. The detailed description of what White calls "the progressive closure of the organizational family" will be particularly poignant to any readers who have been caught up in such painful organizational dramas. The chapter on "Sexual Closure" is one of the most accurate and powerful statements ever written on sexuality as an organizational issue. The no-talk rule on this subject has been broken! The chapters on "closed" organizations tie together for the reader diverse and stressful events in the life of the organization and show how such events grow out of a process that is both predictable and preventable. I am convinced that anyone who reads this book will never look at organizations the same again.

This book is also a primer for managers and supervisors. The last two chapters offer concrete strategies that can be used by the manager to prevent or correct the destructive organizational dynamics described in the book.

While many of the examples and case studies in this book are drawn from health and human service organizations, the concepts and strategies outlined are broadly applicable to organizations in both the public and private sector. The chapter on promoting worker health and productivity in the microsystem should be required reading for all managerial and supervisory staff. In an era where most areas of business and industry are experiencing rapid and turbulent change, this book provides a foundation for managing such change to the benefit of both workers and the organization.

I am convinced this book will become one of the centerpieces in the movement to humanize the workplace.

Russell Hagen
June, 1986

Preface

This is a book about how both individual workers and organizational systems become casualties from excessive demands for adaptation.

This book was born out of confusion and pain. During my early career working in psychiatric and chemical dependency treatment programs, I was struck by the high casualty rate among my peer group of professional helpers. This casualty process ranged from the shattering of marriage relationships to the slow, insidious deterioration of physical and emotional health. Many of these casualties would be particularly painful because they involved people I both respected professionally and cherished as friends. I couldn't understand how a highly competent, committed and compassionate professional helper could become a victim to some of the very problems they were trained to address with their clients. As a professional peer, and later as a manager and organizational consultant, I would feel impotent to prevent this casualty process among workers. These feelings of loss and powerlessness would become the driving forces behind the research upon which this book is based.

The concepts in this book have been in almost constant evolution since they were first developed in 1976. The major influences on this evolution include the following:

- Two formal studies of burnout victims in which I traced the deterioration in the health of each worker and matched their history with the concurrent working conditions and group process within each worker's organization;
- Feedback from professional colleagues and workers from around the country on my early monographs on "organizational incest";
- Feedback from workers and managers from diverse occupational settings who have participated in the author's workshops and seminars, and;
- The application and testing of the concepts through my managerial and consulting experience.

The concepts and strategies, I am sure, will continue to evolve as a result of the publication of this book.

There is an inherent danger in attempting to write a book that deals with complex personal, interpersonal, and organizational issues. This danger consists in the tendency to address complex problems through simplistic formulas that do not apply to the unique resources and constraints of specific organizational settings. In spite of this danger, I have tried to catalogue a number of strategies that can promote the overall health of both workers and organizations. These strategies should serve as guidelines that will require adaptation to the particular needs of your organization. While my early research was limited to health and human service agencies, I have since tested the concepts and strategies in diverse occupational settings and found them to be broadly applicable. I have tried to assess as objectively as possible my successes and failures using these concepts both as a manager and organizational consultant. The proposals in this book reflect both strategies that proved successful and strategies that weren't tested or fell short, not due to the soundness of the strategy, but to my own areas of inadequacy or skill deficiency.

I hope this will be a book that can be an on-going resource for the reader. A detailed table of contents and index and extensive subtitling have been provided to help the reader return to the book and easily find areas of discussion and strategy recommendations. A glossary has also been provided to assist the reader with any unfamiliar terms used in the text.

Since the research began on this book a decade ago, tremendous strides have been made in promoting health and wellness in the workplace. I hope this book will serve as a further stimulus to that movement.

I would welcome the opportunity to receive your comments, your criticisms, and your ideas. Correspondence can be sent to:

William L. White
Director of Training and Consultation
Lighthouse Training Institute
702 West Chestnut
Bloomington, Illinois 61761

Chapter One
Professional Stress: Definitions, Assumptions, and Indicators

The purpose of this initial chapter is to give the reader an understanding of the key terms and concepts upon which our later discussions will be based. The following pages will:

- Define the terms stress, stressor, stress response, professional stress, professional burnout and organizational burnout.
- Identify some preliminary assumptions about the experience of professional burnout.
- Identify both personal and organizational indicators of professional stress.

1.1   Basic Terms And Concepts

Theorists from fields as diverse as internal medicine to cultural anthropology have tried to define and describe the nature of stress and its impact on human beings. The literature of stress is filled with disagreement over the wording of key definitions and theoretical constructs. The following definitions are offered not as a contribution to these intellectual debates, but merely to convey to the reader the meaning of these terms as they will be used in future chapters. The first four definitions are based on the pioneering stress research conducted by Hans Selye (1974,1956).

Stress is the Demand Upon the Human Body for an Adaptational Change

Such demands occur constantly and are of concern primarily when the level of stress exceeds one's capacity to effectively respond. Stress and the body's continual response represent the delicate and intricate mechanisms through which we maintain balance with our social and physical environment. To be free of stress is to cease living. When we say someone is under a lot of stress, we usually mean excessive and unpleasant stress, or distress. When stress is referred to in future chapters, it will mean excessive and unpleasant stress.

1

This book will focus primarily on psychosocial stressors--those stressors that emerge in the relationship between the worker and his or her clients, and those stressors that arise within the emotional climate of the organization. Chapter Nine will outline role stressors that relate to the unique definitions and constraints of one's roles within a particular organization. A stressor is simply a stimulus that causes stress.

The Stress Response is the Generalized and Specialized Reactions or Adaptations of an Individual to Stress.

The generalized nature of the stress response was discovered by Hans Selye (1974, 1956) who pioneered the concept of the General Adaptation Syndrome (G.A.S.). The G.A.S. represents a stereotyped response of the body to stress regardless of the particular stressor. This generalized response occurs in three phases: 1. the alarm reaction, 2. the stage of resistance, and 3. the stage of exhaustion. Each phase has its own concomittant physiological changes. In addition to the generalized nature of the G.A.S., each individual responds in his/her own unique manner to prolonged and excessive stress. This specialized adaptation to stress represents one's own unique style of stress management. Chapter Ten will examine this individual style of stress management and those factors that increase and decrease one's vulnerability to high levels of stress.

Professional Stress is the Demand for Adaptational Change Experienced in the Performance of One's Professional Role.

Professional stress tends to center on demands that threaten self-esteem and prevent effective role performance in the organization.

Professional Burnout is a Deterioration in One's Personal and Interpersonal Performance that is Directly Related to Continued Contact with High Stress Work Environments.

The term professional burnout has come into common usage during the last decade to describe the stress-related deterioration in performance in a wide assortment of occupational groups. Following Freudenberger's early monograph on burnout in 1975, there

2

followed a stream of articles and workshops that applied the concept of burnout to a wide variety of organizational settings and professions. Exhibit 1-A provides just a sampling of articles on burnout that added to an already significant body of literature on occupational stress. It is clear that the term burnout struck a responsive emotional cord in the lives of many professionals from diverse occupational settings.

Organizational Burnout is a Stage of Stagnation and Demise that Occurs When Tasks Essential to the Survival of the Organization Fail to be Adequately Completed Due to the Stress Related Deterioration in Performance of a Large Number of Organizational Members.

This definition implies that organizations as well as individuals may become casualties of the burnout process. A good portion of this book will look at the reciprocal relationship between individual and organizational burnout.

1.2   Assumptions About Professional Burnout

In this section, five assumptions will be briefly reviewed that address the uniqueness, progressiveness, inevitability, importance and complexity of the burnout phenomenon.

The Uniqueness of Burnout   There are aspects of professional burnout that are unique to professions and organizational settings. This means that strategies to address burnout must examine those unique stressors that characterize particular professions. While there may be some similarities in how people experience burnout, those stressors triggering the experience of burnout may be very different for the policeman, the nurse, the pilot, the lawyer, the housewife, or the factory worker. One should avoid simplistic answers or packaged programs to burnout that fail to incorporate strategies that address these specific stressors and conditions.

There are general principles related to managing stress and burnout, for example, that must be refined further to apply to a profession such as nursing. These refined principles must be further developed to apply to particular nursing specialties. Strategies to address burnout may need to be different for nurses

EXHIBIT 1-A
The Application of The Concept of Burnout
To Various Occupational Groups:
Representative Literature

OCCUPATIONAL GROUP	LITERATURE
Physicians	Manber (1979); Madison (1974); Mawardi (1979)
Nurses	Storlie (1979); Shubin (1978) ; White (1981); Friel (1980); Marshall & Kasman (1980); Clark (1980) ; Vachon (1976, 1978)
Medical Social Workers	Allen (1978)
Teachers	Hendrickson (1979); Reed (1979); Dubrin (1979); Weiskopf (1980); Lenhart (1980)
Mental Health Workers/Therapists	Mendel (1979); Larson (1978); Fruedenberger (1979); Warmath & Shelton (1976); Criswell (1979); Van Auken (1979); Garte (1978)
Alcohol & Drug Abuse Counselors	Valle (1979); Freudenberger (1975); White (1978, 1979, 1983); Knauert & Davidson (1979)
Protective Service Workers	Daley (1979); Harrison (1980)
Day Care Workers	Seiderman (1977); Freudenberger (1977); Maslach & Pines (1977); Mattingly (1977); Reed (1977)
Disaster Workers	NIMH (1979)
Police	Maslach (1979); Chamberlin (1978); Haynes (1978)
Lawyers	Maslach & Jackson (1978)
Consultants	Mitchell (1977)
Human Service Administrators	Vash (1980); Veninga (1979)
Business Executives	Ginsburg (1979); Nelson (1980); Tauerwier (1978)

working in a hospital emergency room than those strategies developed for nurses working in an oncology unit or hospice program. Stress remediation strategies for one hospice program may not be fully applicable to another hospice program. The experience of burnout contains elements that are unique to individuals, to professions and to particular organizations. Remediation strategies for professional burnout must be tailored to address those unique elements.

The Progressiveness of Burnout Professional burnout can best be examined as a process rather than an event. While burnout can occur to staff over a relatively short period of time during a turbulent period in the life of an organization, most of the time the process of burnout is progressive and cumulative. It is the constantly high demand for adaptational energy that takes its toll. High levels of stress over a prolonged period of time produce a loss of adaptational energy and increased vulnerability. As the personal health and emotional defense structure of an individual are weakened from prolonged stress, an acute work-related crisis can suddenly trigger a dramatic escalation in stress-related dysfunction.

Hans Selye has called stress "the rate of wear and tear in the body". He believes each person has a set quantity of adaptational energy, that when depleted, cannot be replenished. Stress is thus viewed as an aging process - the progressive consumption of one's adaptational energy. When the intensity and duration of demands become too high and too prolonged, the performance of the human organism begins to deteriorate and develop what Selye calls " diseases of adaptation".

The Inevitability of Burnout It is probably impossible to completely eliminate the experience of burnout. Most people will experience during their career, at least some transient episodes of deteriorating performance that are stress related. While such experiences cannot be prevented, it is possible to develop both personal and organizational strategies that prevent the extreme casualty process created when the burnout experience is prolonged. Strategies can be developed that are capable of decreasing the frequency and duration of these episodes in our professional life. While early stages of burnout are inevitable, we can take responsibility for and control over our organizational structures and group processes to reduce the number of staff casualties resulting from the high stress work setting.

The Importance of Burnout Although the burnout experience is usually spoken of in negative terms, the early stages of burnout may be extremely important in indicating to ourselves areas of needed change and development. The experience may indicate:

- Areas of needed skill development
- A need for time-out periods (vacations, etc.).
- Our need to take the next step in our professional development, e.g., school, job change, etc. in response to feelings of boredom or being trapped.
- Personal needs outside the work setting which are being neglected.
- The need to re-establish a more equitable balance between one's work life and one's personal life.

The symptoms we usually associate with burnout can be viewed as an important internal feedback system. This point will become particularly important in the discussion on personal strategies for managing stress in Chapter Ten.

The Complexity of Burnout If there is one thing the author wishes the reader to gain from this book, it is the complexity of the phenomenon we call burnout. In the coming chapters, burnout will be explained as emerging from the complex interrelationships between the vulnerability of individual workers, conditions and processes in the work environment, and the relationships of both workers and the organization with the outside ecosystem.

1.3 Individual Indicators Of Professional Stress

This section will review in detail, the signs and symptoms that emerge in individuals when demands for adaptation surpass capacity for adaptation. The following indicators of professional stress will be reviewed:

- Health Indicators
- Excessive Behavior Indicators

- Emotional Adjustment Indicators
- Relationship Indicators
- Attitude Indicators
- Value Indicators

<u>Health Indicators</u> Human evolution has provided men and women with remarkable physiological mechanisms to respond to real or perceived threats. These mechanisms are automatic and consistent regardless of the nature of the stressor that triggers them. When we experience a high intensity stressor, the following physiological changes occur almost instantaneously:

- The heart beat quickens, blood vessels constrict raising blood pressure, blood is diverted from the extremities into the muscles, and blood clotting factors are increased.
- The hypothalamus triggers the pituitary gland to produce and release adrenalin and related hormones creating a state of high physiological arousal.
- Signals are transmitted through nerve tissue to alert the lungs, heart and muscles for action.
- The liver immediately converts glycogen to glucose for energy.
- Breathing becomes more rapid, increasing the supply of oxygen for the brain and muscles.
- The body is flooded with a morphine like substance to self-medicate pain.
- All body senses - particularly sight and hearing - become more acute.

All of the above changes are designed to prepare us for physical action, either fighting a life and death struggle or fleeing. While such reactions were very functional in confrontations between cavemen and saber-toothed tigers, they appear a bit extreme for an encounter in a staff meeting or board room. And therein lies the problem.

The constant triggering of these physiological mechanisms - particularly when they are accompanied by no discharge of physiological arousal - can be extremely detrimental to one's health. The cumulative effect of these frustrated automatic responses is to damage many of the major systems in the body and produce a number of stress-related symptoms that can be both uncomfortable and life threatening. This section will not review in detail the mechanics of how this damage occurs. Those interested in an in-depth treatment are referred to two classic works Selye's, *The Stress of Life* (1956) and Pelletier's *Mind As Healer, Mind As Slayer* (1977).

The range of health indicators of professional stress identified in the author's studies included the following:

- Fatigue and chronic exhaustion
- Headaches
- Frequent and prolonged colds
- Ulcers
- Sleep disturbances (insomnia, nightmares, excessive sleeping)
- Sudden weight gain or loss
- Injuries from high risk behavior
- Flare-up of preexisting disorders (diabetes, blood pressure, asthma)
- Muscular pain (particularly in lower back and neck)
- Increased premenstrual tension or missed menstrual cycles
- Bruxism (grinding of teeth)
- Skin disorders
- Excessive sweating and urination
- Cardiovascular disease
- Colitis
- Diarrhea and constipation
- Other gastrointestinal disorders

One might wonder how excessive stress can produce such opposite symptoms e.g., sudden weight loss/sudden weight gain; insomnia/excessive sleeping. The key to this apparent paradox will be discussed next.

Excessive Behavior Indicators Most human beings are disgustingly predictable. The variation in our day to day activities, values, life-style, personal temperament, etc., is very minimal. Such predictability constitutes our identity and helps add security and

8

consistency both for ourselves and those we regularly interact with. Under conditions of high stress, people begin to lose that predictability as behavior moves out of that middle range and becomes excessive. Many people under high stress may develop sleep disorders. For some, sleep is unattainable. They can't get to sleep, they wake up repeatedly during sleep and when they do sleep they awake unrested. For others, sleep becomes the most seductive experience in their life. The alarm goes off and they lay under the covers consciously assessing if some part of their body is uncomfortable enough to allow them a guilt-free call to report in sick and then escape into the warmth and safety of their bed. What both groups share in common is the movement of their behavior from a medium predictable range to an extreme. Some of the examples of excessive behavior noted by stress casualties interviewed in the author's studies are noted below.

Flight Response	Fight Response
Rigid, Compulsive Behavior ⟷	High Risk-Taking Behavior
Lethargy And Detachment ⟷	Hyperactivity
Sexual Dysfunction ⟷	Hypersexuality
Under-Eating ⟷	Over-Eating (food as self-medication)
Passivity & Non-Assertiveness ⟷	Violent & Aggressive Behavior

Excessive behaviors on the flight-response end of the continuum seek to reduce the experience of stress through withdrawal from interaction with the environment. Excessive behaviors on the fight end seek aggressively to remove stressors or seek to overcompensate for the feelings such stressors generate. Persons feeling powerless in the work setting may attempt to demonstrate their potency and increase their supports through frantic sexual activity. Persons who feel emotionally numb from prolonged stress and interpret such numbness as "craziness", may once again discover the experience of human emotions in high-risk situations.

Many of the accidents that occur to victims of high stress are due not only to risk-taking behavior but also to a preoccupation with work stressors. One such victim was playing out a number of stressful work situations so intensely in his head while at home painting his house that he stepped off a scaffolding completely oblivious to the fact that he was painting on the upper story and not on the ground. Sound improbable and impossible? Have you ever been so involved or upset about a situation as you left work and continued to think about it, that you suddenly were startled by the realization that you had been driving your car for five minutes with no awareness of where you were or what you were doing?

Violent and aggressive behavior in response to high stress often starts with people we feel safest with - our spouses, intimate partners or children. It is very frightening to think of the following sequence. Under excessive stress, people are physiologically prepared for violent activity. The expression of that activity is not possible in the work setting and no alternative is provided to discharge that state of physiological readiness. The worker is then sent out of the work setting to go home to his/her family. The worker who feels defeated and powerless in the work setting may use aggression at home in an exaggerated attempt to demonstrate at least one area of life over which he/she does have power and control.

The most common excessive behavior used to counter stress has yet to be mentioned. That is the self-medication of work-related stress with psychoactive drugs. In some organizations one could monitor the aggregate level of stress simply by monitoring increased consumption of caffeine (coffee, tea, colas), nicotine, and over-the-counter medications. There is often a direct relationship between the level of stress and such increased consumption, as well as in the consumption of alcohol, psychoactive prescription medication, and illicit drugs. And of course, this discussion would be incomplete if the author failed to mention one of the most powerful sources of self-medication ever known - chocolate.

The problem with all of these substances is that they work - too quickly and too easily. When we approach such substances as rewards - "I owe it to myself", "It's been one of those days", "The hell with it!", etc. - the experience of self-medication can become

10

very seductive. In fact, self-medication can become so seductive that the victim may begin to develop serious consequences related to his/her chronic self-medication of stress with psychoactive substances.

Emotional Adjustment Indicators Each of us has what John Wallace (1974) has called a preferred defense structure. This preferred defense structure represents the unique style that each of us has developed to manage our emotional life in a manner that insures our safety and helps maintain our self-esteem. As the wear and tear of high stress begins to decrease the strength of this structure over time, the defense structure becomes more fragile and periodically breaks down, producing symptomatic behavior. The fragility of this defense structure is revealed through one or more of the following symptoms:

- Paranoia
- Decreased emotional control
- Fear of "going crazy"
- Feelings of hopelessness and loss of meaning
- Feelings of being cornered and trapped
- Undefined fears and anxiety
- Emotional detachment from work
- Martyrdom
- Increased time daydreaming/fantasy
- Nervous ticks
- Exaggerated blaming of others
- Undefined anger without a target or scapegoat
- Intellectualization

The style of managing emotion reflected in our preferred defense structure helps make us who we are. It provides us a sense of safety and those around us a level of predictibilty about how we will respond in different interactions with them. Under conditions of high stress these elements of safety and predictability are lost. One becomes less in control of when and how emotions will be expressed. From unwanted tears to impulsive outbursts of anger to a fearful retreat into isolation, the experience of burnout eats away at our emotional control.

Relationship Indicators Our response to relationships while under intense and prolonged stress, like the excessive behavior indicators, tends to go to one extreme or the other. At one extreme we begin to emotionally distance ourselves and move out of relationships toward a position of isolation. In health and human service agencies, such a stance can result in the following:

- Emotional distancing that turns a human being into "the coronary in 410" or an account number or some other label.
- Decreased time spent with clients e.g., decreased rounds in a hospital, one hour client appointments that last 15 minutes, etc.
- Responding to clients in a mechanical manner e.g., shifting from a people-changing focus to a focus on people processing.
- Isolation from other workers e.g., less time and verbal interaction with others.
- Use of physical barriers e.g., staying in one's office, shifting more work out of work site, hiding out where no one can find you.
- Social isolation.

At the other extreme, one may become over-involved with clients and co-workers during periods of excessive stress. This may be reflected in the following behavior:

- Developing very symbiotic, dependent relationships with other staff and supervisors.
- Using clients to meet one's own needs.
- Increased anger at clients.
- Increased interaction and conflict with co-workers.
- Increased problems in marital and other interpersonal relationships away from work, including relationships with one's children.

A point that will be raised in much more detail later in the book is the manner in which professional stress begins to spill out and impact one's ability to sustain intimate relationships. It is alarming to see the high number of marital and other relationship casualties that occur to persons going through periods of excessive professional stress. Many of these relationships are shattered and explained away in the rhetoric of "irreconcilable differences" with none of those involved having any awareness of how professional stress has served to disrupt the relationship.

Attitude Indicators   Something happens to the attitudes of persons exposed to prolonged periods of professional stress. It's as if someone, probably God, appointed them to judge all of their peers. Bolstered with grandiosity and spoken with the assurance of the self-righteous, the burnt out professional can talk incessantly about the shortcomings of both the generals and the soldiers. Attitudes vacillate from the hypercritical to boredom, to cynicism, or to expressions of hopelessness.

When an entire organization is going through the stage of high stress and low morale, these attitude changes can take on an extremely contagious quality. The entire communication of the organization may be subverted into the repetitive games of "Ain't It Awful" and "Waiting for Santa Claus". First everyone takes turns sharing the details of how everything is screwed up, with each person contributing his/her latest case example. Then everyone talks about how great everything is going to be when (Fill in the Blank) e.g., they all quit, the reorganization is complete, or when the boss is fired.

Value Indicators   Barring the hormone-induced brain trauma of adolescence and a brief reoccurrence at midlife, most people maintain a fairly consistent set of values throughout their life. When sudden and radical changes in values do occur, it is usually under conditions of very high stress.

Many of the individuals in the author's studies underwent radical changes in their value systems following periods of intense and prolonged professional stress. The changes ranged from conversion to extreme religious or political beliefs to a violation of values and beliefs held important throughout their career. Examples of the latter include the cop who goes on the take after years of refusing to fix even a parking ticket; the teacher who assaults a student out of anger and frustration; the historically ethical therapist who gets sexually involved with a client; and the priest who leaves the priesthood out of loss of faith.

13

This change in values can happen to individuals and it can happen to entire organizations during times of excessive stress. Chapter Five, will describe how an entire organization can experience this conversion of values and beliefs.

1.4   Organizational Indicators Of Professional Stress

The individual indicators of professional stress which were reviewed in this chapter are summarized in Exhibit 1-B. Organizational indicators of professional stress will not be summarized here as later chapters will elaborate these indicators in detail. Exhibit 1-C does provide a brief listing of some of the organizational indicators of stress that will be discussed in later chapters. The next chapter will examine different approaches to burnout by examining how different organizations view and respond to stress-related behavior.

EXHIBIT 1-B
Personal Indicators of Professional Stress

Health Indicators	Excessive Behavior Indicators	Emotional Adjustment Indicators	Relationship Indicators	Attitude Indicators
Fatigue and chronic exhaustion	Increased consumption of caffeine, tobacco, alcohol, over-the-counter medications, psychoactive prescription drugs, illicit drugs	Emotional distancing	Isolation from or overbonding with other	Grandiosity
Frequent and prolonged colds		Paranoia		Boredom
Headaches		Depression-loss of meaning, loss of hope	Responding to clients in mechanical manner	Cynacism
Sleep disturbances-insomnia, nightmares, excessive sleeping (escape)		Decreased emotional control	Increased isolation from clients	Sick humor-aimed particularly at clients and co-workers
Ulcers	High risk taking behavior-auto / cycle accidents, falls, "high risk" hobbies, general proness to accidents and injuries gambling, excessive spending/use of credit	Martyrdom	Increased anger at clients	Attitudes of self-righteousness
Gastro-intestinal disorders		Fear of "going crazy"	Increased interpersonal conflicts with co-workers	Hyper-critical of organization and/or peers
Sudden losses or gains in weight		Increased amount of time daydreaming/fantasy		Expressions of hopelessness and frustration
Flare-ups of pre-existing medical disorders, e.g., diabetes, high blood pressure, asthma		Constant feelings of being "trapped"	Increased problems in marital and other interpersonal relationships including relationships with one's children	
	Extreme mood and behavioral changes	Undefined fears		**VALUE INDICATORS**
		Inbility to concentrate		
	Increased propensity for violent and aggressive behavior	Intellectualization	Social isolation	Loss of Faith
Injuries from high risk behavior		Regression		Spiritual crisis
Muscular pain, particularly in lower back and neck	Hyperactivity			Sudden and extreme changes in one's values and beliefs
Increased premenstrual tension	Change in sexual behavior (sexual dysfunction or hypersexuality)			
Missed menstrual cycles	Over and under eating			
Excessive sweating and urination				
Bruxism (grinding of the teeth)				

EXHIBIT 1-C
Organizational Indicators of Professional Stress

Health Care Costs	Productivity Costs	Issues in Supervision
• Increased sick days • Increased worker compensation claims • Increased on-the-job accidents and injuries • Increase in stress-related health disorders	• Decreased productivity • Damage to equipment from employee sabotage and vandalism • Increase in employee theft • Increased tardiness • Increased frequency of work slowdowns and strikes	• Increased grievances • Extreme employee competiveness over status and turf • Distrust, leading to demands that rights, responsibilities and relationships be formally codified • Scapegoating of organizational leaders • Conflicts over authority

Employee Turnover	Professional Relationships	Quality Indicators
• May show low turnover followed by contagious and high turnover • High level of employee hostility at exit interviews • Increase in employee exit without notice • Increased requests for employee transfers • Disgruntled employees making public accusations about the organization	• Increased interpersonal conflict • Increased interdepartmental turf battles • Emotional detachment • Low morale • "We-they" polarizations, e.g., union vs. management	• Increased consumer complaints about products or services • Increased liability from mal-practice suits • Loss of professional and organizational pride

16

Chapter Two
Organizational Responses to Victims of Professional Burnout

When Hans Selye first introduced the term "stress" into the field of medicine in 1936 through his initial description of the general adaptation syndrome, it generated heated debates that were to last for several decades. Many of the early debates included disagreement over the actual existence of biological stress, criticisms of Selyes' definition of stress, and claims that the term, as an abstraction, lacked utility because it could not be subjected to scientific study. Much of the early resistance to Selye's work was his selection and redefinition of a word as a medical concept that had long been in common usage within the English language.

The response to the concept of stress is not unlike the animated polemics that have accompanied the formal study of the burnout phenomenon. Like the term stress, burnout had been an established part of the vocabulary of many professions long before it became a subject of study. While the early articles on burnout in each of the respective professions were long on general description and short on critical analysis and individual or programmatic strategies, they were generally well received. There followed in each profession, however, a succession of criticisms and debates over problems of definition and scope of the burnout concept and questions regarding the validity and utility of the concept. As we have moved through the "fad phase" of burnout in many of the professions - a phase marked by a multitude of publications, workshops, training seminars, and consulting services - a plethora of definitions and approaches have been advocated that closely resemble the fable of the blind men describing the elephant.

The concept of burnout will be further introduced here not by reviewing the theoretical models of these authors, but by presenting a typology of how burnout is defined in practice through the daily interactions between organizations and their employees. Organizational managers reveal their theoretical approaches to burnout through their organization of the work environment and their responses to stress related performance problems, interpersonal conflicts, and individual casualties of the burnout process. These approaches which are revealed through managerial behavior, but rarely articulated explicitly, are based on powerfully held beliefs and values about human nature and the relationship between people and work. A systematic study of burnout must begin with an examination of these beliefs and values that define responses to burnout in the workplace.

During the past decade, the author has had the opportunity through varied research, training and consultation activities to work with a large number of organizations, particularly health and human service organizations. These opportunities provided a unique vantage point from which to observe organizational approaches to professional burnout and to develop a typology for analyzing these approaches. The proceeding pages, will classify, describe, and critique the following six organizational approaches to professional burnout:

- The authoritarian-moral approach
- The clinical approach
- The cognitive approach
- The training approach
- The environmental approach
- The systems approach

It should be noted that each approach described has repercussions on the victims of professional burnout and on the future incidence of burnout within the organization.

It is hoped this schema will provide managers an opportunity to review their own assumptions about burnout and to assess their supervisory responses to victims of professional burnout. I implore the reader to undertake this self-examination in a spirit of openness and to check one's natural tendency for defensiveness. The criticisms of many of these approaches are based on the knowledge that at different stages of my supervisory career, I have exemplified, hopefully without conscious malice, nearly all of the approaches I now condemn.

2.1 The Authoritarian-moral Approach: Burnout As Bad Character

The authoritarian-moral approach to burnout is reflective of what McGregor (1973) has called the "theory X" philosophy of management. Theory X is based on the assumption that most people dislike work, lack ambition, are essentially passive, avoid responsibility, resist change and are self-centered and unconcerned with the needs of the organization. The role of the manager is thus to direct, motivate, manipulate, persuade, control, reward, and punish the worker to effectively respond to the needs of the organization.

Within the human service organization managed via the propositions of theory X, even the existence of professional burnout is adamantly denied through such flippant phrases as "there's no such thing as burnout, only staff who don't want to work". Behavior indicative of burnout is viewed as emerging from character flaws in the worker. The individual experiencing burnout may also be impugned with malicious motives toward the organization and organizational leadership. Professional burnout is, in essence, seen as a "cop-out" to avoid one's responsibilities or is seen as an act of sabotage against the organization and its leaders. While the authoritarian-moral approach is usually applied to workers on an individual basis, it may also be broadened to encompass stereotyped responses to particular subgroups of the worker population. In this latter case, stress-related behavior of the individual worker is seen as justifying the manager's view of the unreliable and irresponsible character of the subgroup the worker represents, (e.g., women, ethnic and cultural minorities, or older workers).

Organizational managers who typify the authoritarian-moral approach are intensely invested in their work and have great difficulty accepting workers whose time and emotional commitment to the organization does not match their own.

In spite of these leader's extensive investment of time and emotional energy in the work setting, they may work for years before they experience the extreme effects of stress. They are what has been referred to as "stress carriers". These managers externalize their stress to others through verbal reprimands, excessive and unrealistic role expectations, and impulsive and frequently contradictory task assignments. The stress carriers often bolster their own self-esteem at the expense of their employees through repeated variations of the following scenario:

> The stress carrier storms into an office where three workers are engaged in various work assignments, turns to one of the workers and says, "Jane, I need a summary report on _____ (stated quickly, vaguely, and without reference to where the information can be obtained) for a 2:00 meeting tomorrow". The stress carrier rapidly leaves the office not allowing time for clarification. Jane, finding no help from her colleagues clarifying what precisely the boss wants, and unable to get access to him for further instructions, does the best job she can, summarizing what she guesses he wants. At 1:30 the following afternoon, the stress carrier comes into Jane's office and responds with outrage that what Jane prepared was not what he wanted at all, and that he will have to do the work himself.

Such scenarios build up the self-esteem of the stress carrier, are often emotionally devastating to workers playing the scapegoat, and repeatedly reinforce the motto of the authoritarian-moral approach: "If you want anything done; you gotta do it yourself".

The stress carrier is typified by the manager who flippantly boasts, "I don't get ulcers; I give ulcers". The authoritarian-moral approach places impossible burdens on workers and then penalizes them for not being able to stand up under the weight. Organizations characterized by this authoritarian-moral approach respond to burnout victims in a punitive fashion either through disciplinary punishment or by forcing the extrusion of the victim from the organization. This organizational approach produces an extremely high rate of staff turn-over.

There are severe limitations and disadvantages to the authoritarian-moral approach to victims of professional burnout. This approach, first of all, individualizes what is essentially an interactional or relationship problem. The focus on the character of the individual burnout victim camouflages the need to modify the high stress environment, and sustains those organizational conditions that will continue to produce a high rate of professional burnout. This approach also tends to eliminate the communication that would be necessary to reduce stressors and increase supports within the work environment.

The authoritarian-moral approach is also immune to corrective feedback due to its self-justifying moral rigidity and the tendency of the organizational ideology to become self-prophetic. As staff become increasingly burned out from the high stress conditions, they do indeed avoid responsibility, develop malicious attitudes toward the organization, and commit acts of sabotage against the organizational leadership. As the new staff persons enter the organization, they are lauded by the leader for their expertise and all they will accomplish for the agency. As new staff person's performance deteriorates under the high stress role conditions, he/she is scapegoated and extruded like many of the workers that preceded them.

The authoritarian-moral approach provides the ideological justification for the often painful extrusion of workers from the organization. People are used up and discarded within these organizations. The authoritarian-moral approach not only does not effectively respond to burnout victims, its ideology perpetuates organizational conditions that will continue to produce a high casualty rate among workers.

2.2 The Cognitive Approach: Burnout As Faulty Expectations

The cognitive approach to burnout views this phenomenon as emerging from unrealistic or irrational ideas, beliefs and expectations held by workers about themselves and/or their profession. The contradiction between one's notions of how things ought to be, and the realities confronted in the work environment are viewed as leading to a loss of professional idealism, a loss of personal enthusiasm, and the onset of pessimism and hostility. The cognitive approach to burnout is most often utilized to explain the personal changes that occur early in one's professional career.

In the cognitive approach, burnout is often seen as a product of faulty professional socialization. Kramer (1974), and Schmalenberg and Kramer (1976), have eloquently described the "reality shock" experienced in the transition from the nursing school sub-culture to the new and unfamiliar work subculture of nursing practice. Each of these subcultures has a set of distinct values and specific role behaviors that the nursing student and the practicing nurse must perform. The vast discrepancy between the two subcul-tures is a source of intense stress and contributes to the large number of nurses who leave the nursing profession. Valle (1979) has also illustrated this cognitive approach by cataloguing a num-ber of beliefs (myths) that contribute to burnout in the alcoholism counselor.

Organizations that respond to the victims of professional burnout via the cognitive approach attempt to resocialize the worker to bring greater harmony between professional expec-tations and professional realities. Since burnout is viewed as a problem of intellect, the manager's task is viewed as indoctrinating workers with beliefs and expectations that, while reducing idealism, produce a greater level of professional satisfaction and contentment. Some proponents of this approach have adapted concepts from Albert Ellis' rational emotive therapy to address problems of staff burnout. These proponents see irrational beliefs about oneself, one's co-workers, and one's clients as the core problem of burnout and propose that manager's intervene through a "cognitive restructuring" process aimed at altering the "should's", "have to's", "must's", and "don't's" that create conflict between the worker and his/her professional environment. The manager using this approach has relationships that can be characterized as tutorial rather than the punitive role described earlier.

There are a number of strengths to the cognitive approach to burnout. The approach clearly raises the important role of profes-sional education in instilling values, beliefs and expectations that fit the real world. Managerial practices emerging from this approach do impact the incidence of burnout through the estabish-ment of clear role expectations and realistic belief systems for workers. In its response to victims of burnout, the approach also avoids the demoralizing impact of more punitive approaches and avoids stigmatizing the worker as occurs in other approaches.

The disadvantages of the cognitive approach are threefold. By defining the source of burnout as irrational and unrealistic ideas

22

and beliefs, the approach tends to ignore both the emotional vulnerabilities and skill deficiencies that the worker brings to the work setting. A broader criticism of this approach is that it often serves to support the status quo by changing the idealism and beliefs of the workers rather than changing the work environment to more closely match the worker's vision of what could be. A final criticism of the cognitive approach is that it ignores other factors, particularly factors in the work environment, that will continue to produce burnout even after the workers are "appropriately" socialized.

2.3   The Clinical Approach: Burnout As Psychopathology

The clinical approach to victims of professional burnout defines burnout as emerging from individual psychopathology. Perhaps it is only natural that the human services field should take an essentially clinical approach to the understanding of professional burnout. The models, which these workers utilize to understand the emotional and relationship problems of their clients, are inevitably applied to understand the emotional and relationship problems of staff within the work milieu.

The clinical approach to burnout victims by human service organizations is remarkably similar to the response of a family system to an acting-out adolescent. As a particular staff person experiences a stress-related deterioration in performance, the organization identifies the inappropriate behavior and attitudes of the worker (acknowledgment of deviancy). The problem is seen as emerging from the personality of the worker (diagnosis of psychopathology). The worker becomes a problem (identified patient) about which something must be done. The supervisor confronts the worker on his/her current level of functioning and recommends that the staff person seek help (therapy) outside the agency or the supervisory relationship is turned into a treatment relationship. If the worker's behavior does not change, he/she is fired or manipulated out of the organization (the equivalent of institutionalizing the adolescent).

This clinical approach has been noted by a number of other authors. Stotland and Kobler (1965) in their classic study on the *Life And Death of A Mental Hospital* noted the tendency of key staff and consultants of a private mental hospital to begin talking about "treating" the board, "treating" the hospital staff, and "treating" the hospital at a time that severe organizational problems were besetting the hospital. Many of these problems were attributed to the "sickness" of key staff of the hospital. The large number of staff casualties which occurred during the demise of this particular hospital were viewed as problems of individual psychopathology and were not seen within the context of the tremendously high-stress conditions under which the individuals were working. The propensity to individualize organizational problems and the concomitant failure to address major systemic problems in the organization and the organizations relationship with its outside environment played a critical role in the death of the organization studied. Elstein, (1972) in his study of the service reorganization at the Massachusetts Mental Health Center, noted the tendency of administrative staff to use a psychological interpretation to explain conflict between particular staff and the administration. Elstein notes one particular example of a resident who complained to the administration that his current job assignment was impossible to complete. "At first, his complaints were interpreted as reflecting personal psychological difficulties, but when he persuaded his supervisors to try the task themselves, they stopped talking about 'his problem'. "

Another variation of the clinical model is to define dysfunctional responses to stress as a purely medical/health problem. This approach is often used when the victim of professional stress is suffering a number of debilitating stress related health problems. The organizational response is to treat the symptoms of the stress via medical intervention. Such intervention frequently includes the use of sedative and tranquilizing drugs. This approach, in essence, medicates the victim to increase his/her threshold of stress tolerance in order to prolong his/her role performance, while ignoring the primary sources of stress in the organizational environment.

In summary, the clinical approach to victims of burnout defines the problems of burnout as psychological (and/or medical) and utilizes psychological (and/or medical) treatment of the worker as the primary remediation approach.

There are a number of disadvantages to the clinical approach to victims of professional burnout. This approach, like the authoritarian-moral approach, individualizes what is essentially an interactional problem and fails to address the need to modify the high stress work environment. The clinical approach stigmatizes the worker through the diagnostic process. In my interviews with human service workers, it is clear that these workers frequently do not connect what they are experiencing--burnout--to the work environment. Their greatest fear is that they are going crazy. The clinical approach to burnout inappropriately confirms the worst fears of these victims. By focusing the worker's attention on his or her own intrapsychic processes, the clinical approach decreases the worker's ability to mobilize external resources for support at the exact time he or she is in most desperate need of such supports. The definition of the problem as psychopathology increases the worker's feelings of isolation, paranoia, loss of control, and, in short, escalates the symptoms of burnout.

There have been severe casualties resulting from the clinical approach when agencies have taken it upon themselves to confront the worker's problems in a staff "group" or referred the worker into a marathon treatment group. What these agencies failed to realize was that the worker needed a reprieve from the emotional intensity of the work setting, not an assault on his/her already fragile defense system.

Employee assistance programs have been established in many organizations to address problems which result in decreased performance by an employee. These programs may reflect the deficiencies of the clinical approach to the extent that they only address individual factors (psychopathology, medical problems) or factors outside the work setting (family problems, financial difficulties) that affect employee performance. It is much easier, for example, for an employee assistance counselor to identify a problem of alcohol abuse and refer an employee to treatment than to report to management that an employee is using alcohol to self-medicate stress generated from intolerable conditions within the work environment.

2.4 The Training Approach: Burnout As Skill Deficiency

The training approach to victims of professional burnout

defines burnout as a reflection of skill deficiency, particularly skills in the area of stress management. It is assumed that all employees will experience some degree of work-related stress and that some workers lack the skills to manage such stress. Remediation measures include the provision of stress management training to increase the worker's level of stress tolerance and increase the worker's repertoire of stress management techniques. The training approach also assumes that a significant amounts of job-related stress occur from a discrepancy between the skills an individual possesses and the skills the individual needs to effectively perform their particular role within the organization. Skill training that enhances the worker's ability to perform tasks endemic to his/her role in the organization, thus becomes a primary vehicle for addressing staff burnout.

The training approach should be an integral part of any organizational strategy to address professional burnout. There are, however, some limitations to the approach. Training approaches, which focus on deficiencies in stress management skills, may be used to immunize workers against stress generated from very intolerable role conditions. Under these circumstances, the training approach might inadvertently distract the organization from the need to reduce role stress conditions and increase role supports for the worker, and may only prolong the onset of burnout.

Training approaches, which focus on skill development for improved role performance, may be based on a misdiagnosis of the conditions that are responsible for inadequate role performance and the conditions that are responsible for high levels of stress by the worker. There may be conditions in the work environment that prevent the worker from effectively delivering those skills which he or she possesses. The problem may, in fact, be one of unclear or outmoded organizational policies, a lack of role clarity, excessive and contradictory demands upon a worker's time, etc., rather than a problem of skill adequacy. Under these circumstances, skill training will neither improve role performance nor reduce the excessive stress experienced by the worker.

2.5 The Environmental Approach: Burnout As Imperfection In The Organizational Structure

The four organizational approaches to burnout described so far all share one thing in common. All of these approaches define the etiology of burnout within the individual employee and utilize remediation strategies that seek to change the individual in some manner. The next approach ignores individual issues and defines the problem of burnout in the work environment.

Many managers recognize stress-related problems in employees and see these problems emerging from the structure or process of the organization. These managers are constantly tinkering with the organizational structure - changing policies, procedures, and work norms - in an effort to discover the magical structure that gets the work done and makes everyone happy. Anytime an employee reports, "We've really got a problem with ...", this manager immediately begins to think of how to manipulate the environment to address the problem.

During the years that the author's own supervisory style tended to reflect this knee-jerk approach to management, many of the actions taken to address stressors in the work environment increased rather than decreased stress experienced by staff. Most managers want to be seen as capable decision-makers, problem-solvers, and innovators. Perhaps more than anything else, most manager want to be liked by their staff. It is discomforting to discover how such benign intentions can lead to inconsistent, rapidly changing, and stress provoking conditions in the program. Some of the more common problems with this management approach are catalogued below.

Many managers who exemplify the environmental approach to burnout often fail to control the pace of change within the organization. If the reader reflects back upon the definition of stress as a demand for adaptational change, it becomes obvious that we must gear the pace of change to the level of adaptational energy available to staff. This is true even with changes in the environment designed to address stress-related problems. There may be important changes to the organization that should be postponed simply because the staff has already experienced too much change in too short a time period. The persistent change that typifies the environmental approach taps the physical and emotional resources of staff as they attempt to keep abreast of new policies, procedures, etc.

The "system tinkerer" may also neglect one of the most basic principles of system theory: A change in one part of the system inevitably provokes accommodating changes in other components of the system. By manipulating the environment to reduce stressors for one group of workers, this approach may inadvertently increase stressors for other workers in the organization. In short, a change intended as a solution may create more serious problems than the original problem the change was intended to address.

There is also a more fundamental flaw in the environmental approach to stress. The preoccupation with organizational structure and process may divert the manager's attention from the individual worker who is experiencing some level of physical or psychological impairment. Such impairment may require immediate support and/or intervention.

2.6   The Systems Approach: Burnout As Ecological Dysfunction

The five organizational approaches to burnout critiqued in this chapter all oversimplify the phenomenon of burnout by seeing it as caused by a single factor. In this final section of chapter two, the author will begin to outline a more comprehensive understanding of burnout.

The systems approach to burnout defines burnout not as a problem inside the individual worker or as a problem in the work environment, but as a breakdown in the relationship between the individual and the organization.

Biologists study the fragile balance, inter-relationships and inter-dependence between all living things. The systems manager must understand the ecology of his or her organization in a similar manner. The author is very indebted to Jerome F.X. Carroll for the development of this ecological perspective. Dr. Carroll and the author collaborated on a paper (1981) in which we attempted to set forth the major propositions of this systems perspective.

28

This perspective views professional burnout as a complex interaction between:

1. <u>Issues of ontology</u> - personal factors that influence an individual's susceptibility to stress in the occupational setting (see Chapter Ten).

2. <u>Microsystem issues</u>- the prevalence of role stressors and the availability of role supports in one's immediate work environment (see Chapter Nine).

3. <u>Mesosystem issues</u> - problems in the structure (how work is organized) and process (relationships, communication, problem-solving methods, etc.) of the organization (see Chapters Five, Six and Seven).

4. <u>Exosystem issues</u> - turbulence in the organization's relationship with its outside environment and changes outside the organization that have a profound impact on the mission of the organization.

5. <u>Macrosystem issues</u> - political, economic and social changes in the culture that are altering the basic relationship between people and work.

The remaining chapters will demonstrate how these factors are "ecologically nested within one another", and how managers seeking to understand and address professional burnout must recognize and respond to the multiple and reciprocal relationships that exist between the above five elements.

Chapter Three
The Systems Approach to Professional Burnout

As noted in the last chapter, most approaches have sought to examine stress and burnout by focusing either on personal variables or environmental variables. This chapter will begin to explore the phenomenon of burnout by analyzing the complex interrelationships and interdependence of those personal and environmental variables. Burnout will be explored as what Carroll (1980) and Carroll and White (1981) have described as a form of "ecological dysfunction". Burnout will be defined not as characteristics in the individual or conditions in the environment, but as a breakdown or disruption in the reciprocal relationship between the individual and the organization - a relationship that affects and is in turn affected by broader systems outside the organization.

3.1   The Ecology Of Professional Stress

In the following pages, the author will begin to explore the ecology of professional stress by addressing a number of key questions. What factors can be utilized to predict one's vulnerability to professional stress? What roles do organizational structure and internal organizational relationships play in increasing or decreasing vulnerability to professional stress? How do forces outside the organizational setting influence the prevalence and intensity of professional stress?

Figure 3-A graphically illustrates an ecological perspective on professional stress. In this figure, the individual worker is ecologically nested (like an onion) within different layers or levels of social organization. This model depicts the complex and synergistic relationship between individual and environmental variables which can produce burnout. It is hoped that the model will allow the reader to integrate divergent etiological viewpoints that have been utilized to explain the phenomenon of professional burnout. The elements of the ecosystem of the worker are briefly summarized below.

EXHIBIT 3-A
Factors / Relationships Affecting Individual Stress Response

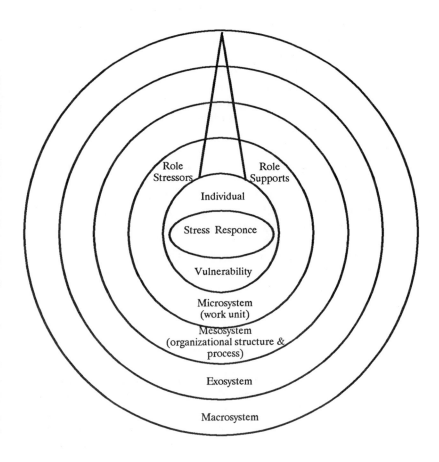

3.2   The Individual

Each individual who begins work in an organization brings with him/her a unique level of personal vulnerability to stress. Some of the factors that make up this level of vulnerability include the following:

- A unique body.
  - genetic endowment (the body's innate, inherited capacity to physiologically respond to stress).
  - developmental history (the number, magnitude and types of illness, physical trauma, or disability).
  - equipment maintenance (the lifetime level of care afforded the body through nutrition, exercise, sleep, preventative health care, absence or presence of toxic habits such as smoking or excessive drinking.
- Prior history of stress management.
- Technical knowledge and skills.
- Values and beliefs.
- Nature and quality of relationships with family of origin and nuclear family.
- Mastery of developmental tasks appropriate to current stage of life.
- Ability to initiate and sustain nurturing intimate and social relationships.
- Expectations and motivations related to work.
- Ability to assert needs and set realistic limits.
- Self-concept related to major life roles e.g., physician, wife, mother, daughter, or friend.
- Unresolved emotional pain e.g., anger, shame, or guilt.
- Current life changes demanding adaptational energy.

Many of the above factors have been mentioned in traditional stress literature as if they were fixed and isolated characteristics. What distinguishes the systems perspective is the belief that most of these characteristics are dynamic rather than static and begin to change as soon as the individual enters the life of the organization.

Let's consider, for example, what happens when a worker brings to a new work environment a high level of motivation and

32

enthusiasm and high expectations for professionally satisfying and stimulating work, only to encounter in the work unit lethargy, low productivity, and "clock-punching". Under these circumstances, a war of adaptation will begin almost immediately. Forces within the work unit will operate to pull the worker's expectations and work values toward the group norm. The intensity of the worker's enthusiasm, on the other hand, may begin to shift and change the group norm. Such synergy marks the dynamic and reciprocal process of adaptation between the individual and the organization.

The synergy can be described through numerous examples. One can bring a self-concept into a work setting and through feedback from the organization have the self-concept confirmed or altered. At the same time one's self-concept is being affected by the organization, this self-concept begins to influence the collective self-concept of the work unit. One can bring to a new work setting a prior history of stress management that relied heavily on the self-medication of stress with caffeine, nicotine, and alcohol. In this war of adaptation, the organization can:

- Reinforce this style of stress management through informal norms that support self-medication via a work unit motto that says "when in doubt, DRINK!" (Shared "happy hour" after stressful days), or
- Diminish the strength of this preferred pattern of self-medication through organizational values/policies that inhibit psychoactive drug consumption, and through mechanisms in the work environment that provide healthier alternatives for managing stress.

In this same war of adaptation, one may influence work group norms so that other workers may have an increased tendency to use self-medication to manage stress ("We've had a hell of a day! Let me buy you a drink before we go home").

The systems perspective dictates that we address not only characteristics in the individual and in the work environment that increase vulnerability to burnout, but also the special chemistry in the reciprocal relationship between the individual and the organization. The systems perspective also demands that we look at what I call the collective vulnerability of organizational members. Collective vulnerability implies that the manager must ask the following questions. Are there shared characteristics of employees that have special implications related to vulnerability to burnout or to the types of organizational strategies that are needed to address stress and burnout? If we were to identify the stress management style of each member of the organization, and then look at this data collectively, what style would dominate? What early warning signs would best indicate a disturbance in the multiple relationships between these individuals and the organization? Are there collective vulnerability issues for the alcoholism treatment program whose staff is composed primarily of recovering alcoholics? Are there collective vulnerability issues for nurses in a community hospital, many of whose spouses have lost or are about to lose jobs to the closed or relocated local industries? Are there issues of collective vulnerability in an organization whose members come primarily from the 35 to 50 (high risk for mid-life crisis) age group?

3.3 The Microsystem

The microsystem is the smallest unit of organization in the work environment. It is the department, division, section, service, unit, or team. The microsystem is that unit of organization and collection of people each individual interacts most intensely with in the performance of his/her role.

There are a number of characteristics of the microsystem that shape the relationship with the individual worker and influence both the level of professional stress in the work unit and permissions and prohibitions on how such stress can be managed by the individual. These characteristics include the following:

- The physical environment containing the unit.
- The goals, objectives, and tasks of the unit.
- Group sentiment (emotional content in co-worker relationships).
- Definitions of power, authority, and control (decision making and accountability).
- Structure (organization of work/division of labor).

- Group norms on how, when and to whom one can communicate.
- The relationships between the unit and other components of the organization.
- The management style and philosophy of unit leadership.
- Equipment and materials.

The microsystem is the primary unit in the relationship between the individual worker and the organization. No matter what kind of values and ideals are espoused by the organizational leader, it is at the microsystem level that these values become reality or empty rhetoric. Many organizations ignore this principle when confronted with the problems of burnout, internal conflict and poor morale. They create new appendages (other microsystems) to the organization such as employee assistance programs or health promotion programs, but do nothing to change the day-to-day conditions at the microsystem level.

There are two basic challenges at the microsystem level, and how these challenges are met will, to a great extent, shape the quality of work life for organizational members. The first challenge is to organize the work of the microsystem - defining tasks, allocating resources, clarifying roles and accountability, defining methods of problem-solving, establishing timelines and outcomes, defining transactions with other units and entities outside the organization, and supervising the flow of activity. The second challenge is to assess which individuals can adapt to and perform microsystem roles, to assess how the microsystem will in turn be effected by each individual, and to develop group norms and values that are consistent with organizational goals and supportive of worker health. The issue of structure allows us to examine how objective conditions in the microsystem environment promote or diminish employee productivity and health. The issue of process allows us to assess and control the degree of harmony or disharmony in the person - microsystem match. Problems in the mismatch of an individual with the wrong microsystem, or microsystem role, can have disastrous consequences both to the health of the mismatched individual and to the group process and health of the entire work unit.

While this special reciprocal relationship exists between the individual and the microsystem, both the individual and the microsystem are involved in broader transactions with the whole organization -- here referred to as the mesosystem. Mesosystem transactions also involve issues of structure and process. A critical function of the microsystem manager is to regulate such transactions and balance the need for healthy cohesion between microsystem members with the need for these same workers to identify with and support the organization as a whole. A balance is sought between the twin problems of the worker identifying passionately with his or her work unit, with no sense of affiliation or support of the mesosystem or the problem of the worker supporting the overall organization while undermining unit goals and leadership.

The management of internal boundaries between the microsystem and mesosystem has tremendous implications on the incidence and prevalence of debilitating professional stress. A major function of the microsystem manager is to sustain the availability of supports for workers in both the micro and mesosystems, while serving as a gatekeeper to control the pace of change (stressors) thrusted on the microsystem by the overall organization. This notion of balancing role stressors and role supports will be addressed in much greater depth in later chapters.

3.4 The Mesosystem

The mesosystem embraces all of the microsystems and constitutes all elements contained within the boundary of the organization.

Factors in the mesosystem that can have a direct influence on the intensity and duration of professional stress include the following:

- The clarity of the organization's mission, goals and objectives.
- The efficiency and utility of the structure of the organization in meeting organizational goals.
- The ability of the organization to adapt to turbulence and changing conditions in the outside environment.

36

- The ability of organizational leadership to manage harmonious and complementary boundary transactions between the microsystems of the organization.
- The nature of the organizational culture-beliefs, attitudes, values, and emotions that govern formal and informal relationships between organizational members.
- The ability of organizational leadership to generate hope, direction, control, and a vision that integrates the activities of the microsystem units.
- The ability of the organization to distribute rewards in a fair and consistent manner.

The ecosystem perspective seeks to understand the chain of reciprocal relationships between the individual worker, the microsystem and the mesosystem. Individual workers influence both the micro and mesosystems. The stress-related disruption of the behavior and health of a single worker increases stress on other workers in the microsystem and may compromise the ability of the microsystem to accomplish work objectives that in turn negatively impacts other microsystems and the organization as a whole. On the other hand, decisions and actions in the mesosystem have immediate ripple effects through the microsystems on individual workers. A mesosystem that has overextended itself by committing itself to objectives that surpass the level of fiscal, technical, and human resources, will inevitably overload the production capacity of the microsystems and, in turn, lead to the stressful role overload of individual workers.

Many classic studies on organizational stress and management have detailed the important aspects of internal structure and leadership activities in the mesosystem. Few, however, have focused on the relationship between the organization and its outside environment, and the impact of the nature of this relationship on the health of individual workers. In the coming chapters, the author will develop the contention that a critical factor in both individual stress and intraorganizational conflict is the organization's relationship with its outside environment and the manner in which the boundary between the mesosystem and the outside environment is being managed.

3.5   The Exosystem

The next layer of life space - the exosystem - contains all the other ecosystems that impinge on the life of the organization and its workers. The exosystem can be divided into two areas for purposes of discussion: those areas of the exosystem that directly impinge on the organization, and those areas of each employee's life that constitute their non-work ecosystem.

The exosystem of the organization includes such important variables as the following:

- The physical environment through which workers, clients, materials and products are transported into and out of the organization.
- The availability of an affordable labor pool with the desired level of technical knowledge and skill.
- Regulatory agencies that govern conditions under which the organization must operate e.g., licensing and accreditation bodies.
- The availability and costs of similar products or services offered by other organizations (competition).
- The availability of capital e.g., levels of federal and state and private funding, interest rates, etc.
- Allied professional agencies.
- Agencies that govern the technical or professional certification of workers.
- Consistency for the demand of the organization's products or services.
- Professional organizations/unions.
- Community attitudes and values that relate to the organization's products or services.

Emery and Trist (1973), and Terreberry (1973), have described the "turbulent field" in which many organizations operate today. If we go back to our definition of stress as a demand for adaptational change, then an organization's response to the pace of change in the exosystem has a profound impact on the level of professional stress experienced by workers. The acceleration of change has created very turbulent fields in which most organizations now live.

As change moves too rapidly in the exosystem, organizations become reactive, and the focus shifts from identified objectives to merely adapting and controlling the demands and contingencies thrust upon the organization by the environment. Alvin Toffler, in *Future Shock* (1970), described in detail this fragmentation and transience of organizational goals and purpose produced by accelerating change in the exosystem.

The acceleration of change in the exosystem has forced the acceleration of change in organizations. The management of the mesosystem / exosystem boundary becomes crucial in preventing the sudden demand for adaptational energy that far surpasses the capacity for change in the organization and its individual workers. As the reader proceeds into later chapters, controlling and managing the pace of organizational change will emerge as a major systems strategy in addressing professional burnout.

A second aspect of the exosystem is the personal non-work ecosystem of each organizational member. This ecosystem includes such components as the family, the non-work social network, the neighborhood, the community, etc. Turbulence in these ecosystems inevitably spills into the work environment just as high levels of stress in the work environment are brought home into the family and social network of the worker. This cross boundary transfer has important implications to the impact of stress both in the work and home environment. A worker's vulnerability to stress increases as he or she experiences simultaneous high demands for adaptational energy both in the mesosystem and in the ecosystem of the family. The family and social ecosystem can also serve as a source of replenishment from work-related stress. Later chapters will describe how closure of the organizational boundary reduces the ability of workers to sustain access to such replenishment and increases the incidence of burnout inside the work system. Later chapters will also detail how work related stress is carried into our personal lives as a disruptive force in family and intimate relationships.

3.6 The Macrosystem

The macrosystem encompasses broader social, political, and economic forces that encompass all of the previously described ecosystem components. Forces in the macrosystem can have both direct and indirect influences on occupational stress. Such forces can include:

- The value attached to various professions as measured by cultural rewards of money and status.
- Broad changes in technology that produce ripple effects throughout the culture.
- Turbulence in the macrosystem e.g., international conflict or war, national fiscal deficit, etc., that create shifts in priorities and the overall allocation of fiscal and human resources.
- Changed values and expectations related to work.
- Broad changes in demography (e.g., movement from a youthful to aging population in the culture, or geographical movement of large numbers of people in the culture).

It should be clear from the above that professional stress and burnout are complex problems influenced by forces at all levels of the ecosystem. Strategies that seek to address the problem of burnout must be sophisticated and target multi-level interventions in the ecosystem. Strategies that seek only to intervene at the level of the individual, or which seek a simple manipulation of one element of the work environment, are doomed for failure.

In the coming chapters, components of this system's perspective will be isolated for much more in-depth analysis. The next five chapters will examine the tendency of many work environments to become "closed organizational families", and the relationship of such closure to the experience of burnout. These chapters will pay particular attention to mesosystem and exosystem boundary transactions as an indicator of organizational health, and as a predictor of the incidence of professional burnout. Chapter Nine will focus in on the microsystem and identity thirteen role stressors that produce inordinate levels of professional burnout. Chapter Ten will examine the role of individual vulnerability in this ecological perspective on stress. In the final chapters the author will attempt to set forth a number of systems interventions aimed at addressing problems of individual and organizational health based on the principles set forth in this chapter.

Chapter Four
The Organizational Family Continuum

4.1 The Organizational Family

The conceptualization of an organizational group as a family system is not new, particularly in the field of residential treatment and more specifically within the field of addiction treatment. The history of child welfare is replete with models which attempt to rehabilitate by replicating the family system. Most of these models designate staff in parental surrogate roles. A wide variety of programs using such catch phrases as resocialization, retraining, reparenting, normalization, milieu, etc., all use a family model in differing degrees to conceptualize part of the treatment process and use staff to perform parental functions. A look at the therapeutic communities in the chemical dependency field shows an even more obvious family model, e.g., clients and staff alike referring to the total treatment community as "the family" and to each other as "brother" and "sister". A great deal of energy has gone into describing what this family model has meant in terms of the relationships between treatment staff and clients. Much less energy, however, has gone into how this model may be used to describe how staff within a given organization are relating to one another.

Family therapists have begun to apply their knowledge of family processes to other human groups. Bowen (1974) has pointed out the similarities between systems in families, organizations, and social systems; Speck and Attneave (1973) have extended the family system model to include broad social networks and described methods to work with such networks; Kerr (1973) has used the triangling phenomenon within families to understand a similar dynamic within a Navy hospital staff; and Minard (1976) has described in great detail the use of family systems theory in organizational consultation. The use of family systems theory to understand organizational group processes begins with the premise that organizational problems, and in particular personal and interpersonal conflicts within a working group, can best be understood and resolved by looking at the operations of the total system rather than the functioning of the individual members of the group.

Events which create ongoing conflict and disequilibrium within the total system will inevitably affect the health of organizational members and their ability to adequately perform tasks crucial to the survival and health of the system.

The term "organizational family" will be used throughout this book in an attempt to conceptualize the organizational group as a family system.

The Organizational Family *Consists of Those Persons Identified as Organizatioal Members and any Other Persons, Who, By Virtue of Frequent Interaction or Influence on Internal Decisionmaking, Constitute the Organizational Group.*

Those persons making up the organizational family will vary greatly from setting to setting. The organizational family may include paid staff, volunteers, consultants, interns, board members, clients, and, under certain circumstances, spouses of the above groups.

As with the nuclear families, one can also speak of an "extended organizational family".

The Extended Organizational Family *Consists of the Professional, Social, and Intimate Relationships of Organizational Members that Serve Collectively to Both Buffer and Link the Organizational Family and the Outside World.*

The extended organizational family may include family, intimate partners, friends and relatives of organizational family members, board members, patrons, stockholders, key personnel from funding and regulatory agencies, and individuals from allied organizations.

Later chapters will examine how the composition of both the organizational family and extended organizational family changes over time, the forces that produce such change, and the impact of such change on the health of the organizational family and its members.

Throughout the remainder of this book, the author will work on the assumption that individuals stay healthy or become dysfunctional in organizations in much the same manner as they do in family systems. From the beginning, we will see that the organizational family contains the same kind of triangulations, myths, projections, taboos, ghosts, heroes, and scapegoats found in the family system. Family systems will be used as a framework to understand organizational health and pathology, and as a vehicle to understand the staff casualty process in organizations.

4.2 Open Versus Closed Organizational Families

Since Von Bertalanffy introduced the concept of "open" and "closed" systems and particularly since his 1950 paper on "The Theory of Open Systems in Physics and Biology" which appeared in *Science* management and organizational theorists have taken the concept of open and closed systems from the physical and biological sciences and applied it to organizational dynamics. The physical science models of closed systems postulated the inherent tendency of a system to move toward maximum homogeneity and homeostasis. (Trist, 1969). Closed organizational systems were characterized as reactive, homeostatic, defensive and resistive of change. (Allport, 1960). More recently, descriptions have emerged of "open-ended" organizational systems which struggle not for maintenance of the status quo, but for growth, change, and ongoing evolution of the organization. (Clark, 1969).

The following discussion will begin to define and distinguish open and closed organizational family systems. To develop this discussion, the author will define a number of key concepts that have been applied to both family and organizational systems.

The understanding of open and closed systems begins with the concept of system's boundary.

A Systems's Boundary Represents That Invisible Circle Which Encloses a System, Separates it From Its Environment, and Distinguishes Members from Non-members.

This systems boundary could be represented by lines on a map separating countries, states or cities. It could be represented by the physical walls of a prison or security installation. It could be represented by powerful social norms that separate and restrict contact between different social groups. In families, boundary may be defined by name and bloodlines. With organizational families, boundary represents the definition by organizational leaders and members on which persons are and are not part of the organizational family system.

Organizational families differ not only in where they draw the boundary of inclusion and exclusion, but also in the quality and nature of the boundary itself. This latter difference includes the issue of boundary permeability.

Boundary Permeability *is the Degree of Resistance Or Difficulty in Making Organizatioal Boundary Transactions.*

It is this issue of boundary permeability that distinguishes open and closed systems. Closed organizational family systems tend to have a very rigid boundary of low permeability that restricts interaction with the outside environment. Open organizational family systems have very permeable boundaries allowing members easy access to other people in the social environment.

Every organizational family manages and controls boundary transactions through gatekeeper roles.

Gatekeepers *are Those Persons Who Control Through the Regulation of the Physical and Social Environment, Who, When, Where, and Under What Conditions Boundary Transactions Can Occur.*

In nuclear families, parents perform this gatekeeping function. In the organizational family, it is managers and their designees who control the frequency and intensity of boundary transactions.

Exhibit 4-A illustrates the gatekeeping functions in an organizational family. In organizations with low boundary permeability (closed systems), the gatekeeping restricts the flow of ideas and people into the organization and restricts the ability of members to develop and sustain professional and social relationships and activities outside the organization. The energy exchange between the organization and the outside environment are reduced

EXHIBIT 4-A

Gatekeeping Functions In The Organizational Family System

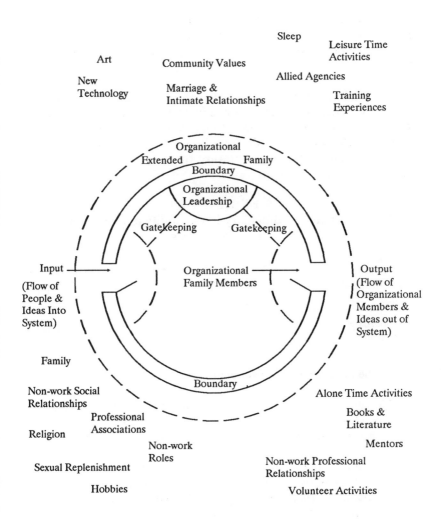

Sleep

Leisure Time
Activities

Art

Community Values

Allied Agencies

New
Technology

Marriage &
Intimate Relationships

Training
Experiences

Organizational
Extended   Family
Boundary

Organizational
Leadership

Gatekeeping   Gatekeeping

Input

Organizational
Family Members

Output

(Flow of
People &
Ideas Into
System)

(Flow of
Organizational
Members &
Ideas out of
System)

Family

Non-work Social
Relationships

Boundary

Alone Time Activities

Books &
Literature

Religion

Professional
Associations

Mentors

Sexual Replenishment

Non-work
Roles

Non-work Professional
Relationships

Hobbies

Volunteer Activities

to the point that more and more needs of organizational family members must be met inside the system.

In contrast, open systems have much less restrictive gatekeeping functions which allow easy interaction between organizational family members and the outside professional and social environment.

Examining the variations between organizational families in boundary permeability and gatekeeping functions, one could construct a continuum of organizational family types based on their degree of closure. The following illustration borrows a couple of terms from family therapy literature to describe three types of organizations along this continuum.

EXHIBIT 4-B
The Continuum of Boundary Permeability in Organizational Family Systems

The Enmeshed Organizational Family	The Self-Regulated Organizational Family	The Disengaged Organizational Family

Low Boundary Permeability

High Boundary Permeability

4.3   The Enmeshed Organizational Family

The enmeshed organizational family represents the most extremely closed system on the continuum. Characteristics that typify this organizational family system include the following:

- Low boundary permeability creating limited interaction between the organizational family and the outside professional and social environment.
- Aggressive gatekeeping functions.
- Excessive demands for time and emotional commitment to the organization.
- Focus on group rather than individual activities and achievement.

- Minimal internal boundaries that provide access to private space.
- Extreme demands for loyalty ("It's us against the world").
- Management style reflecting belief that workers must be controlled by fear, force, or charismatic persuasion.
- Control provided through tyrannical, authoritarian leadership or through manipulated consensus.
- Behavior deviating from norms responded to harshly, to include scapegoating of members from the organization.
- Extreme levels of group cohesion and mutual dependence.
- Implicit rather than explicit organizational family rules.

While there are numerous variations in enmeshed organizational families, all such closed systems share isolation from the outside environment and the high level of cohesiveness between organizational members.

What kind of organizations are usually found at the extreme end of this continuum of organizational closure? Such extreme closure tends to be more frequent in smaller, less complex organizations. Organizations whose nature of work demands isolation, such as prisons, security installations, or psychiatric hospitals, are very vulnerable to such closure. The aggressive, entrepreneur- the successful self-made man or woman -- has a tendency to create closed organizational family systems around themselves. Professions such as law enforcement, the ministry, or medicine in which we have high stress combined with high standards and expectations of personal conduct have a tendency to organize themselves into professionally and socially closed systems. Health and human service workers have a built-in propensity for organizational closure. In this latter example, the level of closure may be related to both the intensity of emotional demands and the degree of stigma or discomfort attached to the clients served by the workers. A hospice unit may be more succeptible to extreme closure than a pediatrics unit. A residential program for sexually abused women may be more prone to closure than an educational program for displaced homemakers seeking entry into the job market. A community mental health center may be more prone to closure than a Y.M.C.A.

4.4   The Disengaged Organizational Family

The disengaged organizational family represents the opposite pole from the enmeshed organizational family. The high boundary permeability, and at times the almost absence of an organizational boundary creates a high level of external interaction and a low level of cohesiveness between organizational members. Other characteristics often shared by disengaged organizational families include the following:

- The absence of a clear sense of mission or goals that bind members together.
- High levels of rationality; low levels of emotional bonding and disclosure.
- Explicitly defined norms and rules.
- Compartmentalization of work resulting in low levels of internal interaction and interdependence.
- Many invisible organizational family members who have been "retired on the job".
- Low level of organizational identity (the whole organizational family is rarely all together in one place).
- Leadership often not physically present in the organizational family or erratically involved.
- Expectations for narrowly prescribed role performance.
- Minimal expectations for loyalty or emotional commitment.

The prototype of the disengaged organizational family system can be found in a large, complex and aging federal or state civil service agency. Many large and complex bureaucracies would fall at the disengaged end of the organizational family continuum.

4.5   The Self-regulated Organizational Family

The enmeshed and disengaged organizational family systems hold in common a rigid and fixed position on the continuum of organizational closure. Neither possesses the flexibility to move forward and backward on the continuum in response to changing needs. It's as if history and inertia have cemented these organizations into a fixed path that allows no deviation or renegotiation on direction.

Between these two poles on the continuum lies the self-regulated organizational family. This organizational type moves back and forth on the closure continuum rarely staying at any point on the continuum for any extended period of time. The self-regulated organizational family is like a living organism constantly shifting and adapting based on changing needs inside the system and based on responses to the changes in the ecosystem outside the organizational family.

The self-regulated organizational family is characterized by the following:

- Changing boundary permeability controlled by organizational leaders.
- Conscious regulation of gatekeeping functions that provides changing degrees of openness/closure.
- Organizational climate seeks balance between smothering intimacy of enmeshed system and the isolation and detachment of the disengaged system.
- Decentralization of power and authority.
- Organizational values and rules explicit but open to negotiation as needs and conditions change.

The most important quality of the self-regulated organizational family is the flexibility to alter boundary permeability to increase the degree of openness or closure. The author will suggest throughout the remainder of this book that such flexibility has a profound impact on the health, vitality, and survivability of the organization and an equally profound impact on the health of organizational family members.

Additional details on the self-regulated organizational family will be explored in the last two chapters of this book when the author discusses interventions to address the more destructive aspects of the enmeshed and disengaged organizational systems.

4.6   The Organization With Mixed Characteristics

Before proceeding into a more detailed analysis of the impact of system closure on the health of the organizational family system and its members, it should be noted that some organizations possess characteristics of both enmeshed and disengaged systems. Some complex organizations, for example, may be broken into departments or divisions, each of which could be described as an enmeshed organizational family. Yet this same organization when looked at as a total system could be described as a disengaged organizational family system.

This point has important implications for our later discussion of system interventions. Strategies in intervening with enmeshed and disengaged organizational families involve moving the organizations away from their polarized positions toward what we have described as the self-regulated family. This is accomplished by altering boundary transactions and increasing or decreasing organizational closure. In an organizational system with mixed characteristics, however, one may need a two-fold strategy, such as moving the overall organization toward more closure while moving the departments toward greater openness.

4.7 The Role Of Boundary Transactions In Organizational / Individual Burnout

The highest incidence of stress-related symptoms, and particularly the incidence of stress-related staff casualties, occurs at each end of the continuum of organizational family closure. A significant relationship exists between the frequency and intensity of boundary transactions and the health of the organizational family and its individual members.

One can find considerable theoretical support for this relationship in the body of knowledge on family systems. If we assume the parallel between family dynamics and organizational dynamics, let's explore what recent literature reveals about individual and relationship dysfunction in enmeshed and disengaged nuclear family systems.

A large number of family theorists and therapists have examined the role of closure as it relates to family health. All of the following concepts were developed by the authors to describe dysfunctional aspects of the closed family system.

- Enmeshment (Minuchin, 1967).
- Fusion (Bowen, 1966).
- Undifferentiated Family Ego Mass (Bowen, 1960).
- Cross-Generation Joining (Haley, 1963).
- Too Richly Cross-Joined System (Hoffman, 1967).
- Family Group Pathology (Schaffer, 1964).
- Connectedness (Hess and Handel, 1959).
- Pseudo-Mutuality (Wynne, 1958).
- Consensus-Sensitive Families (Reiss, 1971).
- Binding (Stierlin, 1974).
- Centripetal Force (Stierlin, 1974).
- Cohesion (Olson, 1979).

All of the above authors would point out that there are times when closure in the family system is healthy and essential. The addition or loss of a family member, for example, requires that the family reduce outside transactions, and come together to redefine itself. The family system, however, that remains fixed at the extreme end of the closure continuum will produce a high level of family and individual dysfunctions. A rigidly closed family system may respond admirably to the needs of an infant only to have that same closure become dysfunctional as the child reaches adolescence and must accomplish major developmental tasks outside the family.

The same principle applies to organizational family systems. The closure required to successfully start an organization from scratch, if continued indefinitely, may undermine the health of organizational family members and sow the seeds for the eventual destruction of the organization.

Family therapists have also noted the high rate of disturbance in the disengaged family system. Where pathology develops out of the enmeshed family from too much intimacy and cohesion, pathology in the disengaged family emerges from too little cohesion and intimacy between family members. The following concepts were developed by family theorists and therapists to elucidate the dysfunctional aspects of the disengaged family.

- Disengagement (Minuchin, 1967).
- Centrifugal Force (Stierlin, 1974).
- Emotional Divorce (Bowen, 1960).

51

- Pseudo-Hostility (Wynne, 1958).
- Schism (Lidz, 1957).
- Skew (Lidz, 1957).

Whereas the enmeshed family may thwart the growth and developmental separation of family members, the disengaged family does not provide sufficient bonding or boundaries to assist family members to meet intimacy needs, develop a value system, or master other key developmental tasks.

In a parallel vein, the disengaged organizational family creates a number of high stress role conditions yet offers few opportunities for relationships or supports to balance such stressors. Many of the role stress conditions that typify the disengaged organizational family will be described in Chapter Nine.

While the author has outlined the continuum from enmeshed to disengaged organizational families, the major emphasis of this book will be on describing the dynamics in the enmeshed organizational family. To simplify terms, the enmeshed organization will be described simply as the closed organizational family. The term "closure" will be used to describe the movement of an organization toward decreased boundary transactions and increased intimacy between organizational family members.

4.8   Incest In The Organizational Family

Hoffman (1976) has reviewed both animal and human studies of incestuous behavior that revealed incest occurring in those situations where the natural developmental separation of family members failed to occur, thus leaving the family unit as the sole arena for the expression of sexual behavior. One finds in the normal family a unique combination of social intimacy and sexual distance between family members. In contrast, the incestuous family combines social bonding (over-connectedness) with sexual intimacy between members. A significant amount of incestuous behavior can thus be viewed as one of the last stages in the progressive closure of a family system.

It was with the above understanding developed in counseling work with closed family systems, including cases of consummated incest, that the author began to see a remarkable similarity between staff dynamics in health and human service agencies and those dynamics seen in these closed family systems. Research on severe burnout casualties by the author only provided further evidence of the relationship between system dysfunction and staff burnout. The conceptual schema used to describe this relationship begins with defining the concept of organizational incest.

Organizational Incest is a Stage in the Life of an Organization Marked by Members Increasingly Meeting Their Personal, Professional, Social and Sexual Needs Inside the Organization.

The next three chapters, will describe the professional, social and sexual closure that can occur in the organizational family. The highlights of this closure process are illustrated in Exhibit 4-C. The next chapters will support the following contentions.

- Stress-related behavior of workers can be viewed as a symptom of organizational system dysfunction just as the psychopathology of an individual can be viewed as a symptom of disturbance in the nuclear family system.
- Workers can sustain themselves in high stress work environments over time only through sources of support and replenishment outside the work setting.
- The closure of an organizational system increases stressors, reduces internal supports, and decreases the ability of workers to develop and sustain sources of support and replenishment outside of the organization.
- Much of what has been called "burnout" is behavior symptomatic of closure in the organizational family system.
- Strategies to address stress and burnout and strategies to address the internal organizational problems in these closed systems will fail if they are unable to reverse the progression of organizational closure.

EXHIBIT 4-C
The Progression of Organizational Closure

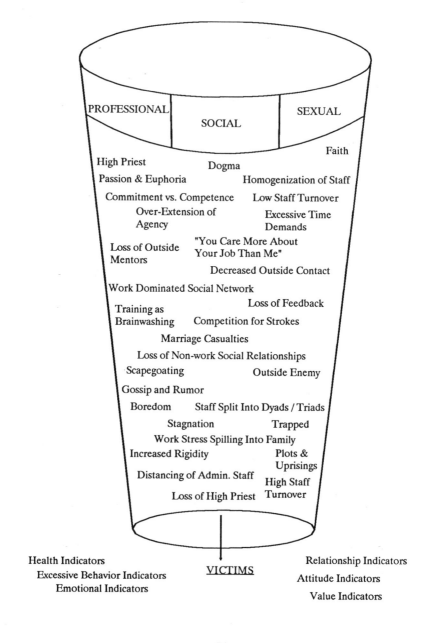

PROFESSIONAL
SOCIAL
SEXUAL

Faith

High Priest   Dogma

Passion & Euphoria   Homogenization of Staff

Commitment vs. Competence   Low Staff Turnover

Over-Extension of   Excessive Time
Agency   Demands

Loss of Outside   "You Care More About
Mentors   Your Job Than Me"

Decreased Outside Contact

Work Dominated Social Network

Training as   Loss of Feedback
Brainwashing   Competition for Strokes

Marriage Casualties

Loss of Non-work Social Relationships

Scapegoating   Outside Enemy

Gossip and Rumor

Boredom   Staff Split Into Dyads / Triads

Stagnation   Trapped

Work Stress Spilling Into Family

Increased Rigidity   Plots &
     Uprisings
Distancing of Admin. Staff   High Staff

Loss of High Priest   Turnover

VICTIMS

Health Indicators   Relationship Indicators

Excessive Behavior Indicators   Attitude Indicators

Emotional Indicators   Value Indicators

Chapter Five
Professional Closure

This chapter will further explore the contention that high incidence of professional burnout can be a reflection of the progressive closure of the organizational family system. Professional closure begins with the assumption that all the professional needs of staff can be met inside the boundary of the organizational family. This closure is evidenced by a reduced contact with persons and institutions outside the family system and a rather predictable progression of problems and experiences that emerge as a result of the closure process.

It is not unusual for a program being organized, reorganized or faced with some major organizational crisis to close itself off from the outside world. Such closure may be necessary for the survival of the organization and the emotional safety of organizational family members. The flexibility and ability to move toward closure in appropriate situations is one mark of a healthy organization. Most organizations, however, also possess the flexibility to shift toward greater openness as needs dictate. This openness reflects the need of the program to further evolve itself based on changes in the outside environment, the needs of organizational members, and, in a service organization, the changing needs of clients.

Many organizations find themselves unable to reverse this closure process. The organization takes on the tone of an overprotective parent sheltering organizational family members from a hostile and threatening world. The "It's us against the world" attitude begins to dominate organizational values and xenophobia-the fear and mistrust of outsiders--becomes a potentially permanent component of the organizational culture. This closure process isolates staff from outside sources of replenishment, increases the physical and emotional demands upon staff, leads to a deterioration in personal and professional relationships, and, in short, sets the stage for individual and organizational burnout.

There were many unique aspects to the closure process of organizations studied by the author. But the most surprising aspect of these studies was the common stages of organizational closure that were repeatedly described by organizations in very diverse fields and geographical settings. The following pages will identify and describe these common stages of organizational closure. It is important that the reader recognize that the onset and full development of these stages of closure are slow (occurring in some cases over an extended number of years) and subtle (phenomenon rarely recognized by organizational family members as crucial events in the life of the organization while they are occurring).

5.1   Dogma And Faith

The first stage of professional closure is the development of a rigid and unchallengeable belief system. Every organization needs a philosophy that communicates the organization's mission, clarifies in broad terms how that mission is to be accomplished, and makes explicit some of the more important values of the organization. In most organizations, the philosophy and its practical applications evolve over time. This evolution occurs due to changes in the external environment, the needs of organizational members, and, in the case of service agencies, the changing needs of the client population. There are, however, situations in the life of an organization where this philosophy gets frozen into a rigid dogma that halts this evolution and refinement of philosophy.

A strong belief system is an integral part of the passion and commitment that characterizes the earliest stages in the creation of an organization. Most belief systems, however, are very time limited. They capture a vision of the needs of a world, a community, or a market and the organization's response to those needs at a fixed point in time. In most organizations, data continues to enter the system that allows the organization to assess these needs as they change and to reformulate the organization's response to these needs. In other organizations, however, this process of evolution and adaptation is missing. The organization gets stuck at its earliest stage of development and the original belief system becomes as rigid and unchallengeable as religious dogma.

This rigid belief system can take many forms. It can be reflected in a company's blind adherence to a single, progressively outdated product line. It can be reflected in the blind acceptance of a single psychological theory through which a counselor will understand and respond to a diverse range of human problems. It can be seen in the selection of narrow marketing approaches upon which a company's future survival depends. It can be seen in the bureaucratic system that is run on tradition and inertia rather than present needs and realities. It can be seen in any organization in which the philosophy or belief system takes on a life and power of its own, unable to be further challenged or changed either by those who created it or those who inherited it.

Nearly all of the closed organizational systems studied by the author were marked by this rigid, unchanging ideology. The mechanisms that served to maintain this rigid belief system include the following:

1. Staff are hired more for commitment to the philosophy than their competence.
2. Staff who challenge the ideology, are extruded from the organizational family.
3. Information that would bring the program philosophy into question is not allowed to enter the system.
4. Staff are allowed limited contact outside the organizational family where they would be exposed to divergent viewpoints.
5. There is a "no-talk" norm that does not allow staff to question any aspect of the philosophy.

5.2   The Director As High Priest / Priestess

When an organization becomes organized around a rigid ideology, the function of the leader changes from the role of manager to the role of high priest/priestess. In looking back over my leadership role in a number of closed systems, my primary function had very little to do with management as it is understood today. My primary functions were to:

- Reinforce and maintain faith in the ideology among organizational family members.
- Establish organizational family member loyalty through personal charisma.
- Tie member self-esteem to the message "you are important because you are part of us".

57

- Provide rituals that allow staff to reaffirm and recommit themselves to the philosophy.
- Preach the faith in the community.
- Serve as the walking embodiment and role model of the program philosophy in my personal and professional life.

The high priest/priestess role may be chosen by an organizational leader as a preferred management style, but more often than not, it slowly emerges out of the collective needs of the organizational family. While any organization during its creation, reorganization, or some other crisis period may temporarily need the role of high priest/priestess, the role becomes fixed in the closed organization. This role, as we will see later, has ominous long range repercussions both on the health of the leader and organizational family members.

5.3 Euphoria

The author would be remiss if he described all of the stages of organizational closure as if they were experienced negatively. The most exhilarating professional experiences of one's life can be experienced in the closure required to build a new organization or program. The early months, and even years, in a closed organizational family system may be experienced more as euphoria than pain. The following remark from a taped interview with a burnout casualty in the substance abuse field illustrates this point:

> I was working 60 to 80 hours per week and loving it. I loved the adrenalin, the knowledge that I was essential to the program, the feeling of commitment, the fantasy that I was the program....It was like a fix - I couldn't get enough or get free of it. I'd go to a movie and find myself making mental lists of what I needed to do the next day. I would be eating dinner and jump to the phone to handle some minor detail I had forgotten. I'd stop by and see other staff of an evening and always talk about (the program). Nothing outside could compete with the sense of excitement I felt during this early period.

All the conditions in the closed organizational family that produce euphoria - the intense bonding of staff, the passion and commitment, etc. - have their darker side when the closure process continues over an extended period of time.

5.4   Homogenization Of Staff

As the organization becomes more closed, staff begin to look more and more like one another. This "sameness" may be based on age, sex, race, lifestyle, etc., but almost always entails the selection of staff with very homogeneous value systems - values that will not conflict with the program ideology.

Open systems tend to create a very heterogeneous staff mix - staff of different ages, levels of experience, cultural and religious backgrounds, working styles, etc. Such heterogeneity helps keep the system open by assuring a divergence of perspectives, ideas, and approaches to problem solving.

Closed systems tend to keep out and/or expel that which is different. Persons in the closed system who are an isolate, e.g., only women, only black, etc., are in high danger of becoming scapegoats and extruded from the organization. This scapegoating process escalates the closure process by eliminating those people who are most likely to inject new ideas and change into the organization. Sameness is reinforced by selecting only staff with similar value systems - a practice assured where almost all new staff hired are from the existing professional and social network of the existing staff. As the organizational family gets increasingly closed, the homogenization may be further intensified by recruiting staff primarily from the extended organizational family, e.g., spouses and other intimate partners, clients, board members, consultants, volunteers, etc.

This homogenization contributes to the further closure of the organizational family by shutting off the flow of new ideas and approaches that inevitably occur in a staff with diverse life experiences. During the early stage of closure, this convergence of staff values and experiences may contribute to group cohesiveness and productivity. As time goes on, however, such convergence leads to the loss of learning, professional stagnation, and feelings of being trapped.

5.5   Commitment Versus Competence

As the organizational family becomes increasingly closed, commitment to the program ideology takes on a higher value than competence both in the evaluation of existing staff and the recruitment of new staff. During one of my tenures as high priest of a residential chemical dependency program, my primary concern in hiring new staff was my judgment of a candidate's anticipated loyalty and commitment to the program. Given a choice between a highly committed candidate and a highly competent candidate, loyalty was consistently chosen over knowledge and skills. There were even times when the highly skilled candidate with broad experience was avoided in favor of a candidate who "would fit into the team" better and who could be trained (socialized) to the program's particular belief system.

As the belief in program ideology becomes more passionately valued in the organizational family, there develops a no-talk norm related to an open questioning of the ideology. In some settings, this no-talk rule is even extended to the point that any criticism of the organization, no matter how constructive, is seen as an act of disloyalty and a personal betrayal of organizational leaders.

5.6   The Making Of A Workaholic

Another common attribute flowing from the professional incest dynamic is the insatiable demands for time and energy upon organizational family members. When a group is involved in an impassioned cause, e.g., a new treatment approach, there are few limits to the expectations placed on members. Most of the closed systems studied by the author had not clearly defined what the organization could and could not accomplish with existing resources. As a result, the organization often ended up trying to "be all things to all people". Staff as a result of this lack of definition either had no job descriptions or had written descriptions which bore little resemblance to their daily activities. The over-extension of individual staff is often merely a reflection of the over-extension of the agency.

The personality of the over-achiever has been extensively cited in the literature on burnout, but little recognition has been given to the organization's responsibility for promoting over-extension of individual members. Consider the following scenario:

> Jane was a superstar while in treatment in a therapeutic community for drug abuse, having completed treatment and moved into a staff position in sixteen months. Over the next two years she took on increasing responsibilities within the treatment center, and it appeared there was no limit to the amount of energy she was willing to devote to the program. During the third year, she began to have a number of physical problems, began to drink heavily, and had repeated "inappropriate" emotional outbursts during confrontations with other staff. She was subsequently hospitalized following an extended drinking episode, resigned her position, and accepted a sales job in her home state. Staff discussions of Jane's situation resembled a clinical review, i.e., "maybe she should have stayed in treatment longer", descriptions of the personality traits that caused her problems, and an "it's really too bad what happened" attitude.

What's missing in the above description is the classic double bind that Jane had been working under for three years. This double bind can be summarized as follows:

1. "You need to slow down and take it easy." ⟷ Increased work responsibilities
    "Give it to Jane, she'll get it done."
    Promises of promotions if the quality (and quantity) of her work is continued.

2. "Why don't you get away for a weekend and visit some friends." ⟵ "I'm sorry Jane, but can you cover the house this weekend? Bob has to go out of town for a funeral."

3. "You need to get a boy friend and some friends that don't work here." ⟵ Scheduled hours and responsibilities left little time, let alone energy, to develop outside of work relationships.

Double binds, like the above, in families, will not uncommonly produce schizophrenia; double binds in the organizational family produce a variety of dysfunctional behaviors that in the aggregate are simply called burnout. Professional incest creates an atmosphere where program interests and ideologies take precedence over human needs, and staff are used and expended in a no deposit/no return fashion.

5.7 Professional Closure And Marriage Casualties

The author has been particularly concerned in his studies as to how the stress one experiences in the work setting spills over and begins to produce a deterioration in the quality of intimate relationships outside the work setting. The over-extension of staff, which is part of the professional incest dynamic, takes its toll in marriage casualties. The incestuous dynamic produces a domino effect. Increased demands and commitment to the organizational family results in decreased energy into marriage and nuclear family relationships. Increased time with organizational family results in decreased energy into marriage and nuclear family relationships. Increased time with organizational family results in decreased time investment in nuclear family. Spouse demands for minimal participation in the marriage increase feelings of inadequacy, and may result in increased escape into the organizational family. The stage is then set for the development of social and sexual relationship between staff who provide each other transient respite from the spouses "who don't understand" them.

Most marriage casualties in closed organizational systems break up with little awareness of how sources outside the marriage have served to drive a wedge in the relationship. It was with a great deal of sadness that many of the persons interviewed in the author's studies looked back after many years finally to see that the conflict in their marriage was exacerbated beyond toleration by outside forces and not by the basic quality of the marital relationship. The frequently heard comment from spouses - "you care more about your job than you care about our marriage" - typifies the torn loyalties for time and emotional energy experienced by members of the closed organizational family.

5.8   The Loss Of Outside Contact

As noted earlier, systems become closed through a decrease in boundary transactions. In the progressive closure of the organizational family, staff begin to lose direct contact with the outside professional world, and there is a decrease in the number of persons bringing new ideas and approaches from the outside. This decrease in boundary transactions takes such forms as those described below:

- There is a decreased access to outside training, usually justified through lack of appropriate budget dollars for this activity.
- Only persons who support the program ideology are brought in from outside for training or consultation. Staff orientation and in service training take on the flavor of a religious ritual or pep rally rather than a focus on skill and knowledge attainment.
- There is decreased contact with one's professional peers through a progressive loss of relationships with other organizations performing similar work. This is justified via extremely judgmental indictments of other organizations (particularly competitors) and professionals. One manager, interviewed by the author after his closed organizational family had just gone through some horribly painful disruptions, stated this stage very articulately when he said: "In retrospect, I think our problems began when we stopped building bridges and started building walls". This manager had summarized in one sentence the three years of progressive isolation that left his program looking more like a cult than a human service organization. For some types of organizations, this isolation may lead to the very death of the organization. The author has seen numerous health and social service agencies become so closed - loss of contact with referral sources and the community at large - that clients couldn't even get into the system. To companies whose survival depends on the marketing of goods and services, such isolation may spell the demise of the organization.

- Staff involvement with professional associations tends to be discouraged, or at least, not encouraged. The high priest or other significant organizational family figures attend regional/national conferences and return to tell staff what's going on in the outside world. Such communication usually involves a filtering process through which any information that conflicts with program ideology is deleted. Some systems may be so closed that staff are not even aware of the existence of outside professional organizations.

This isolation of organizational family members is controlled by gatekeepers - those persons in the organizational family who control who, when, and under what conditions outsiders enter the system and insiders have contact outside.

The importance of this isolation is that all the professional needs of staff must be met inside the organizational family. An individual's professional identity is shaped and maintained inside his/her work setting. When one's professional identity is tied to one organization, vulnerability to professional burnout increases dramatically. The closed organizational family increases this vulnerability by cutting off sources of professional replenishment outside the organization.

This isolation of staff from outside professional and social relationships has particularly dramatic effects for those workers in the human service field working to return clients to more functional roles in their families, neighborhoods, schools, places of employment, etc. We all too often cloister ourselves into professional and social communes barricaded from the outside world and boldly challenge our clients to re-enter the life of communities with which we have long ago lost touch.

5.9   Insulation From Feedback

The loss of outside contact - decreased transactions across the organizational family system boundary - is part of an overall pattern of reduced feedback available to produce change.

Feedback from the community is reduced due to the organization's isolation. As social closure occurs, the whole world of organizational family members begins to revolve around the work setting, further cutting off ties and relationships in the community. Feedback that does reach the program is rationalized away usually by an attack on the source.

Internal feedback is also reduced as the "no-talk" rule about organizational problems becomes the norm. Staff feedback may be written off as a personality conflict, problems experienced by the staff outside of work, etc. In service programs, such as psychiatric or substance abuse services, feedback from clients is explained away clinically through such jargon as "they're testing boundaries", "the client is manipulating", "client is resistant", etc. What all these mechanisms have in common is that the feedback is discouraged, discounted, and explained away so that the factual content contained in the feedback is never addressed to make needed changes in the system.

5.10   The Competition For Strokes

A major premise of this book is that if people are to sustain themselves in high-stress work environments, they must have a network of personal, professional, social and sexual replenishment separate and distinct from the work environment. The closed organizational family breaks down the boundary between personal and work life and decreases one's ability to get replenishment outside the organization. As organizational family members lose these replenishment networks, they become depleted physically and emotionally in the high-stress work environment. This depletion radically alters the availability, frequency, and distribution of strokes (personal affirmations) in the organizational family.

In a relatively open system with replenished staff, strokes are frequent and reciprocal. Its a very simple proposition that says: when I feel good, its very natural and easy for me to feel good about you and express those feelings in verbal acknowledgments. The converse is equally true. When I am depleted and needy, it is unlikely that I can recognize and express my appreciation of you.

In the closed organizational family, the depletion of staff leads to diminished availability of strokes. In the closed organization, strokes are competitive rather than reciprocal. Given the small number of available strokes, the acknowledgment of one person triggers jealousy and resentment in others. It's the assumption that if you're recognized, I won't be. While such an assumption may be the irrational belief of an individual, in the closed organizational family, this assumption may have factual basis.

The competition for strokes further breaks down trust. This once very happy, cohesive organizational family can begin exhibiting such defensive behaviors as:

- Preoccupation with turf (office size, furniture, equipment, etc.) and status (titles, favored relationship with high priest, office location, etc.).
- Demeaning other staff (If they go down the pecking order list, I will inevitably move up).
- Shift to "what can I get for me" attitude, e.g., resentments about salary differences between staff.

5.11   Mirroring, Boredom, And Loss Of Faith

The progressive closure in the organizational family will eventually begin to reveal signs of stagnation in the passion and commitment that marked the early stages of closure. This is inevitable in the closed system. As time goes on, there is a loss of learning in the organization due to the decrease of new knowledge and information into the system.

Loss of new ideas produces a phenomenon called "mirroring" where the intense socialization of staff produces a group of individuals who tend to mirror one another - sharing similar ways of thinking and speaking. Have you ever looked at how members of your organization communicate on key issues and felt that staff took turns spouting the party line - words and phrases that reflect program philosophy? Have you ever sat with a group of co-workers and felt you could predict almost word for word how each person would respond to any question? Have you ever looked back over a period of months and felt like you were in a rut - speaking and performing like a robot with little creative energy or independent thinking involved in your work? Such experiences are common during this stage of organizational closure.

5.12 Burnout As The Loss Of Learning

One aspect of burnout experienced by organizational family members in the closed system is simply the loss of learning. This loss of learning leads to boredom and a very mechanical approach to job performance. Mirroring and boredom lead to a personal and professional crisis as individual workers begin to experience a loss of faith in the program philosophy. It's as if staff begin to see, for the first time, flaws in the philosophy and methods of the organization. Once this questioning of program philosophy begins to be talked about, the loss of faith may be a very contagious process in the organization.

Mirroring, boredom, and loss of faith mark a critical stage in the life of the closed organizational family system. Some organizations use the crisis of loss of faith to open the system and to clarify the mission, goals, methods, and values of the organization and to abort the closure process. Such organizations use the crisis to improve the overall health and vitality of the organization by opening and redefining the structure   and process of the organizational family. For organizations who do not utilize the crisis in this manner, loss of faith marks the beginning of turbulence and increased staff casualties.

5.13 Trapped

It is only natural when one experiences a loss of faith to think about leaving the organization. People experience this all the time and often follow through this thinking by changing jobs without any major personal trauma. This transition, however, is more complicated in the closed organizational family.

There is no guilt-free way to leave a closed organizational family. The issue of allegiance and loyalty is so powerful that leaving is viewed as a betrayal of the high priest/priestess and organizational family members. Many persons who express their dissatisfaction, will be manipulated to stay in the system by promises from the high priest of changing conditions, economic rewards, etc.

As staff members have lost sources of replenishment outside the organization and experienced the emotional depletion from

67

excessive time and emotional demands, their confidence and self-esteem may have deteriorated to the point they question their marketability in other programs. This is complicated further for some workers who have been with the organization long enough that they find it difficult to find another job at a comparable salary. This is particularly true where family/financial obligations will not allow a decrease in salary. Workers in this situation may feel like their very souls have been bought.

The inability of persons to get out of the closed organizational family is obvious by looking at turn-over rates. There is a certain irony in this issue as high staff turnover is associated with burnout. The author has been told repeatedly, "We don't have a problem of burnout here; our staff turnover is almost zero". The fact is, no turn-over is as much an indicator of burnout as excessively high turn-over. Open organizational families have a fairly predictable rate of staff change. Such turn-over is desirable in terms of both professional advancement of staff and the introduction of new ideas and approaches into the organization through new members. In contrast, turn-over in the closed system is extremely low until later stages of closure when there is a contagion of turn-over that may threaten the very existence of the organization.

The emotional and financial chains that keep staff members bound to the organizational family create feelings of being trapped and cornered without choices. The awareness of this loss of choices tends to escalate the experience of burnout in the closed system.

5.14 Projection And Scapegoating

We are at a point in the closure of the organizational family where workers begin to feel something has been lost in the program and start verbalizing feelings of boredom, being "trapped" and their need to "get out". Many of these feelings of disillusionment reflect a wearing down of the collective physical and emotional energy of staff due to excessive time and emotional demands and the loss of outside replenishment.

During this early period of low morale, the stage is set for the selection of an outside enemy or the sacrifice of a victim from within the organizational family.

In the first case, worker dissatisfaction is projected and blamed on an outside person or organization. This outside enemy could be a funding source, a competing program, a regulatory body, a key person or persons on the board, persons who have been critical of the organization in the community, etc. The projection takes the form of extreme preoccupation as indicated by the amount of time spent communicating about the outside enemy. In one organization known to the author ninety per cent of staff meetings for a six to nine month period consisted of stories about the incompetence of the state agency that funded and regulated the program. This blaming helps diffuse some of the pent-up emotion in the organizational family but diverts the family's attention from directly confronting serious internal problems.

The organizational family may also discharge this pent-up emotion on one of its own members. In this situation, a member takes on the role of scapegoat within the organizational family thus providing a needed diversion from much more painful issues within the family. Like the outside enemy, the preoccupation with the scapegoat can expend an enormous amount of time and emotional energy of the organizational family. The intensity of the scapegoating process is in direct proportion to the intensity of the pent-up emotion in the organizational family. Where such pent-up emotion is excessive, the scapegoat may be very painfully extruded from the organization. The scapegoat becomes an untouchable as there is an implicit expectation that staff will break all personal relationships with the scapegoat. When extrusion occurs, there is an aftermath of guilt in the organizational family as members slowly realize that many of the problems they had blamed on the scapegoat continue in the scapegoat's absence. Since the organization won't allow mourning the scapegoat, the scapegoat becomes a ghost that haunts the organizational family. The scapegoating process also increases member's perception of their own vulnerability in the organizational family, e.g., "if it happened to_; it can happen to me." It is my experience that this increased sense of personal vulnerability is a healthy warning sign. The early scapegoats are the first of what can become a long series of personal casualties in the incestuous organizational family.

One reason this casualty process escalates is that the system becomes even more closed following the scapegoating process.

The scapegoats are often the most differentiated from the organizational family system - most likely to introduce new ideas, challenge organizational family norms, break no-talk rules, etc. The loss of the scapegoats thus makes the group even more homogenous and decreases the probability that other staff will want to openly address problems or challenge family norms.

Projection and scapegoating begin to alter the emotional climate within the organizational family. Fear and paranoia dominate the emotional content of the family until the feelings of anger and rage work their way to the surface.

5.15 Fear And Paranoia

Scapegoating breaks the tradition of trust in the organizational family. Members begin to perceive themselves as potential victims and begin taking on protective behaviors. This period, vividly described by persons interviewed by the author as "cover your ass time," is marked by such behaviors as:

- Consciously lining up coalitions of support.
- Memos to record - documenting situations, decisions, etc. in case such written documentation is needed for one's defense.
- Decreased activity and decreased decision-making due to fear of mistakes.

Many of these fears are undefined but are reflected in such worker comments as: "It's like a sense of impending doom looming over our heads", "There's so much tension. I just feel like things are going to explode", "I keep having this dream of needing to run away before something happens," etc.

5.16 Plots, Conspiracies, And Revolts

The slow, subtle process of organizational closure described so far may have transpired over a number of years. In brief review, the program has organized itself around a rigid belief system, become increasingly isolated, gone through a period of almost euphoric missionary zeal, and workers have begun to experience a loss of faith and disillusionment. Staff have become physically and emotionally depleted and are experiencing some increased conflict within the team. Much of the turmoil in the system has existed as an undercurrent. We are now at a stage where this undercurrent is going to break into open conflict.

The organization is now like a bubbling cauldron. When you mix in the ingredients of personal turmoil over the loss of faith in the program, guilt over scapegoated members, loss of professional self-esteem, unresolved resentments, and all the problems of social and sexual closure in the organization (described in the next two chapters), we have an organization ripe for revolution.

The "no-talk" rule related to serious organizational problems is finally broken and conflict breaks into the open. The shape this conflict takes varies widely from organization to organization. Some of the more common variations I have seen include the following:

- A scapegoated (fired) organizational family member makes public countercharges toward the organization and its leaders. Charges may range from embezzlement to gross incompetence to sexual abuse of clients.
- Following months of whispered hallway conversations and secret meetings, a number of organizational family members suddenly and dramatically leave to create a new company or program in competition with the program they are leaving. The history of many consulting firms the author worked with in Washington, D.C., can be traced to such splits in closed organizational families. The zeal of the new organization is fueled more as an act of violence and vengeance than through any entrepreneurial spirit.
- The Director (high priest) is scapegoated internally through open conflict, isolation or sabotage.
- There may be efforts to overthrow the high priest - most often taking the form of secret meetings with board members, funding and regulatory agencies, etc.

71

The high priest becomes a blotter upon which past years of unresolved emotion are projected. The high priest, who has participated in scapegoating of other organizational members, becomes the scapegoat.

5.17 "The Infinite Dance Of Shifting Coalitions"

The conspiracies and open conflict create a tremendously high level of anxiety at a time staff have few supports to handle such tension. There may be constant pressure to choose sides as issues get polarized. There may be a rupture in long standing personal and professional relationships in the program. Staff may be confused by powerful feelings of ambivalence (from rage to deep love and appreciation) toward the high priest and other organizational family members.

As feelings of fear and personal vulnerability increase in this situation, staff take on a number of self-protective defenses. One of the most common defensive patterns, witnessed by the author, is the constant shifting of supportive dyads and triads in the system - a pattern Bateson has described in nuclear families under conflict as "the infinite dance of shifting coalitions". This phrase graphically pictures the constantly changing dyads and triads used to generate transient support and to exchange gossip and rumor. One way to monitor the passage of this organizational crisis is through the reduction in this rapid turn-over of coalitions, and the return to a more stable position of relationships within the system.

5.18 External Recognition; Internal Chaos

It is surprising that the time of the worst internal problems in the closed organizational family may coincide with the organization's greatest external recognition. The isolation of the organization provides a certain level of protection as very little of the internal workings of the organization, particularly related to areas where problems are present, is made known to outsiders. There is also a preoccupation in the closed organizational family that the family look good to outsiders. Very elaborately conceived pageants are prepared to impress outsiders with the work of the organization. A tour of the organization by an outsider is handled like a well-rehearsed play - props well prepared, lines well executed, a good range of emotion expressed, all building to a dramatic climax and the exit of an impressed visitor from the stage. This description is not to imply that the organization is consciously misrepresenting itself. It is simply to portray the frequent incongruence in the external image and the internal reality of the closed organizational family.

A dramatic example of this incongruence occurred in a residential drug treatment program in the early 1970's. The program received a state agency award for outstanding addiction services in the state during a time when the soap opera atmosphere and incestuous organizational dynamics had seriously compromised the quality of client care.

5.19 Increased Program Rigidity

As conditions become more turbulent in the closed organizational family, there is an attempt to administratively tighten the structure to get things back under control. Organizational leaders may take a punitive response to staff they feel are undermining their authority and challenging basic tenants of the program philosophy. Increased program rigidity may also take the form of adding new rules and policies governing staff behavior. This stage is reminiscence of a quote once heard by the author: "The last act of a dying organization is a thicker rulebook". The need for rules to control staff marks a dramatic change in mutual respect, loyalty and the *espirit de corps* that characterized earlier stages of organizational life.

5.20 The Distancing Of Administrative Staff

Through the process of closure, and particularly through the stage of open conflict, the high priest may be experiencing his or her own disillusionment with the program and staff. It is a period in which the high priest is emotionally, and sometimes physically, distancing themselves from other program staff. It is the period that administrative offices may be moved to a location separate from the service facility. More time may be spent by the high priest away from the facilities. The traditionally open door is more often than not closed. More middle management positions may be created to serve as a buffer between staff and the high priest. Informal verbal communication is replaced by more formal chain-of-command communication - a period one person interviewed by the author described as the time of "memo-mania".

Where the early periods of organizational closure may have met everyone's needs, we are now at a time when almost no one's needs are being effectively met in the organization. We have set the stage for a major crisis in the life of the organization - the period when the closed system breaks open.

5.21   The Break-up Of The Organizational Family

During the extreme stages of prolonged organizational closure, there are powerful forces that are beginning to propel the organization to a crisis. It's as if the collective energy of the organizational family has been consumed, and the system cannot sustain itself as currently constituted. Catalogued below are some of the more common scenarios that occur as a result of the organizational crisis.

Variation # 1: The system may use the crisis to re-evaluate and redefine norms and change the structure of the organizational family. In short, the crisis forces an opening of the system. This process can be highly volatile as organizational family members are brought together to address their problems and experiences in the organization. The volatility stems primarily from the pent-up emotion generated by the no-talk norm. The collective expiation of anger, resentment, guilt, etc., although risky (there can be further casualties if not handled carefully), can break the organizational impasse. The organization can redefine itself, re-negotiate relationships and address current needs of organizational family members. This process may create an even stronger organization that is fueled not by zeal but by the collective maturity and wisdom that has come from surviving the closure process. Even though no one may have conceptualized the role of closure in the organizational problems, the open confrontation of current problems and needs instinctively creates remediation strategies that open the system. The organization defines more realistically what it can and cannot do; outsiders are brought into help with some of the problems; staff are given more access to outside training and professional development resources; etc. Later chapters will detail how to facilitate this healing and reorganization process.

<u>Variation 2</u>: The organizational family may cease to exist. The turmoil may be such that decisions are made to go out of business. Probably a more common experience is that decisions and activities crucial to the survival of the organization are not completed or are mismanaged. Everyone in this turbulent period is looking for a guilt-free way out of the organization. If the organization no longer exists, everyone has a way out.

Given that the author has spent most of his adult life hustling money for human service programs, I look back in horror at times I secretly wished a grant crucial to the survival of my agency would not get funded. A high priest can set an organization up for self-destruction when such thinking begins to effect key management decisions. Why would the high priest have or carry out such fantasies? Because the high priest also feels trapped and wants a guilt-free way out!

The most dramatic example of the demise of a closed system was the mass suicide at Jonestown. Jonestown represented the ultimate closed system. When the closure of a system was threatened by exposure from outsiders, mass suicide resulted.

The reader interested in a detailed study of the demise of a closed organizational family is encouraged to read Stotland and Kobler's *The Life and Death of a Mental Hospital*.

<u>Variation #3</u>: The program may experience a contagion of staff turnover. Closed systems may go from almost no staff turnover to the loss of more than half the staff in a four to six month time period. In some cases, particularly where the high priest remains, the program will simply reclose around the same ideology, hire and socialize new staff and replicate the closure process described in this chapter.

<u>Variation #4</u>: The high priest may leave or be extruded. In the absence of the high priest, the program is very vulnerable to reclose around another ideology, select a new high priest and continue as in variation #3 to replicate the closure process.

The fate of the closed system (in later stages) is powerfully influenced by the health and maturity of the high priest. Because of the crucial importance of this role and the character of the person who fills it, we will address the fate of the high priest in more depth.

5.22   The Fall Of The High Priest / Priestess

In more open organizational family systems, the health of the family is not totally dependent upon the health of the leader. There are numerous sources of support for organizational members other than the leader. There are checks and balances that limit the leader's ability to make decisions that could be self-destructive to the organization. There are many areas of the organization that may function autonomously with little if any involvement of the leader.

In contrast to the above, the health of the closed system is contingent upon the health of the high priest/priestess. The high priest can self-destruct anywhere along the closure continuum and alter the stages of closure that have been described. The high priest's ability to function is also progressively impaired by the closure process. The isolation of the organizational family also cuts off sources of support for the high priest. In the midst of this loss of replenishment and feedback, it is easy to see how the whole system can get twisted by the high priest's manipulation of the program to meet his or her needs. Given the absence of internal and external feedback, it is easy to see how there can be a vulnerability for sudden changes in beliefs and values. This isolation can result in very bizarre thinking and decision-making by the high priest. Such decisions frequently take the form of changing values and practices that are divergent from existing community values, and values and practices characteristic of the profession.

The author has been particularly struck by the casualty process among leaders of newly emerging health and social service fields, e.g., hospice, alcoholism and drug abuse, services to abused women and children, etc. While organizational closure is detrimental to the caregivers, we may discover, in retrospect, that it is even more devastating to the leaders of such emerging fields. The emergence of a health care field requires a particular kind of leadership, not unlike the leaders that typify most social movements. Such leaders are profoundly commited, seem to have unlimited supplies of personal energy, are exceptionally articulate, and engender a great deal of support through their personal charisma. They are in essence, organizers and revolutionaries who propose a new vision of more humane and responsive care and concern. How then do such leaders respond to their own stress during the years it may take to see their vision come to fruition? Over time, these leaders' professional and social worlds may become smaller and smaller. They may develop small cadres of converts or supporters who uphold their beliefs and offer them ideological support. They may become increasingly disillusioned as they see "maintainers" coming in to stabilize and standardize the field which the leader created. They may lose touch with the care giving process from which they came. Whether as an intellectual leader in the field or as a director of a service program, these leaders may create closed systems in which to insulate themselves. Cut off from outside sources of personal, professional, and social replenishment, the leader must rely on organizational members for support. The leader's image and charisma, however, make it difficult for staff to actively provide support, express affection, and provide constructive feedback. In such virtual isolation, it is little wonder that the leader's ability to function emotionally, socially, and professionally in the field seriously deteriorates.

There are debts we all owe to our intellectual and professional leaders. One method of repayment is to help the leader get "out of role" to receive our personal respect and our constructive feedback. Such support may reduce the leader's need for seeking shelter in a closed system that may prove destructive for us all.

5.23   Professional Closure And Burnout: A Summary

In the studies on burnout conducted by the author in the late 1970's, the individual description of burnout obtained in interviews from burnout victims was compared with the organizational processes that were occurring during this same time period. The conclusion of these studies was that burnout, in many cases, is the reflection of the progressive closure of the organizational family system.

The incestuous dynamic in the organizational family that becomes professionally closed over an extended period of time:

77

- Reduces sources of outside professional replenishment (We can speak of one aspect of the burnout experience as a loss of learning).
- Limits the worker's professional identity to his/her experience in the organizational family (thus increasing the worker's vulnerability during times of conflict).
- Increases the time and emotional demands on organizational family members.
- Increases role stressors.
- Reduces the availability of strokes available to members in the system.
- Escalates the conflict in interpersonal relationship as members compete to have their needs met in the system.
- Fails to provide permissions and procedures for persons to get out of the system.
- Breaks down the boundary between one's work life and one's personal life.
- Sets the stage for the onset of problematic social and sexual relationships between organizational family members.

This chapter described one aspect of the incestuous dynamic - professional closure - that can occur in the organizational family system. The next chapter will detail how professional closure begins to spill over and influence the social relationships of staff outside the work setting.

Chapter Six
Social Closure

Social closure is a stage in the life of an organization in which members meet most, if not all, of their social needs within the boundary of the organizational system. Professional closure begins to break down the boundary between one's personal life and work life, thus setting the stage for social closure. Professional and social closure often happen concurrently within organizational systems. This chapter will review the major stages of social closure and the impact of this closure on organizational members and the system as a whole.

6.1   Healthy Social Contact

The workplace has, and probably always will be, an arena in which human beings meet social as well as professional needs. The quality and intensity of social/interpersonal relationships is an important indicator of organizational health and can provide workers with powerful incentives for continued identification with the organization. Most organizations strive to create a climate in which social relationships within the organization are both personally fulfilling and supportive of the overall mission of the organization. It is important that organizations provide rituals that allow us to socially recognize the entrance and exit of members from the group, celebrate our affection for one another, recognize individual and collective achievement, and affirm our value as people as well as workers.

Given the above, it should be clear to the reader that the author has no intention of implying that all socializing between workers outside the work setting is either undesirable or unhealthy. In many organizations, these social relationships have clear benefits to both the organization as a whole and to those individuals who enjoy and are nourished in such relationships. The concern of the author is not with the existence of social relationships between workers, but how the <u>diversity</u> and <u>intensity</u> of these relationships are changed in closed organizational families. This chapter will demonstrate how the professional and social closure of the organizational family adversely effects the inner-workings of the organization and increases the vulnerability of workers by cutting off sources of replenishment outside of the work setting.

6.2 Euphoria And Camaraderie: Developing A Work Dominated Social Life

During the earliest stages of social closure, members of an organization spend an increasing amount of time together away from work, but continue to focus all of their energy and conversation on work issues. No matter what topics of conversation arise, the subject is quickly pulled back to issues and personalities in the work setting.

Some workers may have very little social network and simply use the development of a work-dominated social network to fill this vacuum. For staff who have an extensive social network, the process is more subtle. As professional closure reduces the time and emotional energy available to maintain these non-work relationships, they begin to fade away. Many of these relationships are lost without conscious decisions having ever been made to terminate the relationships. We just slowly lose contact. This process is further escalated by the increased expectation of staff to participate in staff-related social activities. Other factors that can work to create social closure include:

- Work schedules which decrease one's ability to maintain contact with existing social relationships.
- The lack of structured work time communications between workers which increases outside of work contact to assure completion of one's role responsibilities.
- On-call responsibilities that never allow one to get "out of role" and that frequently intrude upon and disrupt non-work social activities.
- Role overload that requires significant quantities of non-work time to complete job tasks.
- Distrust of outside agencies/competitors that decreases social relationships with professional peers who are not part of the organization.
- Chronic fatigue and exhaustion that reduces interest and energy available for non-work socializing.

Early stages of social closure in which work-oriented social relationships replace non-work relationships, are not experienced negatively by the organization or by those involved. These social relationships affirm the sense of camaraderie between organizational members, fulfill needs for intimacy and social activity, and increase one's feelings of safety and security in the organization.

There are numerous variations to social closure that increase the bonding between organizational members. Some of these variations include:

● Carpooling.
● Rituals of self-medication (staff meeting frequently after work for drinks or dinner, etc.
● Staff migrating to certain neighborhoods in the city to live.
● Staff choosing to live together.
● Staff getting involved in joint business ventures.
● Merging of varied staff interests into a few regular group activities.
● Sub-groups of staff vacationing together.

6.3   Loss Of Faith And The Social Dominated Work Life

Over time work-oriented relationships begin to replace rather than supplement outside social relationships. Even where some contact is maintained with persons away from work, it is the work relationships that become primary by virtue of frequency and intensity of contact.

When this social closure overlaps the loss of faith stage of professional closure, the nature of outside relationships begins to change. There continues to be a high level of staff interaction away from the work setting, but the focus on work in these relationships begins to change. While there may be some continued focus on personalities and politics, much of the interaction shifts away from work issues to the social activities of the organizational family. As a matter of fact, members spend less and less time inside the organization focusing on work due to the increasing focus on what organizational members are doing with one another outside the organization. It's as if the purpose of the organization is to meet the personal and social needs of staff. Relationships within the program can become social to the point that minimal output is generated by staff. As numbers of staff become socially involved on a regular basis, interpersonal relationships between staff can become so enmeshed that staff spend the majority of their time talking about each other and not about the treatment of their clients and other issues related to the organization.

6.4   The Impact Of Social Closure On Individuals

When one's primary social relationships and work relationships become one and the same, one may suffer from (1) the loss of replenishment outside the work setting, (2) the loss of non-work roles that help affirm one's self-esteem and identity, (3) a distortion of personal values, (4) role confusion in one's personal/work relationships and (5) painful role transitions in the organization.

The Loss of Replenishment Health and human service workers face high demands to meet the intense needs of physically and emotionally impaired clients/families. To be able to sustain such giving over time, requires the ability of each worker to have resources of physical, emotional, social, and spiritual replenishment outside the organization. Regularly replenished through these outside resources, the worker can continue to enter the high stress environment and openly respond to the needs of clients. Lacking such replenishment, the worker will continue to give and give until they are physically and emotionally depleted. In this state of depletion, the worker is very likely to either continue giving - a sacrificial process that will produce serious symptoms of impairment in the worker - or to begin to inadvertently exploit relationships with clients and co-workers to address these unmet needs.

It is a tragic irony that we can daily witness health and human service professionals working with clients on the importance of one's own needs, the importance of developing support systems, etc., at the exact time these workers are self-destructing for failing to practice what they are preaching.

The Loss of Non-Work Roles In the last chapter, we saw how professional closure increased one's vulnerability to stress by limiting one's professional identity and work related self-esteem to experiences within the organizational family of which one is a part.

Other professional roles and relationships are cut off. Social closure escalates this vulnerability by cutting off roles one performs outside the professional and social relationships in the organizational family. The increased amount of time staff spend with each other decreases participation in non-work relationships and roles that reaffirm their sense of self, separate from the work environment. This can be particularly troublesome to the workers who may later find themselves isolated and/or scapegoated within the organization. When one's entire social network is work oriented, such sudden isolation or scapegoating can be devastating.

The Whole World's Crazy Health and human service workers are daily confronted with disease and disorder that is usually kept politely hidden from the public at large. From the physical deformity of the diseased or injured to the prolonged exposure to the products of human neglect and abuse, these workers must balance and reconcile the realities of their work with a broader perspective on life. When one's social network becomes totally work dominated, this perspective is lost. One's view of the world becomes increasingly distorted. The whole world begins to look screwed up and one's life seems like a constant confrontation with craziness and pain. During social closure, things begin to look hopeless as we lose our sense of how healthy people conduct their lives. This isolation, along with the physical and emotional exhaustion produced by organizational closure, may create a radical change in one's personal values and beliefs.

Social Closure and Role Confusion Social relationships with co-workers are natural and inevitable, yet in closed systems the boundary confusion between personal relationships and professional relationships can create discomfort and pain. When persons in our social network also hold roles as co-workers, issues or changes in the nature or intensity of these relationships spill over and influence our professional relationships. Conversely, problems in work relationships can spill over and undermine the quality of social relationships outside the work setting. Given the dual nature of these relationships, confusion can occur on the exact nature of the relationship.

These dual relationships can also go through painful transitions. There are numerous instances where professional peer/ primary friendships away from work are shaken by one of the individual's promotion to the role of supervisor over the others. Such transitions leave the new supervisor responding not only to the stress of the new role, but also the grief and isolation produced by the change in relationships.

6.5   The Inversion Process

A process of inversion can occur during the social closure of human service organizations in which the knowledge and skills that are channeled into client services diminish and the process is turned inward by an intense focusing on the personal and interpersonal problems of staff.   There are numerous factors that contribute to this closure process. A prolonged period of exhaustion from the over-extension of staff during professional closure may overwhelm the personal defense structures of the most vulnerable staff. In an agency committed to serving the mental health needs of its clients, you may see staff develop extreme symptoms reflecting severe emotional stress.   The extensive socializing between staff exacerbates and further exposes these symptoms.

The manner in which the organizational family addresses the emotional and relationship problems of its members may be further reflective of the closure process. Some of the most frequent responses are as follows:

- Clinical supervision turns into a therapy relationship, thus further escalating role confusion and the violation of personal intimacy barriers by the organization.
- The troubled staff person goes into treatment with a program consultant or another staff member of the program who maintains a private practice.
- The troubled staff member is extruded from the organization with no recognition of the contributing role of the organizational environment upon the staff member's dysfunction.
- Mini-staff meetings (informal gossip) are conducted on the status of the affected staff member (see the clinical approach to burn-out discussion in Chapter Two).

This inversion process can also permeate the entire organization and create what could be called a "personal growth" phase in the life of the organizational family. This phase is characterized by staff growth groups, process-oriented training, and the organization of the staff around some well-defined growth ideology. This growth ideology can result in the organization taking on the emotional flavor of a religious cult. Marriage casualties are a frequent by-product of this "growth" phase. As staff are caught up in the artificial intimacy of the closed organizational family, they begin to perceive their marriages differently and raise their expectations of these relationship e.g., "new heights of interpersonal awareness", "communication", "intimacy", "openness", etc. The fact that the social group of the staff is closed provides little perspective on "non-growth" oriented relationships. Marriages become work - a constant processing of feelings and issues. When expectations can't be met, spouses are discarded (often with the support of the organizational family) rather than adjusting expectations. Spouses are sacrificed so that the ideology and values of the organizational family will not be challenged. This collective disillusionment with intimate relationships outside the organizational family also increases the probability of members developing sexual relationships with the other organizational family members e.g., "our spouses don't understand us (we've outgrown them), but we understand each other, therefore...".

6.6   The Impact Of Social Closure Upon The Organization

In a healthy organization, status of members is related to the commitment, knowledge, skills and day-to-day performance one applies to the achievement of the mission and goals of the organization. Social closure disrupts this process. Status and rewards in the organization become based on one's social relationship with organizational members outside the work environment rather than by one's professional contributions. Promotions, merit increases, preferences in time scheduling, choice of work assignments and other rewards are given preferentially to those who achieve favored status in social relationships outside the organization. Overall organizational productivity declines as more and more organizational members are embittered by such favoritism and see little relationship between organizational rewards and job performance.

85

Social Closure and Organizational Decision-Making To illustrate how social closure begins to complicate the organizational decision making process, consider the following scenario.

There is an opening for Director of Outpatient Services in a community-based human service program. Two therapists, Robert and Jane, working in the program, have relatively equal knowledge and expertise, and both have applied for the position. Robert and his spouse socialize regularly with the Clinical Director, who is responsible for filling the position. Jane, on the other hand, has avoided much of the outside-of-work socializing.

If the Clinical Director selects Robert, there is no way possible to convince Jane that the Director's outside-of-work relationship did not influence the decision. If the Director selects Jane, then there are further repercussions in the personal and social relationship with Robert.

A number of other organizational members watch this drama unfold. For them, the decision will communicate important messages about the organization and their future in it. A decision to select Robert for the position could reinforce social closure by communicating that one must cultivate social relationships to obtain upward mobility in the organization. Other organizational members will have feelings about the role the outside social relationships played in the decision, and these feelings will continue to color their relationships with the Clinical Director, Robert and Jane. Even if Robert was chosen because he was the most qualified candidate, the process of social closure undermines the ability to trust in the objectivity of the decision. Robert, Jane and other organizational members will act and generate feelings on their perception, not necessarily the reality, of how the decision was made.

When social and professional roles become enmeshed, organizational decision-making becomes more complicated. This social closure makes decision makers vulnerable to second-guessing and innuendo. The organizational climate becomes permeated with hidden agendas, biases, personal favoritism and secret deals that members believe govern the organization.

The Loss of Direct Communication Social closure escalates the loss of direct communication described in the preceding chapter. As conflict increases, staff of the organization become split into subgroups, and an increasing amount of communication related to the inner workings of the organization occurs in the social setting away from the work environment. Gossip and rumors become staples of trade as members seek information to predict their level of safety and security in the organization.

This loss of direct communication is most dramatic during the latter stages of closure described earlier as the period of loss of faith, scapegoating, and rebellion. Many of us have witnessed the sudden scapegoating (extrusion) of an organizational member under conditions of powerful no-talk rules that prohibited the open and direct discussion of how and why the person was no longer part of the organization. And yet such incidents are processed in excruciating detail in the social subgroups outside the work setting. Persons who cross the social subgroups serve as a vehicle to transfer information and misinformation from one group to another. This frantic level of activity and information exchange in the work-dominated social network is paralleled in the interactions inside the organization by silence and whispers regarding the same event.

The loss of direct communication provides a storehouse of pent-up emotion inside the organizational family. The indirect expression of feeling in the social sub-groups, rather than providing a release for this emotion, only intensifies it. The energy necessary to keep this emotion under control severely limits the flow of information and ideas in the organization and creates very formal, role-prescribed behaviors in such settings as staff meetings.

When no escape valves exist inside the organization, this pent-up emotion may spill out in some unpredictable and potentially uncontrollable ways. Imagine the possibilities when we are at an organizational stage like the above, bring all the organizational members together for something like a Christmas Party, and then add a drug such as alcohol, which will serve to lower the inhibitions and impulse control of those in attendance. One such event occurred at an extremely troubled stage in the life of a professionally and socially closed organization. As the drinking altered judgment and loosened tongues over the course of the evening, the discharge of pent-up anger resentment resulted in incidents of physical confrontation and some serious destruction of property. Under other circumstances it would have been sufficiently volatile to have warranted calling the police except, in this case, those attending the party were the police.

6.7 Social Relationships In Open And Closed Systems

Social relationships between workers in open systems are established out of free choice based on common interests and a desire by two or more people to share time and activities. These relationships form out of individual preference and are not initiated or sustained from the dynamics within the organization. Such relationships are focused on personal interests rather than work issues. These relationships serve to supplement one's existing non-work social network. In open systems, members have easy access across the organizational boundary and the freedom to develop and maintain social relationships both in and outside the organizational family. Furthermore, the open system poses no conditions that inadvertently undermine non-work social relationships.

As noted at the beginning of this chapter, social relationships between co-workers, such as described above, are both desirable for individuals and serve to increase a worker's sense of identity and affiliation with the organization. So how are social relationships between co-workers in closed systems so different that they constitute a serious concern?

Closed organizational systems create a centripetal force that pulls workers toward the center of the organizational family. There are strong supports for developing a work-oriented social network. Conditions in the work environment inhibit the development or maintenance of non-work social relationships. Through the slow, subtle process of organizational closure, more and more time and emotional energy is pulled into the organizational family. First, work-oriented social relationships are added to one's own existing social network. The bonding in these new relationships may be particularly strong because they are forged in the high stress environment of the closed system. Second, non-work relationships begin to slip away. It's not that one makes decisions to stop seeing these people. It's just that the intensity of the work environment deprives us of the time and energy to sustain meaningful contact with them. These people just slowly slip out of our lives. Third, we look around after a few years and nearly all of our social relationships are work oriented.

Social closure (the meeting of most of our social needs inside the boundary of the organizational family) serves to:

- Increase the vulnerability of organizational family members.
- Sever access to sources of personal and social replenishment outside the organizational family.
- Diminish the ability of the organization to accomplish tasks essential to its survival.

The next chapter will examine how professional and social closure will culminate as members increasingly begin to meet sexual needs inside the organizational family.

Chapter Seven
Sexual Closure

It is hard to believe, when one looks at it objectively, that the brief joining of two sexual organs and a few subsequent muscular contractions could wreak such havoc in the life of an organizational group. Since sexuality is such an integral part of our lives (an issue closely tied to our self-esteem, and an issue that greatly influences our relationships with others), it should not be surprising that this same personal issue could have profound repercussions in the life of organizational groups. It should also be no surprise that this issue could create as much misunderstanding and discomfort in the life of organizations as it sometimes does in our personal lives.

Throughout my early years of managing health and human service agencies, I stuck firmly to the position that what staff did away from the work setting was none of my business or the business of the organization. I believed, particularly, that how, when, where, and with whom staff expressed their sexuality (to include with each other) away from the work setting was a personal and not an organizational issue. Any other position, it seemed, would be a gross invasion into the private lives of staff and the inevitable imposition of my personal moral judgments in an area in which I had no right to be involved.

I have learned since those early years that sexuality is more than an issue of private behavior and personal choices. Sexuality is always a dynamic in organizational families just as it is always an issue in nuclear families. Whether unrecognized and/or denied or consciously managed, sexuality has a profound impact on the organizational family culture and the inter-relationships between organizational family members. This chapter will examine the impact of sexuality in closed organizational systems. Our concern with the social and sexual relationships between staff is practical rather than moral and can be stated quite simply as follows:

> Social and sexual relationships between members of a closed organizational family can create staff dynamics that radically alter the workings of the group, reduce both the

quality and quantity of services provided to clients, increase the incidence of personal and relationship casualties, and can lead to the painful extrusion of members from the organization.

7.1 Sexuality As An Organizational Issue

During the last two decades there has been a growing body of knowledge about sexuality in our culture. From Masters and Johnson, to Ann Landers, to How-to Manuals, to workshops on sexual consciousness and to millions of printed and spoken words on love and intimacy, we have individually and collectively been forced to more consciously confront the issue of sexuality then during anytime in history. Within this context, health and human service professionals have been provided expanded knowledge and skills in addressing sexuality, sexual dysfunction, and sexual abuse in the lives of their clients. There is, however, a marked absence of professional literature and discussion on sexuality as an organizational dynamic or a component of organizational culture. This chapter will explore this dynamic. It will be the author's contention that the manner in which sexuality is managed in the staff-to-staff and staff-to-client relationships is an important indicator of organizational health and has a profound impact on the nature and quality of client services.

Most of the examples in this chapter will be drawn from the author's experiences in health and human service agencies. Sexual relationships between members of an organization are obviously not limited to such agencies. We could explore this issue in almost any type of business or organizational setting. However, by virtue of the fact that so much of the work of a human service agency involves a focus on interpersonal relationships, sexual activity in this setting may be particularly problematic to the group. There may also be unique problems in this type of organization due to the types of persons drawn to the work. Some persons are drawn to the human services field not to provide intimate relationships as a service called treatment, but to find and experience intimate relationships themselves. Many persons, whether as career therapists or career "patients", have found that it is only in the emotional intensity of dealing with extreme and tragic problems that they experience intimacy and feeling. Many may have had difficulties experiencing and maintaining personal intimacy away from the profession, particularly in relationships which are sexual. It goes without saying that problems may result as these persons experiment with the intimacy produced from close working relationships within a closed organizational family system.

7.2   Sexual Cultures And Organizational Life

Every organization can be said to have a sexual culture. This culture may be developed through conscious planning, or it may evolve informally, shaped by the attitudes and values of organizational members and, in particular, organizational leaders. Sexual cultures vary widely from organization to organization. The differences in sexual cultures are reflected in:

- Language: Is there permission within the program to talk about sexual issues with staff and clients? Is there a generally accepted vocabulary used to communicate about sexuality, and what values are reflected in the choice of words? Is the language of sexuality consistent with the stated values about sexuality? What is the nature of sexual humor?

- Artifacts: What values about sexuality are expressed by physical objects within the milieu of the program, e.g., paintings, sculptures, photographs, books, magazines, pamphlets, posters, clothes worn by staff, etc.

- Ethics and Values: Are there clearly stated ideals for human relationships? What judgments are placed on the various forms of sexual expression? Does an ethical code governing relationships between staff and clients exist? Does this code prohibit sexual relationships between staff and clients? If not, under what conditions are such relationships sanctioned? Are there formal or informal rules governing sexual relationships between staff? What values are expressed about sexuality to clients?

- Attitudes: What methods of sexual expression are condemned by staff? What attitudes about men, women, and sexuality are regularly expressed by staff? Do the expressed attitudes of staff discourage raising particular issues of sexuality with staff or clients?

● Relationships: How is affection expressed physically and verbally? How are adequacy, self-worth, and competence demonstrated in the work environment? What is the prevalence of sexual gaming and sexual harassment within the work milieu? What types of roles and values do clients see modeled in the relationships between staff?

The sexual culture of an organization constitutes the milieu in which both staff and clients must maintain their self-esteem and adequacy. This culture shapes the interactions among staff and between staff and clients. The sexual culture, much more than the counselor-client relationship, is the message conveyed by the program to clients about sexuality issues.

The sexual culture defines the boundaries of client self-disclosure. Clients rapidly learn what, if any, areas of their sexual lives they have permission to speak about. We are frequently blind to sexual problems of clients, because the sexual cultures within our organizations covertly prohibit the raising of such issues in a serious and straightforward manner.

The incongruency between the sexual culture and the explicitly stated values expressed to clients may have repercussions throughout the program. In cases where specialized services have been developed for women, for example, these services may exist within an overall organizational milieu that continues to discount the specialized needs of women, that forces women into stereotyped sex roles in the name of treatment, and that undermines the power and professional legitimacy of women staff. Clients receive two clearly contradictory messages in such a program. Where the explicit message from the women's service specialist is sexually empathic, the implicit message from the sexual culture of the organization is sexually exploitive. Such contradictions may exist on a number of levels and include a broad number of issues. I have, for example, found it quite remarkable that we can so articulately communicate in meetings with clients the need to slow down, relax, enjoy, explore,

93

and share sexuality, and then address sex in our own lives like it was an emergency appointment squeezed into our frantic schedule.

Sexual issues with clients may also need to be seen within the context of the sexual culture of the organization. Sexual gaming between clients, and client-initiated sexual gaming with staff, often reflects a mimicking of the interrelationships between staff and staff-initiated sexual gaming with clients. For example, when a female counselor is confronted by sexual overtures from a client, it is not surprising to find that similar overtures are occurring between staff and, in many cases, involving the specific counselor. It is equally common in this situation to find male counselors sexually gaming with female clients. The male client is, in effect, exhibiting the behavior that has been modeled to him within the program.

The sexual culture in any organization defines the response to the sexuality we bring to the organization. The sexual culture can also begin to change our own attitudes, values and behavior related to our sexuality. The difference in sexual cultures in open and closed organizational systems will now be explored.

7.3   Sexuality In Open And Closed Systems

It should be made clear in discussing sexuality as an organizational dynamic, that this author does not wish to imply that all sexual coupling between organizational members is somehow pathological, or that all sexual activity within a group results from an incestuous dynamic.

Sexual relationships between members of open systems reflect free choices of individual members, do not flow out of the process of the organizational group, and, in most cases, have very little impact on the organization. There is also, in most cases, no increase in stress on those involved due to the fact that both partners in the relationship work in the same organization. This is particularly true where the person's job roles are not significantly related to one another, and where the personal relationship does not also involve a power relationship, e.g., supervisor - supervisee.

When one superimposes sexual relationships on the stages of professional and social closure described in earlier chapters, you have a very different situation than that described in open systems. Sexual relationships in the closed system often flow more out of the process of the group than from the free choice of the individuals involved. Such relationships flow out of, and in turn, affect the process of the closed organizational family. In the closed system, this sexual activity enters the process of the closed organizational family and alters it. It is not the sexual relationship that is primary, but the meanings and feelings attached to that activity by members of the group. The incestuous dynamic occurs when something within the sexual relationships among group members triggers primitive emotions. Sexual relationships between workers in a closed system create feelings that the staff family has been violated and from that point forward cannot be the same. It is a situation where varying feelings of rage, hurt, jealousy, loss of faith, and in some cases, moral outrage boil up out of group members and begin affecting the relationships within the closed group.

The existence of these relationships, the problems created by these relationships for participants and other organizational family members, and the increase in individual staff casualties concurrent with these relationships, are all symptoms of dysfunction in the organizational family system. Closure in the nuclear family creates an incestuous dynamic that sets the stage for the violation of intimacy barriers and creates symptoms of dysfunction in individual family members. The same process is replicated in closed organizational family systems.

7.4   The Incest Analogy

To those readers not familiar with the family dynamics seen in cases of consummated incest, the author's use of the incest analogy may be both confusing and offensive. This analogy was not chosen out of flippancy or poor taste. The author's contention is that the process of organizational closure described in this book directly parallels the family dynamics often noted (in the professional literature and in my clinical experience) in cases of consummated incest. It was by comparing my clinical work counseling incest victims and their families with my consulting work with organizations that I noted the similarity in group dynamics. In the space below, I have charted a number of these similarities, some of which will be explored in greater detail in the chapter.

AREA OF COMPARISON	INCEST DYNAMIC IN NUCLEAR FAMILY	INCEST DYNAMIC IN THE ORGANIZATIONAL FAMILY
Degree of closure	Family members restricted from outside transactions	Professional and social closure precede sexual closure
	Social closure often precedes consummation of incest	Same
	Outside world viewed as evil and threatening	Same
	Over-protection of family members, e.g., no dating or boy friends of daughters; victims treated with hostility and jealousy	Outside intimate partners of organizational family members may be treated with hostility and jealousy
	Closure may be secondary to family stigma e.g., alcoholism, psychiatric illness, etc.	Closure may be related to stigma (see Chapter Eight)
	Inherent message that all needs of family members can be met inside family	Same
Family Image	Preoccupation with looking good on the outside	Same

AREA OF COMPARISON	INCEST DYNAMIC IN NUCLEAR FAMILY	INCEST DYNAMIC IN THE ORGANIZATIONAL FAMILY
Family Image (cont.)	No talk rules; distrust talking to outsiders about family	Same
	Incongruence between external image and internal emotional reality	Same
Timing of Incest	Father-daughter incest is often preceded by or concurrent with deterioration in husband - wife sexual relationship	Sexual relationships between organizational family members often preceded by deterioration in outside marital / intimate relationships
Type of Relationship	Father aggressor may try to establish pseudo-marital relationship with daughter e.g., courting behavior, daughter's interest in boyfriends seen as infidelity or unfaithfulness	Pseudo-marital relations may be established as part of sexual relations Problems in outside relationships played out in incestuous relationship
Restraining Agent	Lack of an effective restraining agent, e.g., physical absence or illness of mother in case of father - daughter incest	Lack of an effective restraining agent, e.g., absence of anyone with sufficient power to check supervisor as sexual aggressor

AREA OF COMPARISON	INCEST DYNAMIC IN NUCLEAR FAMILY	INCEST DYNAMIC IN THE ORGANIZATIONAL FAMILY
Distortion of Sexual Culture	Violation of intimacy barriers	Same
	Breakdown of sexual privacy and distance	Same
	Consummation of incest last stage of this breakdown	Same
Value System	Value system not sufficient to restrain sexual contact	Same
	Where value system is present, there may be incestuous dynamic without consummation of incest	Where value system is present, there may be professional and social closure without sexual closure
Individuation	All aspects of the incestuous dynamic violate the victims need for individuation, e.g., personal and sexual safety at home to begin the process of of individuation; meeting needs and establish identity separate from the family	Adults may regress from the emotional ingrown atmosphere of the closed organizational, family thus reversing their process of individuation; identity and self-esteem needs are all tied to the emotional life of the organization

AREA OF COMPARISON	INCEST DYNAMIC IN NUCLEAR FAMILY	INCEST DYNAMIC IN THE ORGANIZATIONAL FAMILY
Individuation (cont.)	Aggressor dominates life of the victim / emotional suffocation	Same
Sequential victimization	In father-daughter incest, sons may mimic the behavior of the father and also become sexually aggressive with the victim	Sexual relationships in the closed organizational family rarely occur in isolation; the pattern usually involves multiple concurrent and/or sequential sexual relationships between organizational members
Response of nonparticipants	First denial - "conspiracy of silence"	Same
	Rage, shame, jealousy	Same
	Identification with aggressor or victim	Same
Extrusion	Incest increases the extrusion of individual family members from the family	Same
	Sons who challenge the sexual supremacy of their fathers are extruded from the family	Staff who challenge the sexual supremacy of supervisory / management staff are extruded from the organizational family

The above are just a few of the parallels between the incestuous dynamic in nuclear and organizational families that will be explored in this chapter. One of the most important aspects of this discussion is that the meeting of sexual needs inside the boundary of the family is the last stage in the progressive closure of both nuclear and organizational families. Our concern is not simply with the sexual activity at the end of this continuum. The entire process of closure-each progressive step of this incestuous dynamic-can have powerfully debilitating effects on nuclear and organizational family members and the overall health of these systems regardless of whether the stage of sexual intimacy has been reached.

7.5 Setting The Stage For Sexual Closure

When an organizational family has closed itself off professionally and socially, the eventual meeting of sexual needs inside the boundary of the family is inevitable. But how can this happen? How can changes in the organization actually create conditions that will increase sexual activity between organizational members?

Most persons utilize multiple roles to fulfill their personal needs. For example, during a typical month one staff member might be involved in such roles as father, husband, brother, son, uncle, grandson, lover, friend, club member, neighbor, runner, employee, supervisor, hobbyist, community member, helping companion, a pet owner, etc. Our combined experience in these diverse roles reinforces our identity and allows us to address different needs in different settings with different people. In short, we experience multiple roles and try to establish some boundaries between these roles to keep one or more roles from dominating our lives and restricting those broader interactions through which we meet other important needs. Most people are able to meet a number of important needs in the work place while maintaining a very separate lifestyle through which many other needs are met. There is a clear boundary between their work life and their personal life away from work.

The problem with closed organizational systems is that they begin to progressively break down this boundary between one's personal and work lives. This progressive breakdown is often slow and subtle. Dramatic changes are often only noted when one looks back over a number of years and perceives how work dominated his or her life has become. This deterioration in boundaries can occur in the following manner.

1. Excessive time and emotional demands in the closed organizational family reduce the number of roles workers participate in outside the work setting. Outside activities are reduced. Outside relationships fall by the wayside. As these outside contacts are lost, the worker's identity and selfesteem are increasingly shaped by interactions in the work environment.

2. The loss of outside sources of replenishment leaves the worker physically and emotionally depleted from the high-stress work environment. Given the condition of low personal nourishment and high vulnerability, organizational family member may reach out to each other to meet needs that in the past were met outside of the work environment.

3. The spillover of stress in the closed system into one's personal life may place an unbearable strain on marital or other intimate relationships and lead to a worker's emotional escape back into the organizational family. Problems in outside relationships (creating unmet needs) set the stage for the development of intimate relationships between organizational family members.

4. The violation of intimacy barriers, produced through social closure of the organization, works to break down the emotional distance that usually distinguishes professional and personal relationships. Professional and social closure may also undermine the strength of one's personal value system. Persons with strong personal beliefs on extramarital sexual relationships, for example, may find themselves involved in an extramarital affair with a co-worker when personal values are superseded by the group values in a closed organizational family.

The above conditions set the stage. The reasons for the onset of sexual relationships between organizational family members can be summarized as follows: if the professional closure of the organizational family has restricted professional relationships to other workers in the organization; if social closure has resulted in nearly all social needs getting met with other workers; and if professional and social closure have slowly undermined the existence and quality of intimate relationships outside the work setting, then where else can one address sexual needs if not on the stage of the organizational family?

7.6   Sexual Dynamics And Burnout: The Metaphor Of Impotence

The development of problematic sexual relationships between family members in closed organizational systems seems to occur as part of the burnout process and often occurs concurrently with other symptoms of burnout. This phenomenon should not be surprising if we closely examine the individual experiences of burnout in a closed organizational family.

Impotence can be used as a metaphor for the experience of burnout in the closed system. The slow deterioration in outside sources of replenishment, and the increasing stressors and depletion of strokes inside the system, leaves one, above all else, feeling powerless. This feeling of powerlessness creates the experience of life being shaped by forces over which one has no control-the experience of being controlled rather than being in control-trapped without choices. But if the experiences in the later stages of organizational closure are so personally toxic, why not just leave? First of all, and as noted earlier, there are no guilt-free ways to get out of a closed system. Secondly, and perhaps the most personally devastating, our self-confidence, assertiveness, ability to take control and make clear choices, have all eroded. We have constant fantasies of getting out yet these fantasies do not seem to generate action. There are obstacles to leaving, such as fear of salary cuts and tight job markets and old loyalties that bind us to the organization. This whirlwind of thought and emotion may result in repeated self-denigration over our inability to do what we know we need to do, which further increases our experience of powerlessness. We may, on the other hand, begin exaggerated attempts to demonstrate our potency in the work setting.

It is perhaps only natural that attempts to counter feelings of impotence in the workplace include a demonstration of one's sexual potency. Why does this potency have to be demonstrated in relationships with other organizational family members? Because that is the precise arena where we feel impotent.

The metaphor of impotence may help us understand why during periods of excessive and prolonged stress we see an increase in sexual activity between organizational members, a preoccupation with titles, concern over comparative differences in salaries, conflict over the competence and importance of different departments or professional disciplines, overt and covert struggles for power, and resentments over symbols of status such as office size and location. These are all areas where feelings of powerlessness and worthlessness are countered by exaggerated efforts to be recognized in the organizational family as valued, appreciated and recognized on both a personal and professional level.

7.7 The Non-Sexual Nature Of Sex In The Closed System

The author has made three separate points about sexuality and the experience of burnout that on initial review seem blatantly contradictory. These points are as follows:

1. Two of the common symptoms of excessive and prolonged stress are a decrease in libido and varying levels of deterioration in the frequency and quality of one's sexual relationships.

2. The progressive closure of the organizational system creates a high incidence of burnout and physical/emotional depletion of organizational family members.

3. In later stages of organizational closure, there will be an increase in the incidence of problematic sexual relationships between organizational family members.

There is an obvious question that if the experience of burnout has such a devastating effect on people's libido, then why do we end up with an increase in sexual coupling? This apparent contradiction can be reconciled by pointing out that sexual

103

relationships in closed systems have very little to do with libido and, in fact, may have very little to do with sex.

Below are some of the non-sexual functions sexual relations serve in the closed organizational family. Some of these are elaborated in more detail in the organizational case studies at the end of this chapter.

Sex as Power Dynamic   Sexual competition in some closed systems resembles primitive animal rituals where the most dominant male gets sexual access to females. The human version of these rituals can be played by both sexes with an aggressiveness that justifies our continued placement in the animal kingdom. Sex in this scenario is more a demonstration of power and dominance over others than it is a function of affectional and sexual preference. You may find management staff in any system who will utilize their own formal power in the organizational structure to manipulate the vulnerability of subordinates to meet the manager's sexual needs. In the closed system, the primary need being met in this situation may be the manager's need to have his or her power and position affirmed through the submission and homage of his or her subordinate. The sexual act may be secondary or inconsequential.

Sex as an Act of Violence   A case study at the end of this chapter describes the sexual relationship between an employee and his supervisor's wife during a time of conflict in both the supervisor's marital relationship and also in the supervisory relationship. Occurring in an incestuously closed organizational family, this sexual relationship was more an act of rage and violence toward the supervisor than an act of either affection or sexual gratification.

Sex as Risk Taking   Chapter one noted that one symptom of burnout was an increase in risk-taking behavior. It was further noted that this behavior helped the victim create a transient escape from the emotional numbness of the burnout experience. High-risk sexual choices, the intrigue of arranging sexual meetings, the conspiracy to hide the relationship from other organizational family members, and the fear of being discovered all provide powerful emotional payoffs completely unrelated to the actual sexual relationship. In fact, it is not unusual that it is only through these other payoffs that the sexual relationship can be sustained.

Stripped of these other payoffs, many such relationships quickly end, adding further confirmation that the sexual relationship had little to do with sex.

Sex as Physical Nurturing The loss of replenishment created in closed organizational family systems creates almost desperate needs for physical and emotional nurturing. The loss of outside relationships to provide such nurturing increases the provability that organizational family members will reach out to each other to meet these needs. In such cases, sexual gratification is of secondary importance to the need to be physically and emotionally touched.

Sex for Money and Position When strokes in the closed system decrease and become competitive rather than reciprocal ("every person for him/herself:), sex may become a bargaining chip to purchase rewards of money and positon from organizational leaders. Sexual relationships can simply become units of exchange for purchasing more important commodities within the organization. This type of organizational prostitution is usually short-lived as such arrangements can rarely be kept secret in the close organizational family. This arrangement is almost guaranteed to produce the eventual extrusion of participants from the system-usually as a direct result of the rage of non-participants.

Sexual Partners as Co-Conspirators Closed systems can create, sometimes quite quickly, very powerful relationships dyads. Two workers currently being scapegoated in the organizational family, for example, may quickly reach out to each other for support. They may almost enter a pact as co-conspirators planning defensive strategies and committed acts of organizational sabotage. The relationship, which may be sexual, is completely work-dominated. One member of such a couple, looking back in retrospect, commented to the author on this quality of the relationship: "I remember the whole early period we were sleeping together. We would be having sex and all I could think about was 'If only (supervisors) could see us now'". This sexual relationship emerged out of the process of the group, and it was literally as if they were making love on a stage with other organizational members as the audience. The sexual relationship had little meaning apart from the organizational dynamics in which the participants were involved.

7.8 Internal Boundaries: Predicting The Impact On The Organization

The impact of a sexual relationship between two organizational members can differ significantly depending on what roles the persons involved formally and informally perform in the organization.

One method of predicting this impact is to examine the internal boundaries within the organizational family. Exhibit 7-A graphically displays the organizational family of a sixteen-bed residential adolescent treatment center. This program is four years old and has grown progressively closed professionally and socially over the past two years. The diagram shows three board members and a patron that have contributed to the program's professional closure and socialize extensively with other organizational members. The diagram further shows three management staff (a director and two coordinators) and twelve line staff consisting of two three-person teams of counselors, one three-person team of house managers, and a cook and clerical position. The diagram also includes in the family both current and former clients of the program. (We will discuss staff-client sexual relationships later in this chapter.) Interns, consultants, and ex-staff also hold positions in the outer ring of the organizational family because of their involvement in the professional and social closure but with a reduced degree of time and emotional involvement. Spouses are included because they have become a very visible part of this organizational family due to the extensive staff socializing during the past two years.

The diagram shows a number of levels that reflect formal power in the organization that are separated by internal boundary lines. The double boundary lines which separate clients reflect the special status of clients and the strength of the taboo against staff-client sexual contact.

In general, we can say that the greater the number of boundary lines crossed by those sexually involved, the greater the potential repercussions within the organizational family. We could speculate that the act producing the least reactions within the

106

EXHIBIT 7-A
The Organizational Family: Internal Boundaries

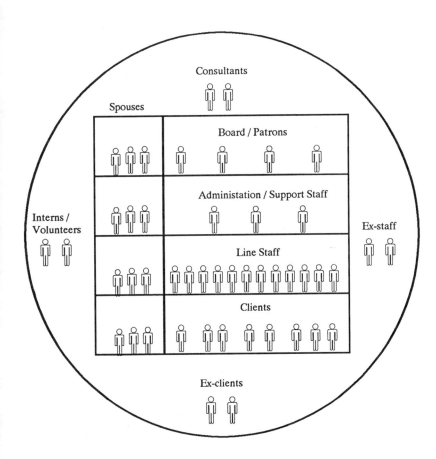

organization would be a sexual relationship between two members at the same level whose daily role functions are only minimally related. A sexual relationship between a counselor and the secretary would have less repercussion than a relationship between two counselors working on the same team. According to our diagram, the sexual relationship having the most system repercussions would be between a board member, a manager, or spouse of one of the staff and a client.

Transactions across these internal boundaries reflect relationships between persons of greater power and persons with less power. This violation of internal boundaries tends to spark primitive feelings that alter the workings of the group and alter the sexual culture of the organization. This is particularly true when management/supervision staff are involved in such relationships.

Another way to examine the potential repercussions of sexual relationships within the organization is to examine dynamically how family roles are replicated in the organizational system. This approach examines which persons, by their personality and function in the system, most closely parallel the family roles of mother, father, uncle, child, etc. A review of the incest taboo within families further illustrates this approach. There appears to be a continuum of the strength of the incest taboo with mother/son incest being the most powerful (occurring mostly in situations where both mother and son are psychotic) Lidy, et.al. 1965, Lusting, et.al., 1966); brother/sister and inter-familial(cousins) incest being the least powerful; and with father/daughter incest in between (Frances, 1976). Much the same continuum can be observed in organizations. For example, in the organization diagrammed in Exhibit 7-A, there were several sexual relationships between organizational family members over a period of years. A relationship between two counselors eventually created some serious problems in their ability to work as clinical team members. The director's relationship with the secretary ended painfully in the secretary's resignation from the organization and a deterioration of the Director's ability to supervise staff (who felt the Director had used his position within the organization to sexually exploit the secretary). There was another relationship, however, that created the greatest emotional upheaval in the organizational family. The cook was the ultimate mother earth. She was older than most of the other staff and was extremely nurturing, i.e. feeding, hugging, teasing, chastising staff to take better care of themselves, etc. In the fourth year of the program's existence, the cook became sexually involved with a counselor who was almost twenty years younger. According to our initial interpretation of the family diagram, this relationship should not have created a profound impact on the organization because both staff operated within the same level and performed different functions. Such was not the case. The knowledge of this relationship horrified and almost emotionally paralyzed the organizational family. Organizational family members could not deal with the personal and sexual needs of the woman who was dynamically the family's mother. Both the cook and counselor were scapegoated and eventually extruded from the family. This episode marked one of the most disruptive and emotionally wrenching experiences in the history of this organizational family.

The next section will look at some of the other irrational forces that shape the impact of sexual relationships between members of a closed organizational family system.

7.9   Cultural Taboos And Sexual Dynamics

There are issues other than the participants' power level and family function that can influence the response to a sexual relationship within the organizational family. Each staff member entering the organizational family brings with him/her a set of personal and/or cultural attitudes that dictate the types of sexual intimacy that are considered acceptable or taboo. Taken collectively, these cultural taboos can have a profound impact on how organizational family members respond to a sexual relationship within the boundary of the organizational family.

One issue that can color such judgments is the respective ages of the staff members who are sexually involved. Where a wide age discrepancy exists, cultural values may add a further weight of condemnation, or at least ambivalence, about the relationship. This is also true when the sexual partners are of different racial/ethnic backgrounds. Ageism and racism can intensify and exaggerate the organizational family's response to an incestuous relationship and may contribute to the extrusion of those involved from the organization.

Cultural taboos may also create a much more primitive emotional response if the relationship of concern is homosexual rather than heterosexual. Listening carefully to the gossip and rumor mill triggered by the knowledge of such a relationship, it is quite clear that homosexuality can trigger a broad spectrum of feelings ranging from confused acceptance to moral or religious condemnation, to the aggressive outrage (reaction formation) of the homophobe.

We have assumed in the above example that the sexual values of the culture at large and those of the organizational culture are the same. There are cases where these values are very incongruent. I am aware, for example, of a women's shelter for abused women in which nearly all of the power positions were held by gay women. Lesbianism was a very strong, but unstated, component of the sexual culture in this organizational family. The sexual relationship that proved the most disruptive to this organization was not any of the lesbian relationships, but the break-up of a lesbian relationship sparked by a heterosexual affair between one of the women and a male volunteer of the agency.

7.10 The Contagious Quality Of Sexual Closure

Once the sexual intimacy barrier is violated in the closed organizational family, there seems to be an escalation in the meeting of sexual needs within the organizational boundary. The progressive closure of the organizational family often produces a contagion of concurrent and sequential sexual alliances.

The frequent socializing between organizational members, in many cases, requires only the disinhibiting influence of alcohol (and other assorted psychoactive drugs) to dissolve the barrier between social and sexual intimacy. The early clandestine violation of this barrier may be followed by the more open, if not blatant, use of the organizational family to meet sexual needs. This transition makes a significant change in the sexual culture of the organization and produces increased permission (and sometimes pressure) for sexual intimacy within the organizational family.

7.11   Gossip And Rumor: Information As Power

The social and sexual closure of an organizational family displaces direct communication with gossip and rumor. The increase in gossip and rumor happens concurrently with the division of the organizational family into the rapidly shifting dyads and triads described in the last chapter. As conflict inside the organization increases and more and more work-related decisions are being made based on social and sexual intimacy, information about who's doing what to whom becomes an important source of power and self-protection. Social and sexual closure and the communication patterns that accompany such closure can turn a professional organization into a soap opera.

7.12   The Incestuous Relationship: Impact On Participants

The development of incestuous relationships within the organizational family can have profound repercussions on the system as a whole and on those participating in the incestuous relationship. This section will outline how the incestuous relationship in the closed organizational family undermines the personal and professional identities of those involved sexually, increases the marriage casualties among organizational family members, and leads to the extrusion of members from the organization. It will be apparent from this discussion that the closed organizational family poses high risks for internal intimate relationships and increases the vulnerability of participants in such an intimate relationship.

When two members of the closed organizational family become a sexual dyad, it is not uncommon for one or both person to lose much of their personal and professional identity. These individuals become a couple. Decisions about their roles in the organization are not made independently. While the partners may seek to manipulate the work environment to sustain their relationship, e.g., work schedules, work assignments in the same area, etc., organizational leaders, who make decisions about one of the partners, are forced to consider the impact upon and response from the other partner. In my earlier studies, it was clear that women in these relationships suffered the greatest loss of identity. Many women that were interviewed noted that once they became sexually involved with an organizational member, other organizational members began to discount their professional knowledge and skills. Some women even felt they had been denied advancement because organizational leaders were uncomfortable promoting the women to a higher position in the organization than their sexual partner.

We have discussed earlier how professional and social closure decreases the time and emotional energy organizational members have available to sustain outside martial or intimate relationships. We have also noted that there are forces within the closed organizational family that will support members terminating outside marital or intimate relationships, particularly when this outside partner has remained aloof and unsupportive of the organization. Given these influences, married organizational family members who develop sexual relationships inside the organizational family are at high risk of sacrificing their marriages. The incestuous relationship within the organization further drains energy that is going into the marriage and may spark the final rupture of the marital relationship. The break-up of a marriage in the closed organizational family is rarely an isolated event. Extreme stages of organizational closure may instigate an epidemic of marriage and relationship casualties. In one program studied, over forty percent of the married staff of a residential program became separated and/or divorced within a one-year period - a period that marked the organization's most extreme stages of professional, social, and sexual closure.

I remember with great poignancy the interviews conducted with couples whose marriages had failed during this process. At the time of the split, most of these couples felt there were deep irreconcilable problems inherent in their marriage relationships. When interviewed some years later, many were still grieving the loss of the relationship. They had come to some awareness that much of the pain and conflict in their marriages was not from the basic relationship, but from the outside changes in their lives over which they had little control. Organizational family members looked back with bitterness as they realized that the loss of their marriage was only one part of the craziness and pain produced by the period of their lives spent in the closed organization.

Sexual relationships within the organizational family increase the loss and extrusion of members from the family. The case histories at the conclusion of this chapter will graphically show the casualty process which results from sexual closure.

7.13   The Married Couple In The Closed System

There may be unique problems for the married couple in the closed organizational system. It was noted earlier that during professional and social closure of the organization, persons in the extended organizational family (e.g., spouses) may be drawn in to the core group. So the married couple in the closed system is not a rare phenomenon. From experiences of married couples in the closed organizational family, the following three observations are offered:

- If the marriage occurred during the time the couple had worked together in the closed system, one or both partners who leave the organization may provoke a crisis in the marriage. It's as if the marriage grew out of the process of the closed group and needs the work setting for the marriage's continued sustenance.
- The closer the functional relationships between the couple in the organizational structure, the grater the strain on the marriage relationship. Power relationships may be particularly problematic as work issues spill over into the personal relationship, and personal issues get played out in work roles.
- A major strain on marriages in the closed system is the inability of the couple to get "out of role" and maintain a separate life away from the work setting. The loss of non-work replenishment in the marriage and in social relationships may result in increased conflict and emotional distancing within the relationship.

7.14   A Redefinition Of Sexual Harassment

The author has had a number of persons during training workshops who have asked if sexual harassment occurs during the stage of sexual closure in the organizational family. The question is an interesting one and can be addressed by comparing the following two situations.

Mary was an administrative assistant to a supervisor of a large social service agency. She had worked for the agency five years and had been quite happy with the position. This contentment was to change with the arrival of a new supervisor. About three months after the new supervisor arrived, Mary became uncomfortable with the supervisor's increasing comments on her physical appearance, questions about her personal life, and what came to be an almost incessant banter of sexual innuendo. Mary's attempts to communicate her discomfort with this situation had little impact. In the months that followed, the supervisor became very "touchy", increased his disclosure of problems about his wife which generally centered on her sexual coldness, and began increasing "working" lunches which Mary was required to attend. During the sixth month after his arrival, the supervisor's sexual advances became quite blatant. Mary's verbal attempts to rebuff these advances only resulted in the supervisor's implied rewards of money and promotion in return for sexual favors. When formal complaints produced no resolution of this problem, Mary resigned from her job.

Very few people would disagree that Mary had been a victim of sexual harassment. The sexual advances were unwanted and continued in spite of Mary's request that such behavior cease. Let's compare this situation to another woman with the same role in a different organization.

Faye took a position as secretary in a community mental health center against the advice of her husband who couldn't figure out why she would want to work around crazy people. Within three years, her intelligence and organizational skills had earned her the position of administrative assistant to the agency director. During these three years she'd found a whole new world of experience compared to her very sheltered upbringing and married life. Her work also changed her social life, as staff socialized frequently away from work. This created some problems as her husband couldn't handle the "weirdness" of most of the staff. They reciprocated by applying a diverse range of diagnostic labels on the husband. During Faye's fourth year of employment, the professional, social, and sexual closure of the organization intensified. Faye was given an opportunity to participate in staff growth groups that demanded a high level of self-disclosure. The director and others commented on her natural counseling aptitude, and it wasn't long before Faye was enrolled in college to prepare herself for a future career change. This was a very exhilarating time for Faye, but also a time of conflict as her husband was coldly unsympathetic to her enrollment in school and her future plans. She increasingly sought support from the director as conflict in the marriage increased. The director became her trusted mentor, constantly providing encouragement and acknowledgment of her personal and professional value. Over the next year, Faye's school schedule, evening staff growth groups, etc., caused increasing conflict at home that was further complicated by her eventual physical and emotional exhaustion. Partially through the counsel of the director, Faye separated from her husband and got a place of her own. Faye had heard, but didn't believe, that the director had been sexually involved with one of the counselors at the agency. The director had never made any sexual advances although there had been times that she wished he would. A month after her separation, she and the director began their sexual relationship - an act in which she was totally willing to participate. She was in love - a fact unchanged by the director's wife and family. Their relationship continued and became common knowledge at the agency. Other staff cooled their relationship with Faye, and she found herself increasingly isolated and dependent upon the director. After four months, the director informed Faye in rather painful terms that he could no longer handle her demands for time, that she put too much stock in the relationship, and that the relationship was over. Emotionally crushed, Faye never returned to the agency. She did not resign as she felt she couldn't face the other staff.

The only major details omitted from this vignette are that the director had been sexually involved with a number of women staff, and that a number of other staff had several outside intimate relationships, and had used sexual intimacy with other staff as a means of emotional support.

In the case of Mary, there was a clear aggressor and a clear victim. The sexual advances were clearly unwanted - a key issue in the traditional definition of sexual harassment. But what about the case of Faye? The roles of aggressor and victim are less clearly defined. There were no <u>unwanted</u> sexual advances. The seduction process was slow and subtle compared to the case of Mary where the sexual advances were blatant and constant. Can the case of Faye be considered a type of sexual harassment, or do we simply say that Faye was a victim of her own adult choices?

It is the author's contention that a definition and understanding of sexual harassment in closed systems must include the phrase "manipulation of vulnerability". A supervisor, or other person with significant organizational power, can isolate staff professionally and socially, overextend staff in ways that deplete their physical and emotional energy, use his/her influence to undermine the outside intimate relationships of staff, and foster dependency in nurturing staff who experience conflict in their outside relationships. If the supervisor then manipulates the vulnerability and dependency of a staff member to meet his/her own sexual needs, then the supervisor has committed a type of sexual harassment every bit as demeaning as the more blatant behaviors we associate with this term.

7.15 Staff / Client Sexual Relationships: Professional Ethics And Personal Needs

Periodically an incident makes headlines which involves a sexual relationship between a doctor/patient, counselor/client, teacher/student, pastor/parishioner, etc. As citizens and professional peers, we respond in moral outrage and demand some level of punitive retribution upon the guilty party. We sit back believing such an act is unthinkable, and that only an emotionally sick or morally degenerate person could so exploit a helping relationship. While such moral outrage is understandable, it offers little insight into how such relationships can occur. It is quite discomforting, for example, to note that many individuals who have been involved in sexual relationships with clients also believed that such an act was ethically reprehensible and unthinkable right up until the time they found themselves in just such a relationship.

A doctor spends extended time talking with a beautiful patient only to run the next series of uncomely patients through the office with assembly line speed. A private therapist fails to terminate the wealthy client for another month because his/her patient load is down and the therapist needs the money. A socially inept counselor turns client relationships into friendships. A teacher devotes special attention to those students who worship his or her intelligence or charisma. A priest uses the confessional for his own titillation. Each of these individuals has manipulated the helping relationship to meet his/her own needs, and yet, each would be blind to the thin line that separates such behavior from overt sexual behavior between themselves and their clients.

Within the framework of Chapter Two, such behavior can be defined in terms of psychopathology or defects in moral character. While there may be some cases where these models are applicable, a significant number of persons who become sexually involved with their clients are suffering neither from serious psychopathology nor an underdeveloped super-ego. The same closure process that creates sexual relationships between organizational family members can also increase the probability and incidence of staff-client sexual relationships.

The exploitation of a helping relationship usually results from the conflict between professional ethics and personal needs. Inadvertent exploitation may spring from a lack of clear ethical standards, but overt exploitation is more likely to occur where human needs block the application of ethical standards. For example:

- I may have a strong ethical belief in marital fidelity and practice that ethic as long as my needs are met in that relationship. The longer needs go unmet in this relationship, however, the greater will be the difficulty maintaining consistency between my ethical beliefs and my behavior.
- I may have a strong prohibition against stealing until my physical hunger and lack of money take precedence over my beliefs.
- The strength of the ethical prohibition against sexual relationships with clients is in direct propor-

tion to one's ability to consistently meet these needs (directly or indirectly) outside of the professional helping relationship.

Participation in closed organizational families creates a broad spectrum of unmet needs and increases the incidence of exploitation of the helper-client relationship. If a program is closed professionally and socially, (meaning the loss of professional and social relationships other than co-workers), a very narrow arena has been created in which all of the personal needs of staff are to be met. Given that clients make up one part of the system in closed organizational families, they can quickly become targets through which staff can fulfill these needs.

If there is a systems perspective, or recipe for staff-client sexual contact, it would include many of the following ingredients.

- Professional and social closure of the organization.
- A physically and emotionally exhausted staff member.
- An organizational structure that does not have built in sources of replenishment to counter the high stress inherent in the helping process.
- A work schedule leaving little time or emotional energy to sustain outside relationships.
- Staff member's marriage / intimate relationship casualty.
- A sexually permissive organizational culture.
- A supervisory structure and process that excludes a review of sexuality in staff-client relationships (the lack of an effective restraining agent).
- A loose structure and boundary on staff-client relationships.
- The lack of a clear and visible code of professional practice governing staff-client relationships.
- The failure of the supervisory process in confronting stages of over-involvement that often precede staff-client sexual relationships.
- The lack of resources to provide male-female co-therapists to work with seductive clients.

If we are concerned about the sexual exploitation of clients by staff, then we need to temper our talk of psychopathology and moral outrage with direct action to shape organizational systems that allow staff to nurture and replenish themselves and provide supervisory mechanisms to inhibit the violation of intimacy barriers in staff-client relationships.

7.16   Organizational Case Histories

This chapter will close with a review of a number of case histories drawn from the author's studies, consulting experience and from interviews with persons who reviewed the author's early monographs on organizational incest. Each case situation will be described briefly and then followed by an analysis utilizing the observations set forth earlier in this chapter. The names have obviously been changed.

Counselor-Counselor Relationship   Jim and Rita had worked together for over a year in a residential drug abuse treatment center. Both were married, but, in each case, the marriage was in a very vulnerable position. Jim and his wife were experiencing some stressful growing pains in their relationship, and Rita and her husband had just moved back together to attempt a reconciliation of the relationship. Since it was early in both of their careers, they were very attracted to the intensity and charisma of this closed organizational family. The intimacy and self-disclosure experienced working as co-therapists made a sexual relationship seem natural and almost inevitable to them. The sexual relationship lasted for about nine months. Toward the end of this time, serious problems occurred in the relationship that detracted from their effectiveness as co-therapists and their ability to work comfortably in their broader team assignments. When the relationship ended bitterly, Rita chose to leave the organization, as working in the same facility with Jim was too painful.

Analysis - This relationship followed a prolonged occurrence of professional and social closure within the organizational family. The closing of the social network coincided with sexual and interpersonal problems experienced in the marriages of both counselors. The excessive time and emotional demands in the closed organizational family further undermined the stability of

Jim and Rita's respective marriages. The extra-marital relationship allowed both counselors to escape from and yet play out issues endemic to their marriages in the work setting. Jim and Rita's relationship became, in essence, a pseudo-marital relationship until its sudden termination. The response within the staff system was quite ambivalent, as a good deal of match making had gone on to get the counselors together, in spite of the fact that both were married (subsequently divorced through the process). Although a good deal of staff time had been taken up by gossiping, moral judgment, etc., the strongest repercussion appeared to be the guilt of the staff. While working for an agency dedicated to strengthening families, they somehow found themselves in a process by which one group member was painfully extruded and two marriages suddenly dissolved. The counselor who left became a "ghost" who continued to haunt the group for some time to come. The overall feelings of the group were summed up by one member who said, "we helped destroy two marriages for our own damned titillation and entertainment".

If we wish to test our incest analogy, we can compare the particulars in the example to Weinberg's (1955) description of incestuous relationships within families.

A. The incest usually occurs in emotionally ingrown families.
B. Incest often coincides with difficulties in the marital relationship.
C. The incest relationship may take the form of a pseudo-marital relationship, and
D. Non-participants may experience guilt as if they have promoted or failed to prevent the occurrence of incest.

Supervisor - Supervisee Relationship This case reviews the history of a sexual relationship between Barbara, a counselor at a family counseling agency and her boss Rex, the agency director. This was Barbara's first professional position following completion of social work training. This relationship began on a guru-follower basis, a stage not uncharacteristic of the early stages of supervisory relationships. When the sexual act was added to the relationship and it became known to the staff, a number of complex dynamics began. The effectiveness of supervision with other supervisees deteriorated as the staff began to question the ethics and motives of the supervisor, and as they began to feel that Rex had exploited the nature of the supervisory relationship. Barbara became extremely depressed when Rex withdrew his attention from her, and she threatened to expose him to his wife if the relationship did not continue. The state of blackmail existed for a short time, and then Barbara chose to leave the organization "for personal reasons". Although the supervisor continued in his position, much of his previous status and esteem within the group had deteriorated.

Analysis - This relationship was what in incest literature would be called a "lust attachment". The isolation of program staff from outside consultation, training events, etc., made it easy for the supervisor to act out his acute case of "prima donnahood" and sexually exploit the supervisory relationship. The supervisor's own professional and social isolation probably contributed to the loss of the usual professional ethics which would have precluded such a relationship with a supervisee. The deterioration of respect for the supervisor and the daily soap opera atmosphere that dominated the program atmosphere for weeks, all but destroyed the provision of services by the team.

Again there are similarities with the incest dynamic in families, e.g.:

A. The development of transient "lust attachment",
B. The lack of an effective restraining agent, and
C. The identification of non-participants with the victim and anger at the aggressor. (Weinberg, 1955)

In both cases reviewed, there is also clear confirmation of how the incest dynamic increases the extrusion of members from the organization - particularly women partners in the sexual relationships.

Supervisor - Supervisee, Non-consummated Incest Peg was a middle-aged counselor who had been traditionally trained and had worked in a highly structured work situation until she took a job with a youth program. The majority of staff were in their twenties, were sexually active with a number of partners, and expressed vocally their feelings about the limitations of traditional marriage. Peg's supervisor, Dennis was a very attractive young man who had sexual involvements of varying intensity with a number of young women on the staff, and responded in an equally seductive manner to Peg. A number of the staff joked about how long it would take before Dennis would get Peg to bed, and it became an unstated goal of the group to "convert" the counselor. Peg, confronted by new ideas, a lack of "professional" structure, increased seductiveness by her supervisor, and her own response to that seductiveness found herself in anxious conflict over her values, her marriage, and her work. As this anxiety escalated, a sudden decision was made as she came into work, turned in her immediate resignation, and left quite distraught.

Analysis - This rather extreme example is used to illustrate that the incestuous dynamic may produce extrusion of staff even when no sexual act is consummated. Here we had the existence of a homogenous group which had become increasingly closed professionally, socially, and sexually. Again there was no effective restraining agent (in fact, quite the opposite), and we see the distortion of values in the sexual culture of a closed organizational family which could turn the seduction of a new counselor into an entertaining game.

Ames et. al. (1954) noted that it is not uncommon to find an incestuous dynamic occurring in the families of runaway girls. In this situation, running away may be a very healthy mechanism on the part of the adolescent girl to protect herself from what is vaguely experienced as a fear of impending involvement with the father. In the above case example, the organizational family produced a middle-aged runaway through the same kind of incestuous dynamic.

Counselor - Supervisor's Wife, Incest and the Extended Family
This relationship occurred in an organizational family in which the social and professional relationships were indistinguishable. For nearly two years the staff (and their spouses) of this agency had extensively socialized with each other. The development of a sexual relationship between Larry, a counselor, and his supervisor's (David) wife Jan, coincided in time with marital difficulties in David and Jan's marriage and intense conflict between David and Larry. Both Larry and Jan later admitted their sexual relationship was more an act of violence against David than it was a mutual attraction on either of their parts. Knowledge of this relationship

was common among staff long before David learned of its existence and resulted in large amounts of time consumed by staff in gossip and rumor. The staff was divided into dyads and triads to secretly share the latest event in this on-going soap opera. When David discovered the relationship, he went to the board and demanded the counselor be fired (It's him or me!"). As might be guessed, the counselor was fired and David also filed for divorce. David left the job and the community after a few months finding it difficult (i.e., humiliation and anger) to continue to work with a staff who had known of the relationship and had not informed him. The fact that this program was left in shambles for months should be evident.

Analysis - This case example illustrates and emphasizes a number of points we discussed earlier in this chapter.

A. Again, the incestuous sexual relationship was preceded by the closure in social relationships of the organizational family.
B. Sexual relationships may develop out of the organizational process as an act of anger at one or more members rather than mere sexual attraction.
C. Rumor and gossip play an important role in the closed organizational family. Information becomes power and a primary means of self-protection.
D. Social and sexual closure inevitably breaks the organizational family into innumerable cliques, dyads and triads and results in what Bateson has called "the infinite dance of shifting coalitions". (Bateson, 1967)
E. Sexual dynamics can rapidly get turned into power dynamics and result in the sudden extrusion of staff.

Switching Partners, The Saga of Synanon   The history of Synanon is not confidential. If has periodically filled the headlines of newspapers and magazines since its founding by Charles Dederich in 1958 as a therapeutic community for the treatment of drug addiction. As the organizational family of Synanon became progressively closed, Synanon evolved from a drug abuse treatment agency to a closed alternative community to a religious cult. Nineteen years after Synanon was founded, Charles Dederich - the recovering alcoholic who was hailed for pioneering a new approach for treating addicts - was arrested in a state of extreme intoxication and charged with conspiracy to commit murder and solicitation of murder. Investigative reporting and court seized tape-recordings penetrated the closure of Synanon and revealed many of the internal practices and changes within Synanon. Anyone interested in closed systems is urged to study the literature on Synanon from Yablonsky (1965) through Mitchell, Mitchell and Ofshe (1980).

For purposes of this chapter, the focus will be on the period in Synanon history from 1975 through 1977. As Synanon moved closer to the status of a cult, Dederich introduced a series of conformity tests that would drive out all but the most committed Synanon members. These tests included mandatory shaving of heads of all members, mandatory vasectomies and abortions and, in late 1977, Synanon couples were required to "change partners". (Mitchell, et. al., 1980)

Analysis - This story has been inserted in this chapter to show how the sexual culture within a closed organization can become distorted and create a wide breach between societal and organizational values. What is amazing in this story is not Dederich's demand to change partners, but the fact that over 700 Synanon members complied with this request. Isolated from the outside world, closed organizational systems have indescribable power to shape the values and behaviors of organizational members. The greater the degree of closure, the greater is this power.

Counselor - Client Sexual Relationship The following three case studies illustrate the earlier discussion in this chapter which noted that sexual relationships between clients and organizational family members can also be part of the closure process.

A counselor (and recovering alcoholic), Don, who had been hired as the first paraprofessional at this agency was discovered to be sexually involved with a female client. Within 48 hours the counselor was fired and left the community. Knowledge of this event leaked into the community and affected the agency's reputation for a number of years, as the client involved was a minor. The organizational process in this case is illustrative and not unlike one seen in family systems with acting out adolescents. Don was immediately identified as the problem of the organization (the identified patient), defined as pathological (we're okay, he's not okay), and extruded. All conversations among organizational group members focused totally on Don's character. Staff morale suffered severely not only because of the community's suspicion of the agency, but also because each member had some vague feelings of responsibility for the matter.

Analysis - What was left out of the above description was the fact that Don had been functioning for months without any supervision in spite of his minimal training, and had risen to the status of a mythical folk hero among his clients. No effort had been exerted to "keep his feet on the ground" by other staff. Don's meeting with clients alone at their homes at night was known and approved of by the agency. All organizational members were aware that Don had no outside-of-work outlets to meet social and sexual needs. Other staff were receiving vicarious pleasure from Don's "hero" status, unorthodox methods, and his seemingly inextinguishable energy.

The vague feelings of guilt and responsibility experienced by agency staff is remarkably similar to Ackerman's (1966) description of a similar process in the family system. Ackerman noted that, when a family member was made a scapegoat and became dysfunctional, other family members experienced a contagion of guilt and a fear that, in retribution, they would experience the same fate.

Again we see the consequence of no effective restraining agent to prevent the consummation of incest in the organizational family.

Key Board Member - Client Relationship: This sexual relationship grew out of a chance meeting by the board member and a client at the treatment facility. Knowledge of this relationship among staff produced feelings of anger and lowered morale, as it seemed the mission of the agency had been tainted. As the counselor, who was seeing the particular client, began pointing out the destructiveness of the relationship to the client, word began to filter down that the board member involved was suggesting a staff cut might be necessary due to finances, and that he felt the particular counselor was the one who should be cut. When the supervisor became aware of the complexities, she directed the counselor to transfer the case to another agency, and she took the information to the director and recommended the board member be confronted. This confrontation did not occur, and the supervisor chose to leave the organization shortly following the episode.

Staff morale suffered severely because of the ethical issues they felt were violated, the organization's failure to confront openly what had happened, and the loss of the supervisor.

Analysis - This relationship occurred in an organizational family which had been closed socially for roughly a year and a half and was already seeing the development of sexual relationships between some members and extended family members (board members, spouses). Although many of the staff were morally outraged at the behavior of the board member and the administrator's failure to confront the issue, none saw that the behavior of the board member was merely an extension of a process nearly all staff had participated in for some eighteen months.

The treatment of the counselor by the board member is reminiscent of Weinberg's (1955) observation that sons who challenge the sexual supremacy of their father (in incestuous families) are treated harshly and may be extruded. Staff who confront the incestuous behavior of administrative/supervisory staff in the organizational family are treated similarly.

High Priest/Client Relationship A number of persons interviewed for this study, remarked that the most severe disruption of the program occurred when the director became sexually involved with a client, or in some cases, a series of clients. The importance of this phenomenon was also noted by a number of reviewers of the author's early monographs on organizational incest. One reviewer commented: "It is very different from the examples of counselor/client sex you discuss in that dissonance noted is far greater.... In one instance, the person at fault was the director of the clinic, and the clinic was even named for him. Staff, who had guessed he was sexually involved with clients, and Board members, who knew of this, found themselves unable to really confront the situation." The occurrence of sexual relationships between director and client often follows a prolonged period of professional and social closure of the staff group and occurs at a time when a number of group members are already experiencing various stages of burnout. The prolonged isolation of the Director from professional peer feedback and accountability contributes to the development of these relationships. (see Zweben and Deitch, 1976)

7.17 Sexual Closure: Summary Of Principles

1. There are significant differences in the impact of sexual relationships in open vs. closed organizational systems.

2. When an organization has become closed professionally and socially, the meeting of sexual needs within the organization is inevitable.

3. Sexual intercourse between two organizational members can be seen as not merely the isolated behavior of two individuals, but an act that flows out of the organizational process of the group.

4. Sexual relationships between members of a closed organizational family may have very little to do with sex, but may be a means of acting out other feelings or needs.

5. The greater the degree of organizational closure, the greater the impact of sexual relationships upon the organization.

6. The closer those sexually involved are to the perceived source of power in the organization, the greater the repercussions in the group.

7. The sexual dynamics in closed systems parallel the dynamics surrounding consummated incest in the nuclear family.

8. Though often flowing from the group process itself, sexual relationships between group members alter the group process and increase the likelihood of disruptive interpersonal relationships.

9. When members of an organizational group become sexually involved, the rate of staff extrusion for those involved increased dramatically (particularly for the women involved).

10. Sexual relationships between organizational members increase the casualty rate of marital and other intimate relationships and contributes to the further closure of the organizational family.

11. Sexual dynamics can rapidly become power dynamics and result in the sudden extrusion of staff.

12. Sexual closure impacts severely on the mission of the organization by breaking the staff team into cliques and by promoting the displacement of direct communication with rumor and gossip.

13. Problematic sexual relationship between organizational family members are part of the burnout process in closed systems and usually occur concurrently with other symptoms of burnout.

Chapter Eight
Why Closure?

The last three chapters have described in detail the professional, social and sexual closure of the organizational family. How this closure occurs and the consequences of such closure on individual workers, and the organization as a whole, have been identified. Before addressing how we prevent or manage the more destructive aspects of this dynamic, it may be helpful to pause and examine why such closure occurs.

In the past ten years, the author has spent a considerable amount of time pondering this issue. Questions such as the following continually surfaced as my work with various organizations was reviewed:

- Are there predictable periods of closure in the life of an organization?
- Are there particular types of organizations or professions that are particularly vulnerable to the closure process?
- What kind of environmental factors work to instigate or enhance the closure process?
- Are there particular characteristics of organizational leaders or organizational members that tend to promote the closure process?

This chapter will review some observations and speculations on these questions.

8.1   When Closure Is Necessary

Closure has been described throughout most of this study as an essentially negative process. The fact is that there are times when closure is essential to the health and survival of an organization. Closure, in general, produces:

- Reduced transactions across the organizational family boundary.
- Increased bonding and intimacy between organizational family members.

- A reaffirmation and commitment to organizational goals and values.

A period of closure may be essential to create a new organization or new program, successfully accomplish a reorganization, or face a major internally or externally produced crisis. Closure represents an appropriate short-term response to maximize internal organizational resources to create change or to respond to change in the external environment. The passion and cohesiveness characterizing the early days of new organizations or social movements is indicative of very functional closure. New organizational leaders may need a period of closure to redefine the organizational family and its values. The company facing radical changes in technology may need a period of closure to plot its response to such innovation. The company, in a life threatening fiscal crisis, may need a period of closure that transcends the historical split between management and labor. The hospital, that is facing a three year accreditation site visit, may need a period of closure. An organization, buffeted by rapid and overwhelming change, may need a period of closure both for the health of the organization and organizational family members. The organization being investigated by a regulatory agency may need a period of closure both for defensive purposes and for a period of self-assessment.

All of the above situations may represent appropriate movements toward organizational closure. The problem occurs when closure continues beyond the point of crisis or beyond the time that closure is needed. Many organizations begin the process of closure very appropriately, but then find themselves unable to reverse the process. Many are unaware that the same process of closure that saved the organization can also destroy it if continued indefinitely. This principle will be crucial in a later chapter where we begin to define the role of organizational leaders as boundary managers - moving the organization back and forth along the closed to open continuum in response to changing internal and external needs.

8.2 Geographical Isolation

Geographical isolation can play a powerful role in promoting professional and social closure in an organization. Such isolation severely limits the boundary transactions (movement of people and ideas in and out of the organization) necessary for a relatively open system. Some organizations, such as a prison or a psychiatric hospital or a military school, are consciously designed for closure with both physical and procedural barriers that limit boundary transactions. Organizations, ranging from those in remote rural areas to those in impoverished areas of the inner-city, may face major geographical barriers to maintain adequate boundary transactions. In other areas, such as the Indian reservation or an urban ethnic enclave, geographical barriers may combine with cultural, racial, and language barriers that collectively sustain the closure of an organization.

8.3   The Personality Needs Of Organizational Leaders

There are organizational leaders who inevitably create closed, incestuous systems wherever they go. This often reflects a blending of both their leadership styles and personality needs.

Such leaders isolate the organization out of their own feelings of insecurity and their needs for power and control. Their ego needs are best fulfilled in the role of a charismatic leader surrounded by followers who seek to lose themselves in a holy cause. Many of these leaders have histories of successful organizational leadership where checks and balances existed from outside the community to keep the leader's personality needs under control. Lacking such checks and balances, the most destructive aspects of these leader's personalities are magnified in the closed organizational system.

A comparison of the evolution of two major self-help movements in the chemical dependency field is illustrative. Alcoholics Anonymous was founded in 1935 and developed an organizational style characterized by decentralized and rotating leadership, personal anonymity, "principles before personalities", and a value system that rejected the accumulation of money and power as an organizational goal. Alcoholics Anonymous built into its recovery principles and traditions, guidelines that would provide checks and balances to prevent the future of the movement from being contingent on the health of a single organizational leader. Alcoholics Anonymous has been successful, not only because of its program of recovery, but also for its organizational structure that prevents the emergence of leaders whose ego-needs could self-destruct the group.

In contrast, Synanon was founded in 1958 by Charles Dederich as the first long-term therapeutic community for the treatment of addiction. The power and decision-making in the organization were centralized in the persona of Dederich. In reviewing the history of Synanon, one could build a case that a leader whose ego needs demanded the power of the high priest role built an organizational structure that guaranteed the fulfillment of this role. As Synanon became progressively closed over time, the checks and balances necessary to keep these ego-needs grounded in reality disappeared. Just as Synanon was created as a reflection of the leader's needs, the deterioration and conflict within Synanon reflected the progressive deterioration in the mental health of its leader.

There are other extreme examples of organizational closure fueled by the personality of the organizational leader. The leader, with a paranoid personality, will inevitably create a closed system with a radical belief system which fuels the fight against real or imagined enemies. In the paramilitary organizations of the right or left, religious sects, and in the single issue political action groups of the 1980's, one can observe closed organizational systems that reflect the personality needs of the charismatic leader.

When the distorted personality needs of leaders and followers intersect in the closed organizational system, individual pathology can become organized into social or political pathology, e.g. terrorism or the mass suicide at Jonestown.

8.4   The Personality Needs Of Organizational Members

Is it possible that certain types of people are attracted to work in closed organizational families? Very few people would question that there are some very irrational forces that influence our choice of intimate partners. Is it possible that some of these same forces could influence our choice of a work setting?

Persons of every personality type could find themselves caught up in the destructive forces of the closed organizational family. Many staff, who work in some of the most extremely closed systems, share remarkably similar backgrounds. A high percentage of these staff members come from very closed family systems. Many come from families that have experienced closure related to geographical isolation, the stigma associated with alcoholism (or other chronic disabling illnesses) or sexual abuse.

Many of these individuals have a long history of involvement in closed organizational systems. It is quite possible that many such persons seek organizational settings that tend to replicate their family system. Such persons may also seek out a role in the organizational family that parallels the role they performed in their nuclear family.

8.5   The Role Of Stigma

As the author reviewed his consulting experience with a diverse group of closed organizations, a central question was what characteristics these organizations shared that could contribute to the closure process. One intriguing possibility was that many of these organizations shared the role of providing services to stigmatized clients, e.g., the alcoholic/addict, the mentally ill, the developmentally disabled, the physically handicapped or disfigured, the aged and infirm, the sexual abuse victim/offender, the dying, etc. This was intriguing because while a great deal of attention has been spent on the impact of such stigma on clients, no attention has been spent on the impact of such stigma on the caregivers.

Stigma can play a major role in promoting the process of organizational closure. Let's consider, for example, how such stigma can promote the development of a work dominated social network.

Several years ago, the author was discussing with a group of hospice nurses how their work affected their social relationships, and why they spent most of their social time with each other. One of the nurses responded for the group as follows:

Imagine yourself at a social gathering, and as people introduce themselves and ask what you do, you respond by
saying: "I provide care for dying patients". Talk about uncomfortable! Nobody wants to look at death! If I tell
people I'm a nurse, they want medical advise on their kids.
If I tell them I'm a hospice nurse, they run away. With each
other, we don't have to deal with that craziness!

I instinctively understood what the nurses were expressing. I
humorously recalled the number of times I had told someone at a
cocktail party that I was Director of an alcoholism program, only
to have the person look at their drink and launch into a defense of
their own drinking or want free advice on the drinking problem of
a family member or friend.

For those of us associated with issues, behaviors, or illnesses
which are misunderstood and to which powerful stigmas and fears
are still attached, we may find barriers to the development of non-
work social relationships. To encounter us is to encounter aspects
of life that produce fear and discomfort in most people.

Imagine the social isolation of the AIDS victim. Would not the
same fear and stigma work to socially isolate the nurse who works
in a specialized AIDS treatment facility? Wouldn't such stigma
promote the development of a predominantly work-oriented social
network?

8.6   The Role Of Status

Status can also work to promote organizational closure. Status
and success can produce a loss of privacy that encourages one to
retreat within the safety of a closed organization. Status and success can produce an arrogance that shuts off the flow of people and
ideas into the organization.

There was a physician group practice that achieved an international reputation for their pioneering surgical techniques. The
success of this organization produced a progression of professional, social, and sexual closure in the organization that would
result in the self-destruction of the practice some eight years following its creation. The demise of this organization left in its

wake, shattered friendships, serious stress related health problems of some of the key organizational members, and a string of marriage casualties.

Political and/or economic power can also produce a level of closure that has far reaching ramifications. A study of the Nixon White House years is illustrative. Such a study would reveal the progressive closure of the White House staff as an organizational system, the lack of reality testing and reduced boundary transactions, the development and persecution of an outside enemy, a scapegoating of those members who challenged the ideology, and a twisting of values that placed the White House staff above the law in a belief that the ends justified the means. The degree of closure is indicated by the length of time and amount of energy it would take to penetrate the organization and unravel the saga that would be called Watergate.

The disintegration of the organizational family and fall of the high priest via Watergate would shake the foundations of our government. But let's consider a more terrifying alternative that could happen in such a closed system. Suppose the outside enemy of this organizational family was not the National Democratic Party, but the Soviet Union. The closure process would prevent reality testing, restrict the flow of objective information to organizational leaders, scapegoat members who propose a more reasoned approach to the Soviet Union, etc. The escalation of conflict emerging from such a closed political organization has horrifying possibilities.

8.7 Xenophobia And Organizational Culture

Some organizational families have a built-in fear and distrust of outsiders as a permanent and major thrust of their organizational culture. This xenophobia can play a major role in maintaining the closure of the organizational family. Examples of such systems include most military organizations, security or intelligence operations, or, at a local community level, most police departments.

This fear of outsiders is also generated in persons from whom we have very high and rigid role expectations. The policeman, the minister or priest, the school teacher, or the local public official may develop closed systems around them as a protection from public scrutiny. The fear that private behavior may not meet often unrealistic public standards fuels the closure of such systems. Such closure helps hide the flaws in our public role models. When in public, these persons are always in role. When with other organizational family members, they can relax and be human.

Our expectations of persons in such public roles also extends to their family life. Professional and social closure help form a wall of protection around the cop whose kid is involved in petty crime, the minister whose daughter is acting out sexually, the psychiatrist with a crazy kid, or the marriage counselor experiencing turbulence in his or her own marriage.

All of the issues identified in this chapter may enhance the movement toward organizational closure. Understanding which factors are at work is essential to developing strategies to open the closed, dysfunctional organizational family.

Chapter Nine
Role Conditions and the Worker
Casualty Process

There are many aspects of the microsystem - the smallest unit of organization in which the worker conducts his or her activities - that can contribute to professional stress. This chapter, will begin with a discussion of the physical environment of the microsystem and then outline a model that examines the relationship between professional burnout and the level of role stressors and role supports in the microsystem.

All activities and relationships in the team, department, section, division or service take place in the context of a physical environment. The qualities of this physical environment can have a profound effect on the level of stress experienced by workers. Some of the most important environmental concerns include the following:

- The amount of physical space per person.
- The layout of physical space, e.g., efficient organization of space, traffic patterns in the physical space and their congruence to needed communication patterns, etc.
- Lighting.
- Ventilation (particularly in industrial settings where materials or processes may produce noxious odors, or in office settings with a high percentage of smokers).
- Temperature (a major issue for the foundry worker pouring iron, or the office worker who freezes in the summer and suffocates in the winter in a building with a poor heating and cooling system).
- Noise level.
- Cleanliness of the work environment, including bathroom and eating areas.
- The quality and quantity of equipment and materials available to the worker to perform successfully his or her job.

A key word in our study of the microsystem is harmony. When

individual workers are in harmony with their environment, very little adaptational energy is required to respond to physical stressors, and energy is freed to devote to the work objectives of the unit. Disharmony occurs when conditions in the physical or social environments undermine the health and comfort of the worker which lowers the energy available for high quality performance. The non-smoker in a small, confined, non-ventilated space with smokers; the secretary in a 90-degree office; the policeman in the mass confusion of the "Hill Street Blues" station environment; the construction worker placed in weather extremes of cold and heat; and the worker in overly crowded, poorly organized space are all examples of disharmony that can disrupt worker health and productivity.

The work environment represents the most basic element of the relationship between the organization and the individual worker. Conditions in the work environment convey the most primary message of respect or disrespect to the worker. Speeches and philosophy statements by organizational leaders which express compassion and support for workers fall on deaf ears when the environment of the microsystem reflects a lack of respect for the physical comfort of workers. One worker captured this principle in the following cryptic comment: "If we're so important to the Company, the least they could do is provide a bathroom that is fit for human habitation"!

9.1   Role Stressors And Role Supports In The Microsystem

This section will outline a model for understanding some aspects of burnout in the microsystem by examining those specific role stressors and role supports that surround each worker in the microsystem. The model is illustrated graphically in Exhibit 9-A.

As an individual enters and works in a particular organization, there exists a number of role conditions which will effect the workers physical and emotional health and their productivity. The relationship between these conditions and the individual worker can be summarized through the use of the following terms.

Role Stressors *are the Number and Intensity of Role Conditions that Threaten and Decrease One's Self-esteem and Decrease One's Ability to Perform Successfully the Assigned Responsibilities.*

EXHIBIT 9-A

The Relationship Between Burnout and Role Conditions in the Microsystem

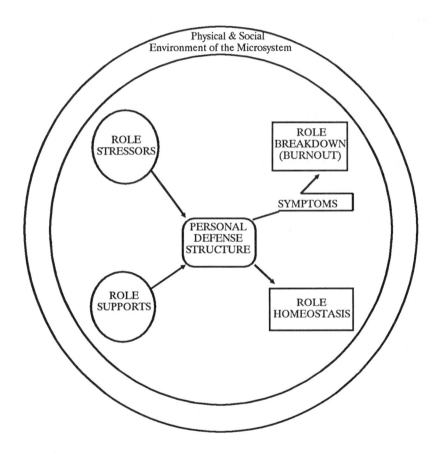

Role stressors escalate the demand for adaptational energy and place a strain on the relationship between the worker and the organization. Examples of role stressors could include safety hazards, excessive work demands, isolation from other workers, or confusion over performance expectations. Thirteen types of role stressors will be catalogued later in this chapter.

Role Supports are the Number and Intensity of Role Conditions thatIncrease Self-esteem and Increase One's ability to Perform Successfully the Assigned Responsibilities.

Role supports serve as a buffer against or a tool to help manage role stressors in the work environment. Examples of role supports could include excellent salary and benefits, availability of high quality and appropriate quantity of equipment and materials to perform one's job, technical and personal support from supervisors, and a high level of personal affirmation and acknowledgment from peers and supervisors. A large number of role support options will be catalogued in the last two chapters of this book.

The Personal Defense Structure is Each Individual's Preferred Pattern of Thinking, Feeling, and Behaving When Confronted With High Demands for Adaptation.

The personal defense structure represents one's personal degree of vulnerability to stress and one's unique style of managing stress. All of us experience both role stressors and role supports regardless of our occupation or type of organizational setting. Both stressors and supports are filtered through our personal defense structure - a fact that makes each person's experience of the work environment different. This is why two people may respond so differently to a similar level of stressors and supports in the microsystem. Those factors that make up this personal defense structure will be detailed in the next chapter.

Role Homeostasis Exists When the Individual Experiences a Relative Balance Between Role Stressors and Role Supports.

The personal defense structure of each individual operates constantly to maintain this balance. When this equilibrium is maintained, the individual performs assigned tasks adequately and suffers no stress-related disruption in physical or emotional health. In short, the individual functions without symptoms.

Role Breakdown Exists When the Individual Experiences A Loss of Homeostasis Due to Changes in Level and Intensity of Role Stressors and Role Supports.

Role breakdown can occur through an increase in stressors and/or a decrease in role supports or through changes in the strength of the personal defense structure. When this defense structure is stretched beyond its capacity for adaptation, the individual worker becomes symptomatic (see chart of indicators in chapter 1) and experiences a stress-related deterioration in work performance.

The above model illustrates three levels of microsystem intervention that can be utilized to reduce the incidence of role breakdown and the toll of human casualties that accompany such breakdowns.

1. We can build programs and services into the organization that increase the strength and flexibility of the personal defense structure, e.g., employee assistance, health promotion and stress management training programs.
2. We can manipulate the work environment to reduce role stressors.
3. We can manipulate the work environment to increase role supports.

Thirteen role stressors are identified in the following pages that lead to role breakdown and the deterioration in the physical and emotional health of workers. Levi (1981) has noted that workers are both adaptable and deformable. Organizations, that sustain the role stressors described in this chapter, prove this point. These role stressors include the following:

- Role/Person Mismatch
- Role Conflict
- Role Ambiguity
- Role Overload
- Role Safety Hazards

- Role Assignment Misplacement
- Role Integrity Conflict
- Role Underload

- Insufficient Role Feedback
- Role Insecurity
- Role Deprivation
- Role Connectedness
  Problems
- Role Termination

The author is particularly indebted in this section to the work of Kahn, Wolfe, Quinn, Snolk and Rosenthal (1964) whose classic studies on organizational stress convinced me that a modified version of role theory would be an effective framework for analyzing burnout at the microsystem level.

9.2 Role Person Mismatch

Role Person Mismatch is the Incongruency Between:

(a) An individual's knowledge and skill level and the knowledge and skill level required to perform tasks of a given role.

(b) An individual's level of stress tolerance and the stress endemic to a particular role.

(c) An individual's style of stress management and the methods of stress management that are officially and informally sanctioned within an organization.

The wider the incongruency in these areas, the greater are the demands for adaptation and the greater the likelihood that the individual worker will experience role breakdown.

A major portion of the responsibility for this mismatch can be found by examining an organization's screening and hiring procedures. An inadequate screening and hiring process can result in the hiring of a worker into a role where skill demands far exceed the skills of the worker. When the worker is then unable to perform at an adequate level, responsibility (blame) for the problem is attributed to the worker and not on the organizational procedures or processes that originally led to the misplacement of the worker.

Common examples of this misplacement include the following:

- Hiring for match with the team rather than match with a particular role (Many times people are hired because of their personality. The applicant has skills that could be used by the organization but is then hired and placed in the wrong role. Interview focus needs to be not only on fit with the organization, but fit [knowledge and skills] for the role).

- Hiring based on scoring on objective tests where knowledge tested has no relationship to knowledge and skills required in day-to-day work performance.
- Mistaking commitment for competence (High passion and motivation to do a good job don't in and of themselves guarantee the knowledge and skill to do the job).
- Making or failing to check out assumptions (e.g., assuming an applicant with an M.A. in psychology can do psychological testing, assuming a recovering alcoholic knows something about alcoholism and possesses skills to counsel alcoholics, or assuming a construction worker can read a blueprint).

This process of misplacement can occur in role changes based on promotion as well as in hiring new employees. The "Peter Principle" (Peter, 1969) which observes that everyone eventually rises to their level of incompetence is, in many organizations, all too often true. Many promotions are made out of a sense of loyalty - a feeling that the position is owed to someone - rather than an objective assessment of skills and the ability of a worker to manage successfully the transition in roles.

The level of stress experienced by the misplaced worker escalates as the discrepancy between real and assumed skills becomes increasingly evident. The misplaced worker may try to overcompensate for the lack of quality performance by increasing the quantity of hours committed to the work environment further taxing the limits of his or her adaptational energy.

The phenomenon of the misplaced worker is an excellent example of the systems principles elaborated in this book. The problem of the misplaced worker cannot be defined in the worker or in the work environment but must be viewed as a problem in the unique structuring of the relationship between the worker and the organization. The impact of problems in this relationship is also not unidimensional - impact of mismatch on the worker. The misplacement of a worker in an inappropriate role feeds back into the system and creates its own repercussions. The under-achievement of the misplaced worker must be countered by overachievement in other roles if the system is to stay in balance. The role/person mismatch escalates the experience of stress for the misplaced worker and for those persons filling roles around the misplaced worker. As coworker stress escalates, there is an increased tendency for scapegoating and extrusion of the worker from the organization. An alternative to scapegoating is the addition of a person (role) to perform those responsibilities of the misplaced person and then retiring the misplaced person on the job (see later description of role deprivation). The misplacement of a worker can thus produce a synergistic effect. The misplacement of a worker may grow out of processes in the microsystem, impact the misplaced person, who in turn impacts the total functioning of the microsystem and increases stress on other workers.

The above descriptions relate role/person mismatch that are due to the worker's knowledge and skill level. Another type of mismatch involves an individual worker's history of stress management and the level of stress inherent in the particular role he/she is hired to perform. Numerous examples exist where role/person mismatch led to serious deterioration in a worker's health, not because of skill deficiency, but because the demands for adaptation inherent in his/her role surpassed his/her capacity for adaptation.

We are talking about a special match between personality, adaptational style, and the level of stress tolerance with a particular job role. Let's consider this role/person match in therapists and crisis workers. While many areas of knowledge and skill overlap between these two roles, the special characteristics of those persons who excel in each role differ significantly. The best crisis workers ever known to the author were adrenaline freaks. They thrived on the action and intensity and lack of predictability of the emotionally volatile situation whether it was on a suicide hotline or domestic violence crisis team. These same individuals often made horrible therapists because the highly structured, one hour per week, long term process of helping people change their lives quite simply didn't provide enough action or stimulation to keep them involved in the process. By the same note, some of the best therapists were less than effective in the crisis situation even though they possessed all the technical knowledge necessary to excel in such a situation. Again the issue is the special chemistry between people and their level of adaptational energy and the adaptational demands of the roles in which we expect them to perform.

Imagine the demands for adaptational energy placed on the first black professional baseball player. Most commentators agree that Jackie Robinson was the perfect choice to break the barrier against black athletes in professional baseball. Jackie Robinson was the perfect choice not simply because of his extraordinary skills as a baseball player but because his level and style of stress tolerance sustained him and prevented his self-destruction when confronted with some of the most shameful examples of racism in the history of professional sports. As more ethnic minorities, women, the handicapped, etc., approach similar barriers in many diverse occupations, this issue of level of stress tolerance, and style of stress management becomes as crucial in the role/person match as the level of knowledge and skills these workers possess.

9.3   Role Assignment Misplacement

Role Assignment Misplacement is the Misplacement of Persons with Excellent Skills in Interior Organizational Positions into Boundary Positions in the Organization, or Vice Versa.

Workers, who hold interior positions in an organization, interact primarily with other members of their microsystem (team, unit, department). Workers in boundary positions interact frequently with other microsystems of the organization and/or have multiple transactions with systems outside the organization.

The role stressor of role assignment misplacement constitutes a special type of role person mismatch. The mismatch often occurs when organizations reward successful performance in an interior role by promoting a worker to a boundary position, assuming the knowledge and skills are transferable. The fact is that boundary roles usually require significantly different skills than interior roles and often require different levels of stress tolerance and styles of stress management.

145

Two examples of this role stressor are illustrative. In the first example, a unit supervisor of a hospital, who provided leadership to other unit personnel related to day-to-day problem solving to provide patient care services, was promoted to a position of department head. This new position required a majority of time interacting with other hospital departments and marketing department services outside the hospital. Rather than focusing on patient care, the new department head was thrown into a world of inter-departmental politics, budget battles, hospital committees, and special task forces to generate new money making ideas to compensate for decreased patient census. In short, the technical patient care skills were not applicable to the new role; the new role demanded areas of knowledge and skill foreign to the worker; the high level of interaction with other departments, specialty areas and the community proved highly stressful; and the personal reward of participating in the healing of injury and illness was lost in the new position. As demands for adaptation escalated, the new department head resigned her position to accept a supervisor of patient care position in another hospital. This example of role assignment misplacement took not only its personal toll, but also resulted in the loss of a highly skilled employee from the institution.

In the second example, a counselor at a residential psychiatric program was promoted to the role of intake coordinator. In his former position, the counselor worked within a tight supervisory structure, had limited professional interactions outside the institution, and experienced knowledge and skill demands primarily related to client assessment and counseling. In the new role of intake coordinator, the counselor was responsible for all initial agency contacts with referral sources, screening and acceptance of clients, and contact with community agencies regarding discharge and aftercare plans. The intake coordinator was to be the institutions bridge to the outside community. This worker, who had performed very well as a counselor, found himself unable to organize the work adequately and keep up with the details of case management without close supervision, found himself disliking many of the community agency personnel with whom he was forced to interact, and found himself constantly in trouble for "forgetting" to return calls, inappropriate admissions, and his inability to market services to keep referrals coming. Facing increasing pressure as he floundered in the new role, the worker resigned from the agency.

In both cases, these workers had established records of successful performance in interior roles of the organization. Both workers discovered in the new boundary positions increased stressors, a loss of old supports, and an inability to transfer skills leading to diminished self-esteem and frustration. Both workers suffered stress-related deterioration in performance as this misplacement continued over time.

9.4   Role Conflict

Role Conflict Exists When a Worker Experiences Incongruous Demands and Expectations From Two or More Simultaneously Held Roles.

Role conflict is probably one of the most frequently described conditions in the literature on organizational stress. Role conflict puts the worker in a no-win position. Incongruent and contradictory expectations from multiple roles means that to meet the expectations of one role is to fail to meet the demands of another simultaneously held role. There are numerous examples of role conflict that could be discussed such as the worker with more than one boss, the shop steward caught between the company on the one hand and the union members he or she represents on the other. Since so much of this book focuses on how work-related stress spills into our personal life and disrupts our ability to sustain intimate and family relationships, our discussion will focus on the conflict between the role of worker and the roles each worker performs in his/her nuclear or surrogate family. The following observations are offered on the nature of this type of role conflict.

Each of us has expectations set for our role performance in the organization, and most of us have expectations for our role performance in a family or intimate social network. Role conflict occurs when the nature of the demands from these roles are such that they cannot be met simultaneously. The units of exchange in all of these roles can be measured in time, productivity and emotional energy. Some obvious conditions in the work environment that create this type of role stressor include the following:

● Excessive demands for time and emotional energy.
● Shift work, (second shift workers who may see very little of their families except on weekends; shift work demands

that conflict with role expectations of wife and mother, e.g., social events, school plays, PTA, little league.

- Excessive travel that prevents regular physical presence with one's family.
- Availability for work emergencies that makes all family activities tentative and contingent on the silence of the beeper or telephone.

Other conditions in the organization that can create and escalate the experience of role conflict may be harder to pinpoint. All the role-stress conditions in this chapter can drastically increase the worker's demand for physical and emotional energy. Under such conditions of high demand, the worker may have little energy left with which to sustain outside relationships and successfully perform his or her family roles.

There are also conditions in the family system that can exacerbate the experience of role conflict. These include any conditions or events that strain the adaptational energy of family members, such as the following:

- A death, disability, acute or chronic disabling illness of a family member.
- The "two-career family".
- Problems endemic to the marriage.
- The single parent household.
- Problems in the care of children.
- Relatives living in the home.
- The relocated family.
- Financial problems.

Many of the marriage casualties of burnout victims in the author's previous studies occurred when role conflict was polarized to the point that either the job or the family had to be sacrificed as there simply was not enough adaptational energy available to the burnout victim to sustain both roles.

9.5 Role Integrity Conflict

Role Integrity Conflict is the Incongruence Between On's Personal Values and the Values Inherent in the Work Environment.

Workers bring values and beliefs with them when they enter the life of an organization, and these values and beliefs may evolve over time through experiences in the organization. The organization also has explicit and implicit values and beliefs that evolve over time through the influence of its members and through interactions with the outside world. When the values of the worker and the organization are very divergent, stress results from the worker's need to bring the organization's values into conformity with his/her own values. At the same time, forces of homogenization in the work milieu seek to bring the worker's values and behavior into congruence with organizational norms. This battle of adaptation, and how it is resolved may have a significant impact on the self-esteem of the worker.

The list of such value conflicts is almost unending - the nurse and physician confronted with hospital administrators more concerned with profits than patient care, the civil service worker fighting cynicism over the political distribution of government contracts, the construction worker concerned over materials and designs that will threaten the safety of future occupants of the building being constructed, the worker in a home for developmentally disabled who observes patient abuse, and the alcoholism counselor who must deny an alcoholic admission to treatment for lack of cash or an insurance card, etc.

The list above is a bit misleading, as it pits apparently ethical individuals against more malign forces in the organization. The fact is that role integrity conflict doesn't include the issue of whose values are right. Stress is not a seeker of truth. It concerns only the degree of discrepancy between individual and organizational values. This degree of discrepancy dictates the amount of adaptational energy the individual worker will need to sustain his/her beliefs and attempts to influence the organization. Each individual, whether healthy or crazy, right or wrong, will seek, at some level, to reshape the organization in his or her own image - which means bringing the organization's values into congruence with his/her own.

The issue for the organization is to determine to what degree it will allow its values and beliefs to evolve and what the role of organizational members shall be to shape this evolution. To the degree this potential process of participation is open, stress is reduced as values tend to move toward the center of the collective beliefs of organizational members. To the extent that the organization closes off participation and evolution of beliefs, stress is escalated by the divergence in individual and organizational values.

For some people this battle of adaptation is more an issue of personal survival than an intellectual debate. For the recovering alcholic counselor, whose own sobriety is based on the beliefs of Alcoholics Anonymous (AA), finding themselves working in a treatment program that undermines this belief system may provoke a crisis of loyalty with potentially shattering consequences. The case study at the end of this chapter shows the results of an organization which drove a wedge between a worker and the belief system upon which the worker's recovery from alcoholism was based.

9.6 Role Ambiguity

Role Ambiguity is the Worker's Inadequate Knowledge of: (1) Role Expectations; (2) Task Priorities; (3) Preferred Methods of Task Completion; (4) Accountability Structure and (5) Organizatioal Rewards and Punishments.

Role ambiguity is a highly stressful condition for workers that usually occurs in organizations that lack the management expertise to consistently define role functions, accountability, etc., or in organizations going through such periods of rapid change and turbulence that such role definitions have been lost altogether.

The following comments typify the sentiments of workers that experience role ambiguity:

- "Look, I can play the game; I just need somebody to tell me what the rules are!"
- "I'm not completely sure who my boss is, and the only way I know what I'm supposed to do lately is when somebody tells me I forgot to do it or did it wrong."
- "I can't win. If I asked her how she wants me to do it (job tasks), she says I ought to know. If I don't ask her, then she comes by and tells me I did it the wrong way. Either way, I look like a fool."

- "You know, I want to go someplace - be somebody, but I can't make sense out of this place. I still haven't figured out if you get ahead here by working hard or sleeping with the boss's daughter."

Role ambiguity is often a sign of the loss of a clear sense of mission, purpose, and goals within the microsystem or the overall organization. This lack of clarity at the top ripples down into a majority of the roles in the organization. Role ambiguity can reflect a holding pattern or loss of direction by an organization whose behavior is represented by the adage, "We won't know where we're going until we get there".

Role ambiguity leads to a loss of security and predictability in the life of the worker. How can I evaluate my own performance in an undefined job? How can I be accountable when I'm not sure who I'm accountable to, and what I'm accountable for? Role ambiguity can trigger stress-related behavior as diverse as angry confrontations to hiding out and a search for invisibility. Both examples reflect the strain placed on the worker's personal defense structure by role ambiguity.

9.7   Insufficient Role Feedback

Insufficient Role Feedback is the Nonavailability of Regular Information on: (1) the Adequacy of Role Performance, (2) the Methods of Improving Performance; and (3) the Adequacy of Adjustment to the Work Milieu.

The lack of adequate feedback to workers in the work environment is a frequent theme among participants from diverse occupational groups who attend stress workshops. Each of us needs feedback and acknowledgment to sustain our performance and self-esteem in any role, whether it be a family or organizational role. When role feedback is absent, we begin to disengage emotionally and seek out new roles that provide self-affirming feedback.

The author observed an amazing example of this a few years ago while consulting with a small civil service agency. During the many days spent with this agency, I observed the following about one of the workers. He maintained a detached, uninvolved

151

demeanor, was silent in the few meetings he was asked to attend, seemed socially aloof, and described his work (in response to questions) in a factually brief manner without emotional affect. The reader might suspect clinical depression, but such was not the case. What was amazing about this individual was the transformation that happened when he left the office area to join co-workers for a coffee break or lunch. He immediately became animated. His voice took on strength and character. He had an incredible sense of humor and was sought out to entertain co-workers with his funny stories and wry wit. He also had numerous roles outside of work which he would describe with great passion and interest. Being struck by this Dr. Jeckyl/Mr. Hyde personality change, the author investigated to find that this individual worked in autonomous, isolated role within the organization, almost totally devoid of any feedback related to his job. He performed a role without measurable outcomes that could have provided self-feedback on performance and thus relied solely on peers and supervisors to convey the level of excellence of his job performance. Completely devoid of such feedback, his interest, excitement and feelings of accomplishment were almost completely extinguished. Lacking such affirmation, he evolved another role in the work setting and created outside roles that reinforced his value and self-esteem. The feedback system in the organization recognized this person as a friend and luncheon partner but rendered him invisible inside the work environment.

Feedback can come in many forms - salary, bonuses, symbols of status, written acknowledgment, awards, verbal praise, the pat on the back (meant literally), objective measures of excellence, etc. The quantity and variety of feedback in the work environment has an important relationship to the experience of professional stress. If we define stress as the demand for adaptational change, feedback is the essential data that helps us shape, modify, correct, or experiment with new behavior to efficiently accommodate this demand. Feedback that is affirming of the person, and specific enough to allow for refined improvement, helps reduce the intensity of stress. Feedback that combines criticism and vagueness can be devastating. Examples of the latter include the following types of supervisory remarks:

- "I'm really disappointed in you. I was really relying

on you, but quite frankly your performance just isn't up to par." (This comment indicts the worker as a person, seeks to elicit guilt, and provides no specific data on what the worker needs to change.)
- "You haven't quite got it yet. Why don't you try again." (The boss doesn't know what he or she wants but they'll know it when they see it.)

Feedback communications can be supportive of worker health and productivity when they enhance the self-esteem of the worker, provide data to support and improve role adequacy, and serve as an early warning of work-related stress problems. Feedback, such as verbal praise, may be crucial in occupational areas where more objective measurable feedback is unavailable, or where the nature of the service guarantees a negative objective outcome. It is easy to conceive of feedback in such measurable terms as sales, profits, production achievements, advances in student achievement scores, deadlines met, number of crimes solved, etc. But what kind of feedback do we provide the manager in a declining industry where even the best management practices may show year end losses rather than profits? What kind of feedback do we provide the physician and nurses caring for the terminally ill patient? What kind of feedback do we provide those workers caring for the profoundly retarded and physically disabled child who with the best of care, will never leave the institution? What kind of feedback do we provide the rescue workers who are called to the horror of a large plane crash where all passengers are dead? When effective mechanisms of social/emotional support and feedback are not present in these situations, highly competent and caring workers can become stress related casualties.

9.8   Role Overload

Role Overload Relates to Excessive and Unrealistic Expectations Regarding the Quantity and /or Quality of Work to be Completed Within a Given Time Frame.

Role overload can have a rapid and profound impact on the incidence of professional burnout in an organization. The excessive demand for physical and emotional energy inherent in role overload takes the workers capacity for adaptation and lowers the body's resistance to disease and injury. Role overload also decreases the strength and flexibility of each worker's personal defense structure. Role overload can also decrease the worker's emotional energy and available time to seek sources of personal and social replenishment outside the work environment.

Role overload is one of the most frequent role stressors in organizations today. Organizations in diverse fields share in common the need to do more with less staff and less costs. Companies are cutting the number of employees, but not the production quotas. Companies are cutting corners by laying off workers (to decrease benefit costs), while increasing regular overtime for those workers that remain. Many organizations are dramatically increasing the use of part-time help to reduce labor costs through decreased benefit obligations. Organizations are overextending workers in an effort to "get over the hump" and generate new business or find new sources of funding. All of these trends confirm the point that overextended workers are often merely a reflection of the over-extension of the organization. Given our understanding of stress, it is inevitable that these trends will impact the quality of organizational services and products, the health and vitality of the organizational culture, and the physical and emotional health of individual workers.

Much of this overload is due to turbulence in the macro and exo-systems. Nowhere is this more evident than in the health care industry, in general, and hospitals in particular. Radical changes in the organization of health care in the U.S., sparked in part by dramatic changes in systems of service reimbursement, have led to the following:

- A dramatic increase in alternatives to inpatient hospitalization e.g., emergi-centers "doc in a box" walk-in physician care in shopping malls, one day surgery, etc.
- Increased acuity of patients with shorter lengths of stay in community hospitals.
- Low hospital occupancies leading to:
  – marketing wars to capture patients.
  – a scramble for new types of patients to fill beds, e.g., psychiatric, chemical dependency, extended care units, etc.

− severe cost containment measures, e.g., staff layoffs, shift to part time workers, use of temporary agencies for nursing coverage, etc.

● The multiplication and fragmentation of institutional goals, with profit surpassing patient care as the primary organizational value.

● An escalation of personal stress and interpersonal and interdepartmental conflict in response to such rapid change.

We could continue the list indefinitely, but the point is that the ripple effect from the macrosystem to the microsystem has left individual hospital workers emotionally spent from the need to care for sicker patients with fewer resources. A person may be dying in a hospital right now in the name of cost containment and efficiency, and the nurse, charged with his/her care, will be too exhausted from overload to feel the pain of the loss.

9.9   Role Underload

Role Underload is the Degree of Tedium Produced from too Few Responsibilities or From the Organization of Work into Mechanical, Repetitive, and Non-stimulating Tasks.

Where role overload produces demands for adaptation from stimulation, role underload produces demands for adaptation from too little stimulation. Monotony and boredom can be as wearing on self-esteem as the experience of excessive and unachievable role demands. In health and human service agencies, stress can be equally intense at both the lowest and highest periods of service demand.

Most workers who experience role underload will either leave their job in search of more satisfying work or resign themselves to their situation by emotionally detaching from their work role while seeking more intense stimulation in roles and activities outside the organization.

9.10   Role Safety Hazards

Role Safety Hazards Reflect the Degree to Which One Experiences Apprehension About Potential Physical or Psychological Harm in the Performance of One's Professional Role.

Shostak (1980), in his excellent work on blue collar stress, noted a 1971 Labor Department study in which workers sited health and safety hazards as their second highest choice of job-related stress. Shostak goes on to cite some alarming statistics that justify the concern of these workers. Consider the following:

- Over 14,000 workers per year die in industrial accidents, and another 100,000 are permanently disabled from such accidents each year.
- The National Institute of Occupational Safety and Health estimates that 100,000 workers die annually from industrial disease, and an additional 300,000 will contract disabling work-related illnesses - such illnesses often created from exposure to radiation, chemicals, fumes and other toxic materials.
- A 1978 study indicated that as much as 20 percent of all cancer in the U.S. is related to exposure to toxic substances in the workplace. (Shostak 1980).

The literature on occupational safety hazards focuses primarily on industrial and manufacturing settings. It may surprise the reader, however, to find that role safety is a concern in a larger number of occupational groups. A few years ago, for example, the author conducted a stress workshop for teachers in an urban public school setting, and, as part of the workshop, asked participants to list and rank the major stressors they experienced in their work. I was shocked to find that fear of physical intimidation and physical assault was ranked as the number one stressor. Role safety issues can be of concern to a wide range of workers from the professional athlete's fear of a debilitating and career-ending injury to the policeman's awareness of vulnerability while speeding to the scene of an armed robbery or domestic disturbance.

It is also important to note that role safety hazards, as a stressor, emerge from the worker's perception or fear of vulnerability regardless of whether such fear is grounded in reality. According to all available data, for example, there is very little risk of health care workers contracting AIDS through the care of an AIDS patient as long as normal sterile technique is used to provide such care. This objective reality does not help explain the current hysteria and fear that can overwhelm health care workers when they confront their first AIDS patient.

Threats to psychological safety can also be a major stressor to workers. Threats to psychological safety can range from the worker in constant fear of verbal abuse from a punitive supervisor, to the human service worker in danger of being overwhelmed by the pain and trauma in the lives of his/her clients, or to the worker whose decisions will have a profound impact on the health and safety of others, e.g., the surgeon, the air traffic controller, or the hostage negotiator.

9.11   Role Insecurity

Role Insecurity is the Degree of Uncertainty In Relationship to One's Future Role in the Organization.

Role insecurity is a stressor that often emerges out of turbulence in the exosystem and macrosystem. Major changes in economic and political policy reverberate down to impact the job security of individual workers. This is an area where such macrosystem issues as foreign competition, interest rates, national foreign policy, and federal and state funding trends, lose their abstractness and directly affect the worker's assurance that he or she will have a job tomorrow. As macrosystem issues create business closings, belt-tightening through layoffs and forced early retirement, reductions in hours worked, etc.; workers experience increased apprehension about their future economic security.

The fear and apprehension about future job loss can be more stressful to some people than the actual loss itself. In systems in which rumors of layoff continue for months and the system of selecting workers for layoff is irrational and unpredictable, role insecurity will take its toll on all workers. Even following the layoff, those workers remaining will continue to feel vulnerable and where "bumping systems" exist, many workers may experience survivor guilt.

Role insecurity can also be produced from internal organizational issues. New organizational leadership, reorganizations, and acquisitions always create varying degrees of worker apprehension about role security depending upon how well such changes are managed.

9.12   Role Connectedness Problems

Role Connectedness Problems Refer to One's Degree of Isolation or Overconnectedness to Other Members of the Organization.

High demands for adaptation occur both when a worker is overconnected to other organizational members, or when a worker is excessively isolated from other organizational members. Earlier chapters explored how the over-attachment between organizational members can break down the boundary between one's personal and professional life, increasing replenishment. In the author's studies of professional stress, there was also a high casualty rate among workers whose role left them extremely detached and isolated from other organizational members. In human service agencies, for example, a high level of stress can be found among workers assigned to outreach roles, or who work alone in satellite offices isolated from the main organization. Such workers often experience the same or higher number of stressors, but have fewer supports by virtue of their isolation.

9.13   Role Deprivation

Role Deprivation is the Sudden or Gradual Removal of All Significant Responsibilities from the Worker.

Role deprivation retires the worker on the job. That such a move would create a loss in status, a crisis in self-esteem and increased isolation from other workers is obvious. When worker's are forcibly retired on the job, they may resign themselves to such a status or, more frequently, begin exaggerated and futile efforts to maintain their visibility and personhood. The defensive response of the worker is construed as further evidence of his or her inability to handle responsible job assignments. The character in Ralph Ellison's The Invisible Man could have been speaking for the role-deprived worker when he said:

"I can hear you say, 'What a horrible, irresponsible bastard'? And you're right. I leap to agree with you. I am one of the most irresponsible beings that ever lived. Irresponsibility is a part of my invisibility; and anyway you face it, it is a denial. But to whom can I be responsible, and why should I be, when you refuse to see me." (Ellison, 1947)

Role deprivation grows out of a number of conditions in the work environment. It may reflect a personality conflict between a supervisor and worker. It may reflect mistakes in role person match which the organization fails to correct. It may also reflect the placement of a burnout worker in an empty role by a supervisor unable to develop a more constructive alternative.

Role deprivation is a common role stressor in disengaged organizational families. One of the reasons civil service systems seem to have an inevitable inertia toward expanding size is that each year a certain number of workers are retired on the job and must be replaced by additional workers to complete the work of the agency.

9.14   Role Termination Problems

Role Termination Problems Reflect the Failure to Provide Permission, Procedures, and Processes to Allow Members Guilt-free Exit from the Organization.

Role termination refers to the process by which organizations bring to a close an individual's responsibilities in a particular role or bring to a close an individual's membership in the organization. We have already noted, in the chapter on Professional Closure, the inability of workers to get out of the closed organizational family with their self-esteem intact. At the other end of the continuum, in disengaged organizational families, the exit of members from the organization could be more aptly described as staff fallout rather than staff burnout. Their exit is no more acknowledged than their presence was, for they have been "invisible" for a long time.

A major component of organizational health is the ability of the organization to allow members guilt-free exit and to provide processes whereby members can leave with a sense of fulfillment and closure on their organizational family experience. It is remarkable how much time we spend on the technology of bringing people into an organization and how little time we spend figuring out better ways to let people out of the organization. Chapter Eleven will explore some ways to facilitate this process that enhance both individual and organizational health.

9.15   Role Stressors And The Organizational Family Continuum

Chapters Four through Eight developed the contention that the level of worker stress increased at both ends of the continuum of organizational closure. It was stated that stress-related casualties were highest in the enmeshed and disengaged organizational family types. This chapter outlined thirteen role stressors in the microsystem that contribute to stress-related casualties among workers. Consistent with this book's perspective on professional stress as a problem of ecological dysfunction, it is important to point out to the reader the relationship between these mesosystem and microsystem issues.

There is a direct relationship between the degree of closure in the mesosystem and role stress conditions in the microsystem. As the organizational boundary becomes too closed and nonpermeable at one end of the continuum and too open and diffused at the other, role stressors in the microsystem increase and the level of available role supports decrease. This chapter will close with a case study that reflects this combined perspective.

9.16   A Case Study On Stress As Ecological Dysfunction

This is a case study of Beth, a recovering alcoholic, who relapsed to active drinking while working as a counselor in an alcoholism treatment program.

Beth had worked as a high school teacher and guidance counselor most of her adult life, until she resigned following the sudden death of her husband in a traffic accident. Beth developed a severe alcohol abuse problem following her husband's death. After more than a year of almost constant intoxication, Beth was hospitalized and subsequently referred to a private alcoholism treatment program. She actively participated in Alcoholics Anonymous (AA) during her course of treatment and became actively involved in AA upon her return to her community. She attended numerous AA meetings and most of her social network consisted of persons she had met within the fellowship of AA. During Beth's third year of sobriety, she took a job as a counselor in a halfway house for alcoholic women and worked there for almost a year until the program was forced to close due to funding problems. During this period Beth participated in numerous alcoholism counselor training programs, completed work on a Master's degree in counseling and developed an excellent reputation as a counselor.

Shortly after the closing of the above program, Beth was hired as a counselor in a year-old outpatient alcoholism counseling center. Her early impressions of the program were extremely positive, as the staff seemed both dynamic and committed. The first signs of problems occurred during her third month of work following an intensive in-service training program for all staff. This week-long training emphasized psychological approaches to treating alcoholism, spoke of "curing" alcoholism, and was extremely critical of the "illness concept" of alcoholism in general, and the approach of AA in particular. The program staff, with the exception of Beth, experienced a type of group conversion to the model advocated by the trainers. Over the next several months, a number of significant events occurred. A large number of staff training events were scheduled for evenings and weekends to train the staff in the new ideology. These sessions were primarily growth groups which emphasized a high level of staff disclosure. These sessions decreased the amount of time Beth could spend in AA activities and were very stress producing as there was a great deal of pressure for her to "deal with the emotional traumas which caused her alcoholism".

Beth's affiliation with AA, and her use of AA principles and philosophies with clients, was subtly but continually discounted and criticized during this period.

As Beth began to experience increased stress concerning her own personal and professional beliefs, she came to rely increasingly on the emotional support of her supervisor. This eventually led to a romantic and sexual involvement which for a period of time provided a welcomed reprieve from the increased stress experienced on the job. Beth, recalling this period, said: "I really believe if it hadn't been for (supervisor), I would have resigned. I knew my thinking was getting screwed up, but that relationship felt so good I didn't believe anything could throw me off balance, and I still felt great about the work I was doing with my clients".

During the eleventh month of Beth's employment, the relationship with the supervisor ended bitterly (at the instigation of the supervisor), and Beth resigned her position and began drinking immediately. Although Beth made numerous AA contacts during the early months following her return to drinking, she had great difficulty maintaining sobriety. At the time of my interview with her, Beth had reestablished herself within the AA program and had maintained continuous sobriety for the last year. She has not, and reports she will not, return to work in the alcoholism field.

Organizational Analysis This analysis is based on interviews with Beth and with three staff persons who worked with Beth during the period described earlier. None of the three staff interviewed still work for the program, and, in fact, report that the entire staff of the center has turned over. Beth was the first of many casualties which resulted from the very serious internal organizational problems that were to plague the agency. Beth unknowingly entered what the author has earlier called an "incestuous organizational family". The program had become progressively closed off from the outside professional and social world and the "conversion" of the agency to a new faith system and the emergence of the Director as the high priest, would only intensify this closure process. Beth's relapse took place in the context of very turbulent internal program relationships and a concurrent escalation of stressors and loss of supports experienced by all staff.

The probability of Beth functioning effectively within the agency described should have been very high. She had four continuous years of sobriety, formal training and education in alcoholism counseling, a year's experience in counseling alcoholics, and an extensive network of personal support outside the agency. And yet, within eleven months, she become victim to the very problem she was hired to address in her clients. The stresses placed on Beth within this agency can be catalogued as follows:

A. Contradiction in Personal / Program Beliefs (Professional Closure, Role Conflict, Role Integrity Conflicts)

Beth experienced constant contradictions between those personal beliefs which supported her continuing sobriety, and those beliefs espoused by the program on the nature of alcoholism and the recovery process. This stress was intensified by the following double message received from other program staff:

"You do excellent work" with ⟵⟶ "You shouldn't emclients (in which she emphasized   phasize AA so much." principles learned through her AA experience).

B. Breakdown of Personal Supports for Sobriety Social Closure / Role Overload)

The program's subtle disapproval of AA, and the increasing time demands on evenings and weekends, both decreased Beth's ability to maintain her previously active participation in AA. This was further exacerbated in later months, by the time spent with the supervisor and an increasing expectation for socializing with staff away from work.

C. Breakdown of Personal Defenses (Role Safety Hazards)

The mandatory participation in staff growth groups, which required that Beth verbalize the emotional traumas of her life, severely weakened the defenses that had served Beth well in her period of sobriety. This breakdown of defenses left Beth very emotionally vulnerable.

D. Bonding to the Agency (Sexual Closure, Role Connectedness Problems)

Beth's relationship with the supervisor marked her final bond to the organizational group and her loss of outside supports. Beth's increased reliance on the supervisor for support in the face of increased stress allowed the supervisor to exploit the relationship for sexual purposes. (The supervisor had also been sexually involved in a similar manner with other women staff.)

E. Replication of Earlier Emotional Trauma

The sudden termination of the relationship with the supervisor replicated emotionally Beth's earlier loss of her husband and came at a time when she had few defenses left to cope with such a loss. Having lost other sources of coping, Beth regressed to the use of intoxication to medicate her emotional pain.

This case study shows how forces in the mesosystem (organizational closure) and forces in the microsystem (role stressors) can interact with individual vulnerability to produce a stress-related casualty.

Chapter Ten
Predicting And Managing Individual Vulnerability

Most of this book has examined how conditions and processes in the organizational environment influence the health of the individual worker. This chapter will look at those personal characteristics each individual brings to the work environment, and how such characteristics influence one's vulnerability to professional stress. A number of strategies will also be reviewed that can reduce one's vulnerability to stress-related disorders. The chapter is not intended as a comprehensive primer on individual stress management. Many authors, e.g. Pelletier (1977), much more capable in this area than the author, have already completed this task. The chapter is, however, intended to provide a systems perspective on the management of professional stress that is often neglected by other writers on the subject.

10.1   Factors Influencing Individual Vulnerability

If we are to develop strategies to decrease worker vulnerability to professional stress, it is essential that we isolate the major factors that contribute to such vulnerability. The following pages will explore eight factors that can increase or decrease one's vulnerability to professional stress. These factors, which are illustrated in Exhibit 10-A include the following:

- Genetic and developmental history.
- Prior history of stress management.
- Stage of life.
- Values, beliefs and motivations.
- Professional training.
- Life changes.
- Social and family supports.
- Role boundary management.

EXHIBIT 10-A

Factors Influencing Individual Vulnerability

WORKER

STRESSOR

STRESSOR

STRESSOR

INDIVIDUAL VULNERABILITY

Physical (Genetic and Developmental) History

Prior History of Stress Management

Stage of Life

Values and Beliefs

Professional Training

Social and Family Supports

Life Changes

Role Boundary Management

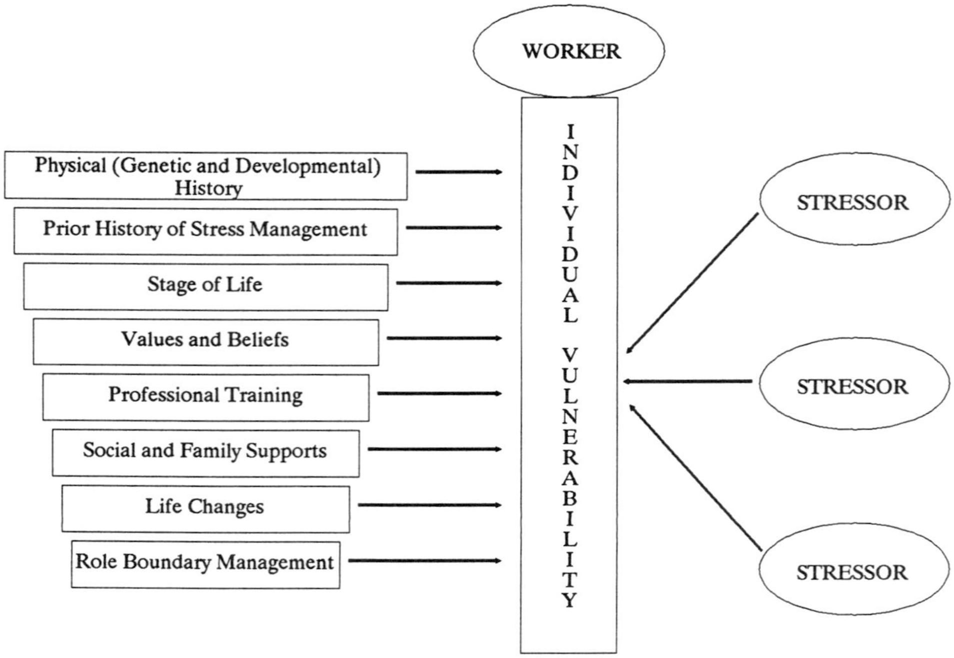

10.2   Your Body (Genetic and Developmental History)

The human body is a miracle in its range and capacity for adaptability, and yet the intensity and duration of such adaptation takes its toll on the body as it would on any such piece of intricate machinery. It does not, however, exact this toll consistently from person to person. There is a wide variation from person to person in the body's capacity to respond to stress.

Each of us is provided, through the roulette of human genetics, a unique body that, except in the case of identical twins, differs in both its physiological capacity for stress and in its physiological responses to stress. While there are generalized responses to stress that most humans share - what Selye (1956) has called the General Adaptation Syndrome - the degree to which the body responds to stress by altering blood supply and pressure, sharpening the acuity of the senses, altering adrenaline production, etc., differs from individual to individual. Such genetically predetermined differences may shape both our tolerance to stress and the unique areas of physical vulnerability to prolonged and excessive stress. Prolonged stress will attack the weakest link in the body's system of physiological defenses.

Understanding one's unique vulnerabilities, those weakest links, requires a knowledge of our unique physiology and both the genetic and developmental influences that shape that physiology. The cardinal rule of stress management - know thyself! - begins with knowledge of our body. For some of us, knowledge of genetic influences is as easy as reviewing our maternal and paternal family histories. One can simply ask: what organ or organs of the body are most vulnerable in my family history. Are there certain types of illnesses to which my family is particularly vulnerable? What conditions led to the death of relatives in my maternal and paternal family tree? Family trees dominated by the incidence of heart attacks and strokes, cancer, diabetes, gastrointestinal disorders, alcoholism, etc., can provide important information about physiological vulnerability.

Following conception, environmental and developmental influences work to increase or decrease this genetically shaped vulnerability to stress. Our physiological equipment may be enhanced through careful and regular maintenance or may be undermined by disease, illness, injury, or life styles and habits of daily living that produce excessive wear and tear on the body. These genetic and developmental factors often mesh together in ways that spell human disaster, e.g., the person with generations of deaths from cancer who begins smoking and then smokes excessively to self-medicate stress, or the person with generations of coronary heart disease whose lifestyle increases this vulnerability.

In the early 1900's, temperance lecturers used to place a brain damaged alcoholic in front of the lectern while they spoke. The alcoholic served as a living example of the horrors of demon rum. The author has often had the impulse to copy this technique in his stress seminars. Imagine poor Joe fidgeting impatiently in front of the lectern clearly overweight and underexercised, glassy-eyed from an infinity of 60-hour work weeks and no vacations, washing down double cheeseburgers and fried potatoes with a beer, chainsmoking cigarettes between bites - all while sitting under a diagram of his family tree showing four generations of deaths from cancer and heart disease.

The emerging field of holistic medicine has forged a definition of health as a state of harmony between body and mind and one's physical and psychosocial environment. The recognition that the majority of debilitative illnesses in this country are preventable, when that harmony exists, is sparking a revolution in our thinking about health and illness. Out of our historical emphasis on medical technology and specialization, people are reclaiming ownership of their bodies through a growing preventive health movement. This movement is producing a growing body of knowledge about how to decrease our vulnerability to the stress-related illnesses of modern civilization. The following pages will catalogue how one can decrease one's physical vulnerability to professional stress.

Body Maintenance There are three broad strategies for decreasing one's physical vulnerability to professional stress. These strategies include:

(1) establishing habits and rituals that provide regular repair and maintenance of our physical equipment so as to support rather than undermine the body's natural capacity for responding to stress,

(2) learning techniques that actually alter and improve the body's physiological response to stress, and

(3) developing an assertive role in advocating our own health needs in the work environment.

The first strategy is designed to reduce the wear and tear on the human body and also to enhance the body's own internal mechanisms for day-to-day repair of body tissue. All effective programs of stress management address the issues of nutrition and exercise.

Diet is an essential component of effective body maintenance. By consciously controlling the types of food we take in, we are able to improve the body's efficiency and longevity. Many people under excessive stress lose touch with the needs of their bodies and fall victim to undereating or overeating. Undereating deprives the body of fuel to perform its complex functions and deprives the body of essential ingredients for self-repair. Overeating, particularly chronic overeating, which results in obesity, places an excessive strain on one's physical equipment. This eventually can result in such conditions as diabetes, kidney disease, high blood pressure, and heart trouble.

Diet can have a profound influence on the availability of adaptational energy. When the body is working efficiently, energy is freed to interact with our physical and social environment and meet other human needs. Poor diet reduces the availability of such energy and also shapes the emotional affect with which we respond to the outside world.

The attractiveness of quick-fix gimmicks is more a symptom of stress than a productive option for developing a more healthy and fulfilling lifestyle. Persons who need to decrease their vulnerability to stress by altering their weight and pattern of food consumption are cautioned against fad diets and exotic approaches to weight reduction. Nutritionists in most local hospitals are now available for consultation to develop more permanent changes in diet.

Exercise is another essential component to reduce one's physiological vulnerability to stress. The body's total physiological

169

response to stress is designed to prepare the individual for a high level of assertion through a fight or flight response. Since neither fight nor flight is a viable option for most workers, stress provokes a level of physiological arousal that has no outlet. The physiological chemistry that prepares the body to respond to stress becomes toxic in the face of inaction and over time will produce the wide array of physical problems that Selye (1974) calls "diseases of adaptation". Exercise thus becomes the essential vehicle to discharge this level of arousal and allow the body to return to a more normal state.

In addition to this direct link with the stress response, exercise also improves the overall health and efficiency of the body and expands one's tolerance and capacity for stress. Other essential components of body maintenance include the following:

- Utilizing dentists, physicians and other health care providers for preventative health maintenance through regular checkups.
- Developing regular and physically replenishing sleep habits.
- Developing rituals of self-care, e.g., women checking monthly for any lumps in their breasts.
- Eliminating toxic habits, e.g., smoking, excessive consumption of caffeine, alcohol, and prescription and over-the-counter medications.
- Utilizing effective safety behaviors, e.g., seat belts.
- Developing and nurturing relationships that allow one to be touched and to touch for physical and/or sexual replenishment.
- Consciously controlling risk-taking behaviors, e.g., speeding.
- Developing general rules of behavior that prevent physical over-extension, e.g., avoiding the consistent 60-80 hour work week.

The second strategy of reducing physiological vulnerability to stress involves learning techniques that can actually alter the body's responses to stress. These stress management techniques are becoming an essential part of modern medicine. Most of these techniques, ranging from biofeedback to various meditative techniques, can actually save lives by altering the normal physiology of the body.

EXHIBIT 10-B
Techniques & Rituals That Alter the Body's Physiological
Response to Stress

Aerobic Exercise Training. Aerobics is a systematic exercise program developed by Dr. Kenneth H. Cooper that is aimed at improving overall health through the strengthening of the cardiovascular system. A number of companies who have discovered the high risks of heart disease and heart attacks among their managers have introduced aerobics as part of their occupational health program (Cooper, 1977).

Autogenic Training. Autogenic training is a technique popularized by Johannes Schultz (1959) that combines autohypnosis and a series of physical exercises to produce deep relaxation.

Benson's Technique. Benson's technique is a simple breathing exercise and meditation technique developed by Herbert Benson of the Harvard Medical School. Detailed instructions on the use of the technique are described in The Relaxation Response (Benson, 1975).

Biofeedback. Biofeedback is a technique that utilizes a number of instruments (e.g., electromyograph to measure muscle tension) to provide feedback on a number of complex physiological processes. Through such feedback, its proponents hold that an individual can learn to modify these processes. Advocates of biofeedback recommend it in the treatment and prevention of anxiety and a number of stress disorders (Brown, 1977).

Clinically Standardized Meditation (CSM). CSM was developed by Dr. Patricia Carrington. CSM, involves an easily learned technique for meditative relaxation. Detailed instruction on the use of the technique can be found in Freedom in Meditation (Carrington, 1978).

Jogging. Jogging as sport, pastime, and as a technique for stress reduction is currently very popular. Jogging can provide a physical release for pent up stress and tension and can also serve as an excellent time for introspection and reflection.

Progressive Relaxation (PR). PR is a technique developed by Dr. Edmund Jacobson that involves the progressive relaxation of body muscles to prevent and treat stress and anxiety. The technique is easily learned and is described in Progressive Relaxation and Modern Treatment of Tense Patients (Jacobson, 1929, 1970).

Tension Reduction Exercises. There are a number of tension reducing exercises, such as Tai Chi Chuang and Yoga, that can be effectively used to reduce muscle tension and stress.

Transcendental Meditation (TM). TM was introduced into the United States in the 1950's by Marharishi Mehesh Yogi and has since received substantial popularity. Proponents of TM describe the benefits of this particular meditation technique as including the increase in one's ability to manage personal and professional stress. TM is being used experimentally in the treatment of stress related illnesses, drug abuse, ulcers, high blood pressure and cardiac conditions (Hemingway, 1975).

Exhibit 10-B catalogues a number of the more popular techniques. These techniques are highly recommended for persons already experiencing stress-related physical problems or who are at high risk for the development of such problems. However, a word of caution to the reader is in order. Proponents of some of these techniques assure you everything from complete freedom from anxiety to entrance into the promised land. Carefully sift through the sales pitches and decide which particular techniques can be of personal benefit to you.

The third strategy to reduce physiological vulnerability to stress involves advocating for your own health needs within the work environment. Such advocacy requires skills in asserting one's own needs, and a style in negotiating for one's needs that can be effective in one's unique work environment. Conditions in the work environment that threaten your physical comfort and/or safety must be confronted. Conditions, ranging from overcrowding, to exposure to toxic substances, to unsafe equipment, to exposure to extreme temperatures, must be assertively confronted rather than passively accepted. When it comes to conditions that threaten physical comfort and safety, every worker must become an activist or pay the physical price for his or her silence.

10.3   Your Prior History Of Stress Management

Each of us brings to the work environment a unique history and style of managing stress. This style reflects enduring characteristics of our personality, a constellation of preferred defense mechanisms we use to maintain our self-esteem and unique areas of personal vulnerability.

There are a number of aspects of a preferred defense structure that can work to increase one's vulnerability to stress. These aspects include:

- The inability to verbalize emotion or show weakness.
- A rigid, fixed response to all stressors, e.g., anger, isolation.
- Patterns of stress response that escalate stressors and cut off of social supports, e.g., blaming others, displacement of anger on others, overproduction, and grandiosity.

- A rigid belief system, in which all issues are seen as black and white.
- A propensity for thought and affective disorders when under excessive stress.

If we are to decrease our personal vulnerability to work-related stress, we must develop ways to increase the strength and flexibility of this preferred defense structure. The following are some suggestions in this area.

<u>Personal Defense Structure/Organizational Match</u> It is essential that we recognize what types of work environments will be most conducive to our emotional comfort and health. Choosing an organization is not unlike the process of establishing and maintaining an intimate relationship. When the chemistry is right, the rewards to both the worker and the organization can be immense. When the chemistry is bad, the pain and turmoil in this relationship can disrupt the organization and undermine the health of the worker.

This issue of person/organization match begins by examining the congruity between one's personal style of managing stress, and the explicit and implicit directives on how stress is to be managed in the work environment. This relationship will have a great deal to do with the individual's risk level of burnout in the organization. For example, an individual with a very good history of stress management could enter an organization that wouldn't allow the individual to use those prior successful methods of managing stress and could further fail to provide any alternative methods of stress management in the work environment. In such a case, the worker could become a stress-related casualty in spite of his/her past history. Conversely, workers with a poor style of stress management may do very well in an organization that won't allow them to use the old style and provides alternative methods of stress management.

When economy and job availability allow, one should select an organization as carefully as you would select a spouse. The consequence of these choices on your health and happiness may be equally important. The ability to make this match assumes one has taken the time to examine his/her own personal style of managing stress and his/her own areas of personal vulnerability.

Knowing Your Early Warning Signs Each of us has a unique early warning system that indicates our personal defense structure is approaching a level of overload. It takes a conscious effort, however, for most of us to learn what our early warning signs are and to sensitize ourselves to recognize when they are occurring. Scan Exhibit 1-B in the first chapter and see if you can identify what category of indicators you are most likely to respond to under high stress. Are you most likely to exhibit health symptoms, increases in self-medicating behavior, changes in relationships, etc. Then see how specifically you can identify the earliest indicators of excessive stress. You may also want to ask family, friends or co-workers how they can tell when you are under stress. They may provide helpful data on a number of stress indicators of which you are unaware.

The importance of recognizing these early symptoms can't be over-emphasized. All the stress management techniques in the world will be useless if we can't identify when we need to use them. These symptoms represent an internal feedback system that tell us when we are reaching the limits of our physical and emotional defenses. To ignore such symptoms is to invite serious physical and emotional illness. These symptoms may also indicate:

- Areas of needed skill development.
- A need for time-out periods (vacations, etc.).
- Our need to take the next step in our professional development, e.g., school, job change, etc., (in response to feelings of boredom or being trapped).
- Personal needs outside the work setting which are being neglected.
- The need to reestablish a more equitable balance between our work life and our personal life.

Expressing Emotion The ability to express human emotion decreases our personal vulnerability to stress and strengthens our personal defense structure. This is a skill many of us have to learn or improve upon as adults, particularly for those of us who came from families in which such emotion was not expressed.

Learning to verbalize emotion discharges the feelings and physiological changes that accompany strong emotion allowing us to return to a lower level of physiological and psychological arousal. When such emotion cannot be expressed or is discharged in an uncontrolled manner (e.g., rage reactions), the failure to manage our emotions can lead to a breakdown of our personal defense system and a disruption in our interpersonal relationships.

This ability to manage emotion is particularly important to the health and human service worker. The primitive emotions stirred by working with the abused, the diseased, the dying, the disabled, and the deprived must have an outlet. The worker, incapable of discharging this emotion, rather than helping victims, becomes a victim.

Identify when, where, and with whom you can safely ventilate feelings elicited from your work experiences. Utilize co-workers and persons outside your specific organization. Expressing deep emotion, like other areas of communication, becomes easier with practice. Take the risks of sharing. If this is a particularly difficult area for you, you may want to seek out some specialized training in affective communication skills.

Utilizing Counseling Services One of the problematic aspects of professional stress is the difficulty in identifying whether one's emotional turmoil is primarily due to stress in the work setting, to unresolved emotional issues, or to problems endemic to one's intimate and social relationships. There are a broad spectrum of counseling services that can help identify and resolve the sources of our emotional pain.

Professional counseling can be of great assistance in examining and strengthening our own personal defense structure. As we come to understand this defense structure, we are able to achieve a much higher degree of self-acceptance and personal fulfillment. The patience and tolerance that can come from such self-examination makes us much easier to be around, which, in and of itself, begins to reduce some of the self-provoked stressors in our life.

Pace Setting Our physiology and personal defense structure combine to provide each of us an optimum pace at which to conduct our day-to-day activities. A major part of managing stress is to control and to shape events around us in order to operate at that optimum pace. Trying to operate at someone else's optimum pace can be disastrous. Maintaining a pace consistent with our biological nature reduces the physical wear and tear of stress. We must recognize whether we are a turtle or a race horse and act accordingly. While each has value, to ask the turtle to model the race horse (and vice versa) would be patently absurd. When selecting professional roles, we need to match both the pace and style of the role with our own biological nature.

Limit Setting A major contributor to personal vulnerability to stress is the inability to set limits on oneself. Recognize the limits of your knowledge and expertise. Learn to say "I don't know". Recognize the limits of your physical energy and how these limits change. Learn to say "No, I can't" to additional role responsibilities during periods of low physical energy. Recognize the limits of those situations you cannot emotionally handle alone. Learn to say "I need help." Recognize the limits of your emotional endurance. Learn to say "I need time for myself." Clarify the priorities between your responsibilities to work and your responsibilities to those you love outside of work. Decide under what conditions you must clearly say "Their needs come first."

Limit setting is a behavior that requires a belief in the legitimacy of our own needs and the skills to assert these needs in our interactions with the outside world. These assertiveness skills do not come naturally to many of us, particularly for those of us who have been programmed for most of our lives to respond to the needs of others. For us, assertiveness training may be an important stress management technique to acquire.

There are a number of approaches to assertiveness training which include the methods popularized by Manuel Smith (_When I Say No, I Feel Guilty,_ 1975). A significant amount of professional stress is exacerbated by our inability to use assertive behavior to set limits, protect our own needs, and avoid being manipulated into positions and roles that we find unbearable. Assertiveness training provides a vehicle to develop and practice assertive communication skills.

Using Time-out Periods Time-out periods are rituals that allow us to step out of stressful role demands and replenish ourselves. Learn to take regular breaks during the day to replenish yourself--sit and relax, go for a walk, etc. Utilize vacation, mental health days, and compensatory time to physically and emotionally nurture yourself.

Laughing Your Way To Health Laughter is one of the most important signs of both individual and organizational health. Laughter recognizes our need to play, to stop taking ourselves so seriously, to celebrate life, and to celebrate our affection for one another. Laughter demands that we slow down enough to observe and appreciate the lighter side of our day-to-day interactions. Cultivate the healing power of laughter.

10.4 Your Stage Of Life

Daniel Levinson, in his classic study *The Seasons of a Man's Life, (1977)* and Gail Sheehy in her bestseller *Passages (1976)*, have both outlined the problems, concerns and needs that characterize different developmental periods of our life. Their studies have made the term "midlife crisis" a household word.

These studies provide important information to us, because they show how our personal vulnerability to stress can change during different stages of our life. Whether it is the young adult first entering his/her profession, or the middle-aged manager or the worker looking to retire in two years, each persons response to the stress will be partially shaped by the unique developmental tasks characteristic of their age group.

Knowledge of these Developmental Issues This can be an important tool in understanding our vulnerabilities and in altering our style of stress management to fit our unique needs and lifestyle at different periods in our life. The middle-aged manager who is suddenly aware of his/her own mortality, who is mourning his/her lost youth and missed opportunities, and who is reevaluating his/her values and career goals, may experience these changes as very close to his/her fantasy of what it is like to go crazy. Understanding and anticipating these changes can smooth the process and increase the strength of our defense structure while going through these developmental stages.

10.5   Your Values, Beliefs And Motivations

Values and beliefs can play an important role in determining one's vulnerability to professional stress. In a survey the author helped conduct some years ago of hospice nurses working with terminally ill patients, the majority of the nurses indicated that their personal and religious beliefs provided an important resource for managing stress in the care of the dying. Each of us must develop a set of values and beliefs that reconcile us to the realities we confront in our professional life.

Seek Spiritual Replenishment   Seek out opportunities with coworkers to explore and discuss values and beliefs and their relationship to your work. Establish rituals that reinforce and nurture these values and beliefs through sharing with others. Whether religious or non-religious, these value systems help reduce our vulnerability to stress. During times of rapid change and excessive demands for adaptation, these rituals help keep us grounded. It is under such turbulent conditions that it will be most important to have the ability to say: "This is who I am and this is what I believe".

Sort Out Professional Motivations   It is not unusual for many of us to discover ourselves in a job or profession that we did not choose. In some cases, the profession may have been chosen for us by our family. In other cases, we may have simply fallen into the profession by accident or financial necessity. Sometimes these accidents work out and we are very satisfied in the type of work we are doing. A more common experience, however, is the person who finds himself experiencing added stress because of the mismatch between his/her professional role and his/her personal needs. In interviews with burnout victims, the author has heard the following phrase repeatedly: "I didn't want to be a teacher (or nurse, or policemen, or minister, etc) anyway"! The use of career counseling can assist us in determining whether we should seek a change in area of specialization, or whether we might be more personally satisfied with work in a completely different area.

Examine Our Personal Motivations and Expected Rewards These can also help us determine our vulnerability to professional stress. In Exhibit 10-C, I have included an illustration based on the work of Vachon (1978), as an example of how different motivations

EXHIBIT 10-C
Motivational Factors Influencing One's Stress Response in the Care of the Dying [*]

MOTIVATION FOR WORKING WITH THE DYING	STRESS RESPONSE
Accidental or out of convenience	Emotional involvement with patients minimized; stress experienced from lack of knowledge and feelings of professional inpotence; As emotional involvement increases, so do emotional risks.
"In-thing"/wish to affiliate with charismatic leader	Stress increases dramatically as one discovers dying patients are not "all young, beautiful, and articulate people who are longing to spend their dying months talking about their philosophy of life and death" (Vachon, 1978) and as the human chinks appear in the armor of the charismatic leader.
Intellectual appeal	This scientific approach may break down as person becomes emotionally involved with patients. As intellectualization breaks down, the worker is highly vulnerable.
Sense of "calling"	The missionary zeal may result in overcommittment and over-involvement with patients. The worker is very prone to physical and emotional exhaustion.
Past personal experience with death	Previous unresolved grief may result in overidentification with dying patients. Workers overinvolvement with patients produces emotional depletion and conflicts with other staff.
Suspicion that one will develop the disease	Overidentification with the patient. Highly vulnerable when a number of patients die in short period of time.

[*] Adapted from M.L.S. Vachon's "Motivation and Stress Experienced by Staff Working With the Terminally Ill" (Vachon, 1978)

179

can influence our stress response. This example shows how various motivations influence the vulnerability of hospice nurses to professional stress experienced in the care of the dying.

10.6 Your Professional Training

Professional education and training can increase or decrease one's vulnerability to professional stress depending on whether such training,

- provided the necessary knowledge and skills to perform professional role responsibilities;
- provided adequate preparation for the emotional demands of the profession;
- provided information about the nature of organizational systems one would be working in; and
- provided methods of problem solving that were adaptable to changing technology and conditions in the work environment.

The most basic element of professional stress remediation is to bridge the gap between the knowledge and skills that workers possess, and the knowledge and skill demands placed upon them in their professional roles. Change is occurring so rapidly in most professions that nearly all workers experience stress related to knowledge and skill deficits.

There are a number of strategies that can reduce our vulnerability in this area. These could include:

- Self-study through reading journals and texts that keep us abreast of new technology in our field.
- The return to a formal program of academic study.
- Affiliation with professional associations and professional meetings.
- Attendance at workshops, seminars, and other continuing education opportunities.
- Cultivating professional mentors both inside and outside one's work environment.
- Visiting other organizations and professionals to discover and share new ideas and approaches.

One of the biggest handicaps to using such strategies is a belief by workers that professional development is an organizational rather than an individual responsibility. The author frequently hears: "We can't do those things because our training budget has been cut". I strongly recommend that you take responsibility and control over your own professional development, even if that means you use non-work time and personal finances to support it. After all, its your level of stress, your self-esteem, and your potential career advancement that is at stake. View the organization as a partner in your professional development rather than a benefactor.

It is also helpful to try to match professional development activities as closely as possible to those stress provoking areas of knowledge and skill deficiency you experience in your professional role. Self-examination and the use of supervisors, colleagues, and mentors to help identify and correct skill deficiency experienced in the performance of one's role is a crucial aspect of reducing one's vulnerability to professional stress.

In the health and human service fields, there is another deficiency often not addressed through our preparatory training and education, and that is, how to manage the emotional pain often inherent in such work. I remember vividly my first such crisis. There was a client I had counselled and grown very close to as part of his one-year stay in a long-term residential chemical dependency program in which I worked. Following several months of abstinence following his discharge, the client relapsed following the break-up of his relationship with his girlfriend. While intoxicated he crawled in the back seat of a car to sleep and was arrested and jailed for auto theft. During the night, this young man hung himself while still in a state of intoxication. Before committing suicide, he had pinned a note to his clothing in which he asked his parents to reach me to make sure I would be at his funeral. The news of this event was overwhelming to me early in my career and precipitated several weeks of soul-searching as to whether I could or should stay in the field. My professional training had prepared me in terms of technical skills, but it had done nothing to prepare me for the repeated losses I would experience while working with alcohol and drug-dependent individuals. My training prepared me with a full arsenal of skills to assess and respond to the emotional needs of my client, but only superficially prepared me to manage my own emotions during the process.

A number of experiences that can help prepare one for such crises. These include:

- Peer support groups for clinicians.
- Therapy or analysis to explore one's own areas of emotional vulnerability.
- The use of supervision to clarify and work through biases, personal agendas, and issues that can increase our vulnerability (and decrease the service quality) in our helping relationships with clients.
- Critical incident training in which more experienced clinicians provide structured opportunities for us to rehearse emotionally critical situations that arise in the counselor-client relationship.

10.7   Your Level Of Life Changes

Another factor that influences our individual vulnerability to professional stress is the overall pace of change in our life. Much of our knowledge in this area is based on the research of Richard Rahe and Thomas Holmes (1967). These researchers studied the relationship between the pace of life changes and the onset of major illness. Using an instrument called the social readjustment rating scale, Rahe and Holmes numerically scored major life changes, such as deaths, separations, marital and legal difficulties, and changes in day-to-day lifestyle, to come up with a total score of life change units. They found that the probability of onset of major illness rose significantly as one's life change units increased.

If we look at stress as the demand for adaptational change, it is clear that the pace of such demands could speed up to the point where it surpasses our capacity for adaptation and results in the onset of stress-related physical and emotional problems. A big component in any strategy of stress management thus becomes how to control the pace of change in our life. Examining our demand for adaptation and our level of supports to absorb such change can allow us to slow or speed the pace of change. This is illustrated in Exhibit 10-D. This figure illustrates the four possible combinations in level of stressors and level and supports, and the implications of each combination on one's vulnerability for stress-related problems.

EXHIBIT 10-D
Planning Change Matrix

High Stressors	High Supports	Your life is delicately balanced. Unexpected change or stressors could provoke serious stress related problems. Work diligently to balance stressors with nurturing people and activities. Set limits and listen to your early warning signs.
Low Supports	Low Stressors	You are understimulated. First develop new relationships then escalate change. Good time to take on challenges and responsibilities as long as support system is developed first.
You are in a position of high vulnerability. Reduce demands on your time and energy and slow the pace of change. Use caution in making major life decisions. Stress management techniques may be essential to avoid illness.	You are in a position of low vulnerability. You have adaptational energy available to increase change and stimulation in your life. It is a good time to take on new challenges	

Effectively coping with stress in our lives can be improved by the conscious management of the pace of change and by working to enrich our level of social supports. If, for example, we find ourselves in a position of high stressors and reduced supports, we can reduce our vulnerability by cutting back non-essential obligations, setting limits on taking on added demands, and using our energy to rebuild sources of support.

10.8 Your System Of Family And Social Supports

The major sources of support to affect professional stress need to be built into the same work environment in which the stress is generated. This belief doesn't change the fact that many organizations fail to provide such supports and that one's family and social network often are the only buffer or intermediary between work-generated stress and the physical and emotional consequences of excessive stress. Lacking such supports in the work environment, many of us must have a network of replenishing relationships and activities outside the work setting to ameliorate the effects of stress experienced on the job.

It is the author's assumption (in the health and human service professions), that if we are to continue to give emotionally to clients, we must be able to leave the work setting and emotionally replenish ourselves through nurturing relationships and activities. When such replenishment occurs, we can continue to enter the work setting and give emotionally of ourselves to clients in need. When we fail to get such replenishment, we continue to give and to give until we are empty - an emotionally numb and spent victim of burnout.

Given the above, it can be seen that the development of a replenishment network is an important, if not essential, aspect to reduce one's vulnerability to professional stress. In my studies of burnout victims in closed organizations, those staff lacking this replenishment network were most likely to become victims to severe stress-related physical and emotional problems. The concern with the process of organizational closure is the fact that such closure disrupts one's ability to establish and maintain a replenishment network and thus increases vulnerability for burnout.

The reader is invited to assess his/her own replenishment network by completing the diagram in Exhibit 10-E using the following sequence of instructions.

The Replenishment Network Diagram consists of six circles in which you will be asked to list the names of people or activities.

(1) Beginning with the top circle, list the names of three people who you would consider professional peers, with whom you share ideas about work, and from whom you receive emotional support while discussing work-related issues. The catch is that none of these people can be employed at the organization in which you work.

(2) Dropping down to the first circle on the right marked "Family Supports", list the names of three people from either your nuclear family (husband, wife, son, daughter, etc.) or family of origin (mother, father, brother, sister, etc.), from whom you receive the most emotional support and personal affirmation when things are very stressful for you at work.

(3) In the lower circle on the right, list the names of three people with whom you regularly socialize and from whom you receive positive affirmation about yourself in non-work roles. None of the people listed should have any affiliation with the organization in which you work.

(4) In the bottom circle, list three leisure-time activities that are self-nurturing. The activities listed must be things you do alone.

(5) In the bottom circle on the left, list the names of two people (mentors) who you look up to, see yourself following in their professional footsteps, and who provide you guidance in your professional development. These persons may be from either inside or outside your current workplace.

(6) In the upper-left hand circle, list the names of three people who provide you with the most assistance, affirmation and emotional support inside your current organization.

EXHIBIT 10-E
Replenishment Network Diagram

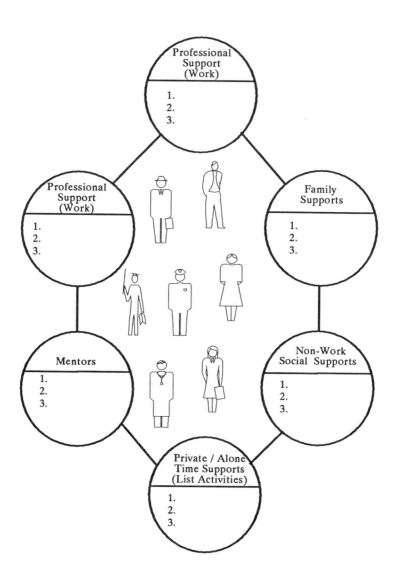

Professionals from all over the country have filled out the replenishment network diagram as an exercise in the author's training seminars. Based on this experience, I would like to share some observations about each component of the diagram. Organizational concepts from earlier chapters will also be integrated into this discussion. What the reader should focus on are those areas of the diagram that were most difficult for you to complete.

Professional Supports (Non-Work) Workers who have difficulty filling in this circle often come from professionally closed or geographically isolated organizations. When all of our professional supports and our professional identity are tied to our organization, vulnerability to professional stress increases dramatically. Imagine the trauma of being the scapegoat in this situation when all of our professional relationships are with co-workers inside the organization.

We can decrease our vulnerability by developing professional peer relationships that transcend our organizational boundary. We can consciously expand this network through building relationships with professionals in allied agencies, building new relationships through attendance at seminars and workshops, or through active participation in local, state, and national professional associations. The key here is to have a network of people who affirm our professional competence and value even when such value may be undermined in our organization.

Family Supports This circle is fairly easy for most workers to complete. It can become difficult, however, for the persons who are single or divorced, persons geographically or emotionally isolated from their family of origin, or for those persons whose family relationships have become more a source of stress than a source of support.

We can decrease our vulnerability to stress in this area by:

- Creating a surrogate family, if none exists. (See discussion of the next circle)
- Nurturing our family relationships to assure they continue as relationships of reciprocal support.

- Intensifying our energy in rehabilitating a toxic marital relationship or terminating the relationship.

Non-Work Social Supports For individuals without substantial family support, this circle becomes critical in reducing vulnerability to stress. It is through this circle that such individuals can create a small network of intimate relationships that can function as a surrogate family.

Many workers may have difficulty in completing this circle if they lack skills in initiating and maintaining social relationships, or if they have recently moved to a new geographical area. Difficulty in filling this circle can also reflect organizational dynamics. Workers in organizations that have gone through a process of social closure or workers who experience role overload, may have difficulty sustaining non-work social relationships.

Workers under excessive levels of stress, who have family supports but minimal non-work social supports, may be placing undue strain on their family. One of the reasons there is such a high marriage casualty rate of workers in professionally and socially closed systems is that the family becomes the sole blotter to absorb work-related stress. Workers from such systems spill work-related stress into their families while at the same time they bring insatiable needs for support into their marital and family relationships.

Non-work social relationships allow us to affirm our value and broaden our identity beyond the work role. Such relationships provide a clear time out period from work-related issues and provide a cushion of acknowledgment and support as a buffer from work related stress. A work-dominated social network can be seductively pleasurable when things are good at work. But if things get bad, the workers may suddenly find themselves isolated, alone and vulnerable.

We can decrease our vulnerability to professional stress by avoiding a work-dominated social network and by cultivating nurturing relationships and roles totally unrelated to our profession and our work environment.

Private/Alone Time Supports Alone time supports consist of activities or rituals that allow us to step out of all our life roles and interactions and to center ourselves by experiencing who we are outside of such roles and relationships.

When our work-life becomes frantic and spills over into an equally frantic personal life, we may find ourselves experiencing something just short of terror if we finally come to a standstill alone. Developing pleasurable and self-nurturing activities, done alone, allows us to catch up with ourselves and decide if we like what we see, and, above all, respond to our own needs and desires rather than the needs of others.

Mentors With the possible exception of workers very early in their career, this is often a difficult circle for workers to complete. It seems many of us outgrow our mentors or discover they have clay feet and somehow don't seem to find new mentors. A mentor can be a powerful source of affirmation and support that many of us need. Beyond our early career, it takes conscious work to find and cultivate mentor relationships. As important as such relationships are, they cannot be measured in terms of frequency of contact. A mentor may be seen only a couple times a year, but each visit can fire one's enthusiasm for new learning for months.

Organizational dynamics can also influence our choice and access to mentors. In closed systems, most workers will list a mentor from inside the organization (usually the "high priest/priestess"). The lack of boundary permeability in such systems restricts the access to outside professionals who could become mentors.

Professional Supports (Work) This is probably the easiest circle for most workers to complete. There seems to be supportive alliances developed by most workers even in those organizations that combine the highest level of aggregate stress and the lowest level of built in supports. The exception to this is workers who experience the conditions we earlier described as "role underload" and "role deprivation", or the worker who is the victim of a scapegoating process.

Looking at the Whole Replenishment Network The author feels very strongly in the ability of a network of nurturing relationships to counteract the more dire consequences of excessive stress. This conclusion is based on my study of stress-related casualties. Before closing this discussion of replenishment networks, I would like to describe briefly some shared characteristics of a few people interviewed by the author who seemed almost invulnerable to the untoward effects of stress. A shared philosophy of these individuals was revealed in a comment made by one worker in response to my question: "what would be the thing you would most hate to have written on your tombstone"? The answer came without hesitation: "Here lies John. He spent most of his life with people he didn't like doing things he didn't enjoy". These apparently invulnerable individuals had stripped themselves of the "shoulds" and oughts" that drive many of us into filling our lives with unfulfilling activities and impulsively agreed upon obligations. They also shared a rich network of people they loved and by whom they were loved. They had quite simply refused to participate in relationships they experienced as unrewarding or toxic. When asked what they would do differently if they only had six months to live, they responded that they would do very little or nothing differently and would spend the time very much like they had the last six months.

The detachment from toxic relationships, the development of a nurturing network of professional, social, and family relationships, and the cultivation of self-nurturing activities is clearly a powerful antagonist to professional burnout.

10.9   Your Role Boundary Management

A major portion of this book has addressed how stress experienced in the work environment spills over into our personal life and disrupts intimate and family relationships. While such spillover is often given momentum by forces in the organization, it can also reflect an inability of the worker to establish and enforce the boundary between one's work life and one's personal life.

We have already discussed some recommendations related to this boundary management such as the devlopment of multiple and varied life roles and the avoidance of a work-dominated social network. One of the most important additional strategies of boundary management is the development of decompression routines.

Decompression routines are rituals that signal to ourselves and others that one part of our life is ending and another part is beginning. These routines represent a "rite of passage" from our work life to our personal life. These rituals immediately follow our exit from the work environment and precede our re-entry into active participation in personal or family life. These rituals (e.g., jogging, taking a hot bath, reading the newspaper, etc.), allow us to diffuse the emotional energy from work and enter our personal lives in a more relaxed manner. In the absence of rituals of decompression, pent-up energy and feelings may be discharged upon our family and friends in ways that undermine these relationships.

10.10 Controlling Your Relationship With The Organization

The author has tried to present in this chapter a broad overview of strategies and techniques that can reduce one's vulnerability to professional stress. A major theme that emerges from this review is that we can each take responsibility and control to shape our relationship with the organization. By nurturing and taking care of ourselves, we can give our best to the organization. At the same time we can demand the organization's respect for the physical and emotional needs we experience while in the work environment. When the organization is insensitive to these needs and all efforts to negotiate more humane responses fail, then it is time to leave the relationship. Reduced vulnerability comes from our ability and assertiveness to negotiate mutual needs as an active partner in our relationship with the organization, and, ultimately, from our power and freedom to terminate this relationship.

Chapter 11
Systems Interventions: Boundary Management

Earlier chapters of this book reviewed how the failure to confront the issue of stress can have far reaching repercussions on the overall health and vitality of an organization. Responding to the issue of stress can create opportunities to increase worker health and productivity, improve the reciprocity and mutuality in the relationship between workers and the organization, and enhance the overall ability of the organization to achieve its mission and goals. Failure to confront the issue of stress can be measured in lowered productivity and morale, the continual drain of technical knowledge and skills from the organization, increased interpersonal conflict that undermines organizational objectives and the escalation of direct costs in stress-related utilization of health care benefits. In spite of the above, very few organizations have made a systematic analysis and response to the issue of work-related stress. In the remaining two chapters, a number of organizational strategies to address this problem will be catalogued and discussed.

11.1 Creating A Comprehensive Strategy

Organizational efforts to address stress are generally plagued by a lack of comprehensiveness and a lack of continuity and follow-through over time. Many organizations feel they have responded to the issue of stress if they have an employee assistance program or host an occasional stress management workshop. In other organizations, responses to stress may be fragmented and uncoordinated between various organizational departments. In others, stress may be a fad topic one year which generates a wide variety of activities, only to become a non-issue the next year.

A systematic response to work-related stress requires the development of a comprehensive plan developed with the participation of workers at all levels of the organization and implemented with the full support of organizational leadership.

One model of strategy development, that can be used success-fully, combines the use of outside consultants with an internal task force. The task force is made up of organizational members who represent various departments, disciplines, and levels of authority. In settings which utilize unionized workers, the task force will be most successful as a joint management-labor venture. The task force is given the mandate by the organizational leadership to iden-tify the nature and extent of work-related stress problems and to formulate both short and long range strategies to address the problems. Outside consultants are hired to help facilitate the over-all work of the task force, to help collect data, to assist the task force in getting ideas converted into a cohesive written plan, to conduct work on behalf of the task force such as identifying strategies and programs used by other organizations, and to assist the task force in implementing an approved plan.

A comprehensive plan to address work-related stress should encompass, through needs analysis and strategy development, all the levels of the work ecosystem discussed in Chapter Three. Ex-amples of the issues to be addressed by the task force include the following.

The Individual   One function of the task force is to assess the personal vulnerabilities and personal costs of work-related stress in the organization. Looking at individual workers in the ag-gregate, can one ascertain information about the collective vulnerability of the work force? The task force may examine the following:

- Are there medical problems that workers in the organization are particularly prone to contracting?
- Are there unique aspects of work stress inherent in the professional disciplines employed by the organization?
- Are workers in the organization prone to any par-ticular type of dysfunctional stress responses, e.g., self-medication, suicide, etc.?
- Does the unique age composition of employees have any implications on vulnerability to stress?
- Given the nature of the organization and work roles, are there any individual characteristics that would make a worker particularly vulnerable to stress?

193

- Given the answers to the above questions, are there particular programs the organization could implement to reduce the individual vulnerability of workers?

Examining the above questions can help tailor a strategy that fits the unique needs and vulnerabilities of the employees of a particular organization. A police department, that collected data on the above questions, concluded that their overall program needed to include employee assistance components that focused on education and intervention on the problems of alcoholism, marital problems and suicide. Another organization, composed mostly of men thirty five years of age and older, looked at their casualty data and concluded they needed to do something to reduce employee risk of cardio-vascular disease. The latter organization's overall strategy included components to reduce individual vulnerability through such areas as dieting, exercising, smoking cessation, and training in stress management techniques.

The Microsystem A major focus of the task force is to identify those sources of stress workers experience within their work unit. This data can be collected through surveys, one-to-one or small group interviews, or through larger employee forums. The task in this area is to identify and prioritize the intensity of stressors in the physical environment, stressors in the organization of work roles, stressors in worker relationships, and areas that require the development of additional supports. The next chapter will catalogue a number of strategies aimed at the microsystem.

The Mesosystem At this level of analysis, the task force examines stress within the context of the total organization by examining issues such as the following:

What costs to the company are attributable to stress-related problems? (An analysis of employee benefit utilization, e.g., health care costs, sick time, etc., can provide some startling data in response to this question.)

- Are there stressors resulting from a lack of clarity of organizational goals and objectives?

- What stressors are a result of conflict between units of the organization?
- Is there sufficient closure to give employees a sense of mission, purpose and direction?
- Is there sufficient openness to allow members easy access to meet professional and social needs outside the organization?
- Is the pace of change within the organization congruent with workers' capacity for adaptation?
- Are their mechanisms built into the work environment to respond to stress casualties and facilitate the return of these workers to health and productivity?

The Exosystem and Macrosystem   In the final level of analysis, the task force looks at how conditions and events outside the organization affect the level of stress of organizational members. This level of analysis is designed to help anticipate, identify and plan for organizational change.   If a hospital task force, for example, examines this level and projects a 30-per cent drop in inpatient bed utilization and a 20-per cent cut in inpatient staff over the next five years, then the task force may need to examine not only new directions in the level and setting of service delivery, but also how the hospital is to go through such institutional change in such a way as to minimize stress on the employees and assure a consistent quality of patient care through the process.   Whether the macrosystem analysis indicates dramatic growth or reduction, a plan needs to be developed to control the pace of change and to support staff through each stage of change.

The combined mandate of organizational leaders, the task force and the outside consultants is to capture on paper and implement a comprehensive plan to address worker stress.   The plan should be capable of addressing stress at the multiple levels described and to do so in a manner consistent with overall organizational objectives and within the fiscal and human resource constraints of the organization.

11.2   Creating A Continuum Of Support

The author has frequently been asked: "If you could begin to intervene at one place in the organizational hierarchy to impact stress-related problems, where would you start"? After more than a decade of experimenting with such interventions, the answer today without hesitation would be that the most critical focus of attention should be with an organization's central leadership and its supervisory/managerial continuum. While there may be isolated components of a comprehensive plan that are amenable to quick resolution, such as the elimination of some environmental stressors, the success of most comprehensive plans rests on the initial work with supervisory staff. The reason for this focus is two-fold. First, the managers will bear major responsibility for implementing organizational strategies of stress remediation. Their ability to control boundary transactions makes the manager essential to mesosystem strategies. The managers' abilities to control the level of stressors and supports at the work unit level makes them equally important to microsystem strategies. Secondly, the implementation of these strategies hinges on the ability of managers to utilize sources of emotional and social support to manage their own work-related stress. It is not only the point that managers need to serve as role models regarding stress management and problem-solving, it is the fact that managers who handle their own stress poorly will have neither the desire nor the adaptational energy available to implement organizational strategies to reduce worker stress.

In the health and human service organization, for example, there ideally exists a continuum of support within the service environment. Clients and their families are provided service and support by direct-care workers, who are in turn provided technical and emotional support by supervisors, who are in turn supported by the organizational administrators. Stress-related problems at the top of this continuum ripple down the hierarchy resulting in increased stress-related problems of direct care staff and decreased quantity and quality of client service.

A key component of organizational strategies to reduce professional stress thus becomes the training of supervisors and managers. This training begins with a personal analysis of the manager's own response to stress and then builds on knowledge and skills to manage stress in the work environment. At a minimum, such training should include:

- Personal and organizational indicators of excessive stress.
- Opportunities for the manager to assess his/her own style of stress management.
- Personal strategies and techniques to improve the manager's capacity for adaptation.
- Supervisory strategies to identify and reduce role stressors.
- Supervisory strategies to increase role supports.
- Supervisory strategies to respond to victims of excessive stress.

11.3 Gatekeeping And The Art Of Boundary Management

While there are a whole range of organizational strategies capable of reducing stress-related casualties, the remainder of this chapter will focus on one major type of strategy. A major portion of this book examined the relationship between excessive stress and the permeability of organizational boundaries. It was contended that stress-related casualties were high both in the enmeshed organizational family with its rigid, non-permeable boundary and in the disengaged organizational family with its diffuse, almost non-existent organizational boundary. The self-regulated organizational family was described as the ideal healthy system due to its flexibility to move toward either greater openness or closure depending on the changing needs of organizational members and changing conditions outside the organization.

Managers are the primary gatekeepers in any organization. It is their decisions that determine the ease with which, or the pace at which, ideas and people from outside cross the boundary and enter the organization. It is also their decisions that determine who, when, and under what conditions organizational members will cross the organizational boundary to make professional transactions with the outside world. Much of this gatekeeping function is done by instinct with little conscious thought or design. It is clear from the concepts outlined in earlier chapters that such boundary management has a profound impact on the level and intensity of professional stress experienced by organizational members. As managers, we need to learn how to consciously utilize the boundary management function to promote the health of both individual workers and the organization as a whole.

By regulating boundary transactions, the manager can increase or decrease the pace of organizational change, intensify or diminish the level of professional stimulation, tighten or loosen intimacy bonds between organizational members, increase or decrease overall demands for adaptation, and inhibit or promote access to outside sources of replenishment. The manager has the capability of moving the work unit back and forth along the continuum from closure to openness based on an assessment of the needs of the organization and the collective needs of workers.

There are clearly times that both individual and institutional needs dictate that the manager reduce boundary transactions and increase organizational closure. The newly created organization must have a level of closure to complete the tasks of building the internal organizational structure and to allow workers time to define themselves as a group. The agency, which is reorganized or is directed by new leadership, needs a period of closure to redefine itself and clarify its future directions. An organization, quaking from too rapid change, needs a period of closure to restabalize itself and allow members a reprieve from the over-stimulation of rapid change. The work unit in which members have been over-extended due to vacation schedules, sickness, unfilled positions, etc., may need a period of closure to reduce demands on workers and allow the unit to catch up to its production expectations. These are all conditions that can be consciously analyzed by the manager and responded to by regulating boundary transactions. As these situations stabilize and institutional and worker needs change, the manager can then alter this gatekeeping function.

There are also particular events in the life of an organization that dictate decisions by the manager to open the system through increased boundary transactions. Decreased sales of products, or utilization of services combined with increased competition, may demand opening the system to achieve heightened visibility. The growing community agency may have to increase boundary transactions if it is to successfully launch a capital fund drive. The organization, which seeks to redefine its service program due to dramatic changes in the client population, may have to increase boundary transactions to find new ideas and new technology. The organization whose goods and services are no longer in demand, may need to increase boundary transactions, if it is to survive, by diversifying to meet the changing needs and desires of consumers. The organization, that has become trapped in the process of professional, social and sexual closure, will need to increase boundary transactions if it is to avoid the disastrous consequences of prolonged closure described in earlier chapters.

The gatekeeping functions of the manager include regulating both external and internal boundary transactions. In more complex organizations, for example, a major part of the manager's role may involve shaping the nature, intensity and frequency of interactions between his/her work unit and other work units of the organization. Regulating such internal boundary transactions can have as important an impact on controlling the level of worker stress as the external boundaries discussed above.

11.4 Preventing Dysfunctional Closure: An Overview

In Chapters Four through Eight of this book, the propensity of small health and human service agencies to become closed organizational families was discussed in detail. The repercussions of such chronic closure on the health of the organization as a whole and on the physical and emotional health of organizational members was also noted. The next few sections of this chapter will outline a number of organizational strategies designed to prevent such closure.

Strategies aimed at preventing the professional, social and sexual closure of organizational systems need to be designed to fit the unique characteristics of the organization and the unique characteristics of an organization's work force. Strategies developed for a manufacturing firm may differ significantly in detail from strategies developed for a police department or an insurance company. The strategies outlined below are specifically designed for health and human service agencies. They have been developed out of the author's experience with hospitals, community health care agencies, chemical dependency treatment programs, community mental health centers, child welfare agencies and community corrections programs.

There are, however, general principals common to all strategies aimed at preventing organizational closure. All such strategies seek to:

- Assure the mutual boundary transactions of ideas and people between the organization and the outside ecosystem
- Control the level of cohesion and intimacy between organizational members.
- Enhance the access of organizational members to outside sources of professional and social replenishment.
- Control and limit those forces in the work environment (e.g., role overload) that break down the boundary between the worker's professional and personal life.
- Build into the work environment mechanisms that facilitate and support change but also control the pace of change.

11.5   Preventing Professional Closure

Professional closure begins with the assumption that all the professional needs of staff can be met inside the organization - an assumption enforced through gatekeeping functions that inhibit staff developing and sustaining professional relationships outside the program. The following strategies are designed to change that assumption and reverse gatekeeping activities.

<u>Avoiding The High Priest Role</u>   High priests create or enforce dogma, cultivate dependence of followers, and build walls within which the rituals of worship can occur. While some organizational leaders may consistently seek out high priest roles based on their personality needs, many high priest roles evolve, over time, based on the collective needs and unique chemistry within the organizational family. Many managers dislike themselves in such roles but are unsure both of how they got in the role in the first place and how to get out of it. While there are numerous times in the life of an organization that may require charisma and powerful and decisive leadership, the creation of a more permanent high priest role is a major contributor to the progressive closure of the organizational family.

To those organizational leaders wishing to avoid or get out of the high priest role, the following recommendations are suggested.

A. Recognize that organizational family members need a high priest, usually under conditions of high stress and low supports. Under conditions of low self-esteem, emotional depletion, and escalating demands for adaptation, workers will trade their freedom and autonomy for the safety and security provided by the high priest. Reducing stressors and increasing supports decreases the collective need in the organizational family for the high priest role. The microsystem strategies outlined in the next chapter may prove exceptionally beneficial in this area.

B. Decentralize power and decision-making within the organization. Authoritarian styles of leadership are very congruent with the high priest role. Moving to more participative styles of management, and broadening the distribution of power and accountability for decision-making, decreases the dependence of workers on the centralized leader. By increasing the power of other workers, the awesome power that can accumulate within the role of the high priest is decreased.

C. Model boundary transactions. Cultivate sources of professional support and development outside the organization. Conditions, where the personal affirmations of the leader come solely from the loyalty and devotion of subordinates, reinforce the high priest role. The manager, who visibly utilizes outside consultants, seeks new ideas from outside the organization, and develops an outside network of professional support, will find staff much more willing to do the same. Such activity works to humanize the role of the leader and avoids the image of omniscience that characterizes the high priest role.

D. Identify where you can facilitate or acknowledge decisions rather than make decisions. The over-involvement of the high priest in organizational decision-making reinforces low self-esteem in workers and prevents their professional maturation. The effective manager delegates and rewards appropriate levels of decision-making throughout the organization. By helping others think through the process of decision-making rather than making decisions for them, the effective manager decreases worker dependency and increases the capabilities and self-esteem of subordinates. By discovering those situations in which the role of consultant is more appropriate than that of decision-maker, the effective manager avoids the seductive power of the high priest role.

E. Learn to say, "I don't know". The high priest is all-knowing, never makes mistakes, refuses to reveal his or her human frailties, and generally enforces expectations of perfection from workers in a punitive fashion. The manager who seeks to avoid the high priest role can do so by learning to model such phrases as:

- "I don't know. Let's find out."
- "I don't know much about that. I'd like for you to do some research and let me know what you discover?"
- "This is one of the areas as a manager that's most difficult for me."
- "I made a mistake in that decision. Next time we face that situation, I think I'll have a much better idea of how to handle it."
- "That's the decision I'm thinking about, but before I go ahead, I would really like to know what all of you think."

Such communications model honest self-disclosure; give workers permission to make, talk about, and learn from mistakes; reinforce learning rather than perfection as an organizational value; and counter the omniscience of the high priest role.

Adding New Members to the Organizational Family Perhaps the most significant boundary transaction the manager controls is the selection of persons to become members of the organizational family. The manner in which the recruitment and selection of new members is managed can significantly influence the level of professional closure in the organization. It was noted in Chapter Five that the homogenization of staff was a critical early stage in the onset of professional closure. The recruitment of staff from the existing social and professional network of organizational members, the selection of staff based on their ability to "fit in" and the homogenization of staff selection by age, race, sex, training, values, and lifestyles, all contribute to the progression of professional and social closure in the organizational family.

While the primary selection criteria for new members should remain the procurement of needed knowledge and skills, there is still room within this standard to make selections that broaden the heterogeneous nature of the organizational family. Cultivating diversity in the backgrounds of staff not only improves the quality of services to very heterogeneous client populations, it also provides a rich kaleidoscope of perspectives and ideas that work to enhance professional stimulation and creativity and inhibit professional closure.

Early attempts by the manager to diversify the composition of the organizational family must be done with the awareness of the following two points.

- Under conditions of high stress, groups will always have a tendency to isolate, scapegoat and extrude those members who are most different from the majority.
- New members from diverse backgrounds coming into the organizational family may need increased supports to insure their professional and social inclusion.

The Code of Professional Practice   The establishment of a code of professional practice can serve as an important instrument in managing organizational stress and preventing organizational closure. The overall function of the code of professional practice will be first outlined, as there will be numerous references to it in the later discussion of other strategies.

If an organization is to assemble a heterogeneous staff and then open up the flow of new ideas into the organization, there needs to be some mechanism that serves to establish the behavioral boundaries within which staff are expected to operate. It is strongly recommended that each health and human service organization establish just such boundaries through the creation of a code of professional practice to which all organizational members are held accountable. Such a code serves multiple purposes that include:

- The explicit definition of organizational values.
- The protection of the health and well being of consumers of the organization's services.
- The enhancement of public safety.
- The protection of the health, integrity and reputation of both individual staff members and the institution as a whole.

The code of professional practice establishes standards of behavior related to the following:

- Personal conduct (definitions of any moral or legal standards to which staff will be held accountable).
- Professional conduct (e.g., guidelines on adherence to institutional policies, representation of credentials, publishing, research, potential areas of conflict of interest, etc.).
- Conduct in client relationships (standards related to confidentiality, civil rights, physical and sexual abuse, etc.).
- Conduct in staff relationships (standards governing peer relationships, methods of problem solving, etc.).
- Conduct in professional peer/agency relationships (standards governing relationships with outside professionals and agencies).
- Conduct related to public safety (standards governing situations that must be brought to attention of managers e.g., reports of physical and sexual abuse, threats of suicide or violence to others, etc.).

Such standards should be developed with full worker participation, should be reviewed with all new employees and periodically with all existing staff, and should be reviewed and refined periodically.

Now, with this background, how does the code of professional practice work to prevent professional closure of the organization?

The code provides an opportunity to define expectations for the frequency and nature of professional boundary transactions by staff. For example, the code can state that:

A. The agency does not have the resources to meet all the professional development needs of its employees. Staff are therefore strongly encouraged to seek outside opportunities for continued knowledge and skill development.

B. Professional development activities, to include activities outside the organization, are not an optional benefit but a non-negotiable expectation of all staff.

C. Given that the organization does not have the resources to meet all the critical needs of clients, staff shall be expected to utilize, through referral and collaboration, the full network of health and human services to aid clients.

D. Staff relationships with other professionals and agencies are strongly encouraged and should be marked by openness, respect, and an appreciation for workers with other areas of expertise and interests.

Such statements in the code of professional practice, reinforced consistently by managerial behavior, not only legitimize, but mandate professional boundary transactions by staff. Such policies break down the isolation, myopia, and the "it's us against the world" stance of the closed incestuous system.

Exclusive Versus Inclusive Program Philosophies A key element of the closure process is the organization of the health and human service system around a rigid and unchallengeable belief system or treatment philosophy. Rigid treatment philosophies and approaches are very attractive to organizations whose staff have an inadequate level of knowledge and skill and to organizations which experience excessive levels of stress. The reason for this attraction is that rigid belief systems generate fixed and mechanical responses to clients that reduce the amount of thought and decision-making required of staff. Rigid client admission criteria can be established that screen out a lot of people organizational members don't like working with, expose those clients accepted to treatment by recipe, and then measure success more by whether the client accepted our belief system (i.e. religious conversion) than by whether services were of benefit to the client. When clients get better, it is a program success that justifies the truth of the belief system. When clients don't get better, it's a client failure, and the clients are blamed. There is a certain amount of truth in the above scenario anytime there is an attempt to fit a very heterogeneous client population into a narrow, exclusive treatment philosophy.

A major strategy in the prevention of professional closure is the development of an inclusive treatment and program philosophy. Such philosophies can be summed up by the old adage "different strokes for different folks". More technically, these philosophies suggest that most human problems can spring from diverse and multiple etiological causes and that treatment approaches may be very different depending on the unique needs of the particular client. While such philosophies may create more humane and effective responses to a broad spectrum of clients, the use of such a philosophy requires a greater level of knowledge and skill on the part of staff and greater levels of adaptational energy to implement such individualized treatment.

Every organization needs a philosophy to integrate and make sense out of the activities of organizational members. What is important in preventing the professional closure of human service organizations is the following four points:

1) The philosophy must be broad enough to encompass the diverse needs and problems of the client group.
2) The philosophy must be flexible enough to allow exceptions in prescribed methods of treatment, when to do so is in the best interest of the client.
3) There must be mechanisms of feedback and self-examination that allow the philosophy to evolve and change over time in response to changing needs of clients and the development of new knowledge and technology.

4) Inclusive philosophies require higher levels of day-to-day support if workers are to sacrifice rules and rote behavior for the more difficult task of individualized assessment and service planning.

Planning Change Closed systems are known for their inherent resistance to change. Strategies to avoid such closure inevitably entail building mechanisms into the organization that facilitate needed change, allow member participation in the planning of such change, and control the pace of change.

Cataloguing the array of planning technologies that can assist in this process of evolutionary change in the organization is beyond the scope of this book. There are, however, some aspects of this planning process that can be helpful in preventing professional closure. While most organizations have advanced to the point of building in employee participation in the planning process, many still neglect important elements of the planning process that can represent significant professional boundary transactions. Professional closure is offset by cultivating multiple mechanisms of feedback into the planning process. These mechanisms can include:

- The use of technical experts from the field that can provide data on trends and new technology.
- The use of an internal study group or consultants to conduct a professional literature review on trends in the design, organization and funding of services.
- Client questionnaires or client advisory groups.
- A formal survey of community referral sources to solicit feedback on process and outcome of past service delivery and anticipated future needs.
- A bold approach of proposing a joint planning process with the agency's primary competitors.

The key elements of the planning process that relate to professional closure are: 1) the belief that change has positive value if it enhances the mission and goals of the organization; 2) the use of the planning process to increase feedback into the system through boundary transactions; and 3) an analysis of the level of supports and the pace of change required to sustain the quality of service delivery and protect the health of workers through the change process.

Tearing Down Walls/Building Bridges In Chapter Ten, the author noted how xenophobia, the fear of outsiders, can become a rather permanent component of organizational culture and drive an organizational family into professional and social closure. At other times, such isolation grows out of the commonplace interplay of egos, turf issues, competition, and conflict between community agencies. This process not only is a disservice to the clients allegedly being served, but also is destructive to all the agencies involved and to their respective staff members. Strategies designed to reduce professional closure encompass any plan designed to promote inter-agency collaboration and to increase the ease with which professionals can cross the boundaries of their respective organizations and interact with one another. Strategies that create joint planning, service and case coordination councils, shared training resources, staff exchanges, etc., all serve to decrease professional closure.

Strokes for Boundary Transactions In professionally and socially closed systems, organizational rewards are distributed more for commitment, allegiance to the high priest and for one's social affiliations than for competence and performance. Professional and social closure can be prevented by the clear message that money, status and other rewards in the work environment will be distributed based on one's performance. Furthermore, part of the performance that will be evaluated, is one's boundary transactions in seeking professional development activities and in establishing positive relationships with other health and human service providers in the area.

The Implementation of a Comprehensive Human Resource Development Strategy The most important vehicle for preventing professional closure is unquestionably the design and implementation of a comprehensive human resource development strategy. Such strategies are just now coming into popularity with progressive organizations and are creating a whole new field of human resource development (HRD) specialists. Historically, the training and professional development areas have been viewed as a luxury in health and human service agencies and have often been the first areas slashed in the name of cost containment.

The major issues that have been raised by organizational leaders in opposition to HRD strategies are the twin obstacles of time and money. Neither issue is substantive upon close examination. It is incomprehensible that an organization could take the position that there is not sufficient time available to assure that staff have the knowledge and skills to provide the highest possible quality of services to clients. Any organization that honestly takes such a position is hopelessly over-extended and needs to reexamine what level of services they can and cannot provide with existing resources. Such short-sightedness will eventually undermine the health of both clients and staff. While comprehensive HRD strategies do require a significant financial investment, some HRD components, such as training, can be significantly expanded with a minimum of financial investment and a lot of creativity. Consider the following example: A hospital department with 24 employees experienced a cut in the training budget to $1500 per year - an embarassingly low investment in the staff's knowledge and skill enhancement. Having $62.50 per year to invest in training for each staff person forced such creative options as the following:

- Staff met and agreed that more people would be able to get out for training each year if the unit would implement a cost-sharing policy in which part of each training activity would be paid for by the hospital and part would be paid for by the staff member attending.
- Unit managers negotiated with some state conference organizers to trade conference presentations by some staff in exchange for free admission for additional staff.
- The unit began to conduct workshops for a fee for other organizations and used this additional income to supplement the training budget.
- Each staff member, scheduled for an outside workshop was responsible for returning and conducting an inservice for other staff on the workshop material.
- The unit traded inservice training presentations with other agencies without cost to either.
- The unit utilized site visits to other programs as a professional development activity that required only mileage costs.

This should illustrate the point that training activities are possible even in the worst of financial conditions if there is a strong organizational and staff commitment to pursue this goal.

Comprehensive HRD strategies have a potent effect on reducing professional closure by providing opportunities for staff to meet professional needs and develop a professional identity outside the organizational family. HRD components, that can work to prevent and diminish professional closure, include the following:

1) Career Planning. The manager can assist staff in career and professional development planning and then match, where possible, both work assignments and training opportunities to the worker's career goals.

2) Development of career ladders and career paths. Organizational positions can be structured to provide a career ladder or path within the agency. Professional development activities can be designed to increase opportunities for upward and lateral mobility both within and outside the organization.

3) Academic education. The organization can provide financial support for work-related academic work and such other supports as supervisory encouragement, flex time to attend classes, leaves of absence for internships, etc.

4) Assistance with professional certification. Organizational support in the form of study groups for certification exams can be provided as a source of support and encouragement to staff who seek advanced credentialing.

5) Clinical consultation. The use of outside clinical consultants, who represent a variety of backgrounds and areas of specialized expertise, can provide a significant resource for professional development of staff. The use of such consultants represents a significant boundary transaction due to the increased flow of ideas and the ability of the consultants to provide a source of outside affirmation for staff.

6) Affiliation with professional associations. By encouraging and supporting staff affiliation with state and national professional associations, managers can help staff develop a professional identity and develop professional relationships that transcend the boundary of the organization.

7) Inservice and offsite training programs. Both inservice and offsite training can provide important boundary transactions that work to decrease professional closure. The inservice training program should not be designed to merely confirm and reinforce program philosophy and methodology. A varied inservice plan, that even includes presentations of modalities strongly opposed by the program, may prove exceptionally stimulating and professionally broadening. Offsite training is crucial to prevent the isolation of workers from their field.

The fact that HRD strategies, such as training, increase the knowledge and skills of staff and improves performance is an important but not exclusive benefit. As a manager, the author often sent staff to outside training events in which learning was not the primary goal. Training events and other HRD activities may provide benefits that at times may be more important than knowledge and skill acquisition. HRD strategies can serve to:

- Provide staff nourishing time-out periods from the high stress work environment.
- Facilitate the development of an outside professional peer network.
- Create access to the development of mentor relationships outside the organization.
- Provide staff personal and professional strokes from outside resources.
- Break down the myopia of the closed organizational system, and,
- Maintain an action set that includes the use of outside resources for upgrading and problem solving within the system.

HRD strategies represent a potent force in the prevention of incestuous organizational closure.

<u>Termination: The Act of Letting People Go</u> It was noted earlier that a shared characteristiics of closed organizational families was the inability of members to leave the family guilt-free. The forces that bind members to the organiation are so powerful that individuals must leave the same way adolescents separate from closed family systems - they act out and are extruded or they run away. A major strategy in the prevention of professional closure is the development of permissions, procedures and processes to allow members healthy and guilt-free paths out of the organization.

Knowing how to separate and say good-bye is a particularly difficult area of interaction in our culture. The relationship between the worker and the organization is treated like a marriage. A tremendous amount of time is spent in the screening (dating), recruitment (courtship), selection (marriage), and initial orientation (honeymoon period) of the worker. However, when it is discovered down the road that the needs of the worker or the organization are no longer being met in the relationship (irreconcilable differences), the efforts to figure out a way to terminate the relationship in a spirit of honesty, mutual respect, and emotional maturity are marked by awkwardness and failure. This phenomenon is true even in healthy organizations. In closed organizations, such problems in separation take on pathological dimensions. When irreconcilable differences develop in one's relationship with a closed organizational family, options are limited to submissive dependence or fighting one's way out of the organization. You can leave, but not without an emotional price.

Preventing organizational closure requires building mechanisms into the work environment that allow members to exit from the organization with a sense of fulfillment, with a sense of completion and with their self-esteem intact. Such mechanisms seek to protect the health of the exiting member and the organizational family through the termination process. Healthy termination strategies include the three earlier mentioned components: permissions, procedure and processes.

A. <u>Permissions</u> Workers can be told as part of their initial orientation and as part of their on-going professional development planning that no one expects them to remain

212

employed eternally with the program, that the program can assist them in making their next professional step, and that their exit can be planned in such a way as to enhance their feelings about the job experience and to minimally disrupt the flow of services to clients. A commitment to staff can be made that the manager can help them through feedback on types of work the manager thinks they would do well in, serving as a professional reference, flexibility in granting time off for interviews, and using professional contacts to help them indentify job leads. This position recognizes that there are highly legitimate needs such as money, broadening one's professional experience, and career mobility that may make leaving the organization not only desirable but necessary. The alternative to this position is the prolonged presence of a worker in the organization who is poorly motivated, is probably providing client services with minimal enthusiasm and whose negativity may be contagious to other staff. The alternative to such openness also includes the disruptive quality of the "secret mission" approach to job hunting by staff that is rarely ever secret. What the manager can ask, in return for such clear permission and assistance in exiting the organization, is that the worker continues to provide high quality client services right up to the day he/she leaves.

B. Procedures In health and human service organizations, procedures need to be developed which allow for a phased termination process between the exiting staff person and his or her clients. These procedures should build into the termination process a progressive decrease in responsibilities, the smooth transfer of responsibilities to other staff or the staff member's replacement, and the close supervision of termination with clients.

The development of step by step procedures of termination meets the organization's needs to maintain its efficient completion of work tasks through the transition period. It also provides daily evidence that the person is in fact leaving. This latter function of termination procedures works to counter denial of the impending separation and the tendency to act as if the person isn't really leaving, right up to the point they walk out the door.

C. <u>Processes</u> The termination of relationships within the organizational family, like any significant loss, can trigger primitive group emotions. Such responses capture the whole range of ambivalent feelings that surround the exit of a significant member from the organization. The range and power of such emotions, when not appropriately expressed or channeled, can prove extremely disruptive to the health of the organizational family. Providing members guilt-free exit from the organization requires that rituals be built into the period of termination that facilitate the reciprocal emotional detachment between the worker and the organization.

The group process surrounding terminations can aptly be described as a <u>grief and mourning process</u> characterized by stages similar to any response to the loss of a significant person. These stages roughly approximate the following:

Stage 1: Denial that the relationship is ending.

Stage 2: Denial plus physical symptoms (loss of appetite, sleep disorders, feelings of emptiness).

Stage 3: The experience of emotion (sadness and anger).

Stage 4: Identification with the person who is leaving (wanting to go with the exiting person).

Stage 5: Beginning of emotional separation from the person, and,

Stage 6: Reintegration (return to one's previous level of emotional functioning).

This grief and mourning process occurs simultaneously within the health and human service organization at three different levels. The worker leaving the program is going through these stages in response to the loss of the program, the staff, and clients. The staff group is experiencing this process over the loss of one of its members. The exiting staff member's clients are also experiencing their own sense of loss. When rituals of emotional separation are not provided, workers and clients get stuck at various stages of the mourning process with potentially destructive consequences to all concerned. The following common scenario is illustrative:

A counselor in a closed organizational family (community mental health center), after more than a year of feeling trapped, finally resigns. The counselor's supervisors respond to this news with guilt trips and open hostility, clearly communicating to other members that the counselor's resignation is a rejection and betrayal of the organizational family. The counselor responds by releasing a year's pent up emotion in verbal criticisms of the program and its leaders, handling terminations with clients poorly, and exiting on extremely short notice. The spill over of emotion to the counselor's clients results in a number of them acting out self-destructively. The counselor's alliance with other counselors during the short termination process sets them up to verbalize similar negative feelings about the program. Within three months two of the other counselors have resigned.

In the above illustration, a counselor stuck at stage 3 (the expression of emotion) is forced to remain angry to get out of the system. Clients, also stuck in stage 3 are, acting out due to the incomplete termination process. The other counselors stuck in stage 4 (identification with the person leaving), leave the organization. The mismanagement of the termination process in this example shows how the absence of grief and mourning rituals can disrupt the health of the exiting worker, escalate the loss of hope and acting out by clients and create a contagion of staff turn-over.

Rituals of termination that seek to promote the health of the organizational family and the exiting member can include such activities as the following:

- Make repeated verbal reference to the impending exit of the member from the organization. This functions to break down denial.
- Explicitly identify the short and long range implications of the loss. Answer each person's concern of "How is this going to affect me"?

- If the exiting member is a manager, quickly identify interim authority and the process and timeline to reestablish more permanent leadership.
- When a supervisor announces his or her resignation, address the safety and security needs of subordinates by immediately increasing their access to the next higher level of organizational authority.
- Phase down the exiting members activities and responsibilities. Decreased responsibilities will speed the transition from professional role relationships to social relationships between other workers and the exiting member.
- Establish the transfer of support in key relationships in which the exiting member is involved. With clients, consider moving to co-therapy to ease the client's loss of one counselor and enhance relationship building with the new counselor. Identify the workers to whom the exiting member provided the most emotional and technical supports. These workers may need increased supervisory contact to help manage their loss.
- Allow the expression of anger from members, (e.g., "I feel like you are abandoning us."; "It's such a bad time for you to leave"; etc.), but protect the exiting worker. Help the worker process such aspects of termination. Try to prevent the worker from personalizing the anger by explaining that such feelings are a normal part of the process of ending significant role relationships.
- Build in time for individual good-byes. Make sure the exiting worker is available for contact by other organizational members. At all costs, avoid the situation when the worker resigns and immediately leaves the work environment; or resigns, immediately takes two weeks vacation, and is gone without contact with other organizational members.
- Provide some form of final ceremony that marks the final step in the termination of the relationship between the worker and the organization. Such ceremonies or rituals mark a clear, visible com-

munication that the person is no longer a member of the organizational family.

- Build into the final ceremonies other nurturing activities that meet members needs (e.g., eating, drinking, playing, laughing, hugging, etc.)
- Provide some group activities immediately after the termination to allow the organizational family to redefine itself without the exited member.

The strategies in this section have focused on how to prevent professional closure by shaping how new members come into the organization, how professional boundary transactions are maintained and increased, and how to allow members guilt-free exit from the organization. The next section, will outline strategies to prevent the social and sexual closure of the organizational family.

11.6   Preventing Social And Sexual Closure

The social and sexual closure of organizational systems often grows out of the reduced boundary transactions, increased stressors and decreased supports inherent in professional closure. The strategies, that have already been outlined to prevent professional closure, thus become an integral part of the overall approach to preventing social and sexual closure. Additional activities and approaches that specifically influence the existence or nature of social and sexual relationships between organizational family members include the following:

Role Modeling of Managers Supervisory staff provide, through their behavior and interactions, the model for interpersonal relationships within the organizational family. Given the fact that the whole nature of health and human service work generally takes place in the context of interdisciplinary team relationships, this managerial function has profound implications on the health of the overall organizational family, and the quantity and quality of client services. Important elements of this role modeling function include the following:

A. Life space boundary management. Does the manager have a clear boundary between his/her work life and his/her personal life? Does the manager model through

217

his/her life-style the need for personal and social replenishment outside the work setting? Managers, who don't possess and model such boundaries, are much less likely to either reinforce or respect such boundaries in their subordinates.

B. Limits of self-disclosure. Does the manager set limits on his/her level of self-disclosure to other organizational family members and thereby communicate that there are areas of one's life both outside the reach of organizational members and inappropriate to bring into the organizational family? The manager, as well as the clinician, can utilize the self-disclosure in the human service setting more for his/her own self-growth and emotional healing than to respond to the needs of clients. Does the manager respect intimacy barriers of other organizational family members by refraining from over-involvement in member's personal problems. Does the manager avoid creating emotional dependence in subordinates by being overly intrusive or serving more as a therapist than a supervisor?

C. Limit on socializing. Does the manager refrain from developing a work-dominated social network? Does the manager create competition and conflict based on his or her inclusion or exclusion of staff in social relationships? Has the manager reinforced an in-group and an out-group within the organizational family based on social relationships outside the program?

D. Management of one's own sexuality. Has the manager refrained from involvement in seductive and sexual games or relationships with other staff? Supervisors who have been involved in sexual relationships with other staff become impotent to confront problems arising from such relationships between other organizational family members. Does the manager model the message that one can work closely with, care deeply about, and have sexual feelings about another staff person without these resulting in sexual activity? Has the manager modeled non-exploitive interactions with clients? It is difficult for the manager who has had clients do favors for him/her or bought a car from a client at cost to confront a staff-client sexual relationship. The manager has already inadvertently communicated that it is O.K. to exploit a client relationship for one's own benefit. Is the manager comfortable enough with his or her own sexuality to talk to staff about sexuality and make sexuality an issue in clinical supervision?

Orienting Staff to Problems in Social and Sexual Intimacy Another aspect of preventing social and sexual closure within the organization is to orient all new and existing members of the organization to the potential problems that can emerge in the social and sexual intimacy between staff. New members can be oriented as part of their initial orientation to the agency by the supervisor. Heightening the awareness of these problems for existing members can be facilitated in either an in-service discussion or workshop format.

Such information probably does very little to prevent the actual development of problematic social and sexual relationships between staff. The development of such relationships spring from much more primitive needs that are probably only minimally modified by cognitive processes. The goals of providing such information thus become:

- Opening up permission to talk about intimacy issues in supervision both as it relates to staff-staff and staff-client relationships,
- Providing words and labels to help staff understand what is happening when problems in such relationships do occur, and
- Providing a clear communication that social and sexual relationships between organizational members will be confronted as a supervisory issue anytime such relationships spill into the work environment and impair either worker performance or team relationships.

The Code of Professional Practice Revisited Some organizations address the problems of social and sexual closure by incorporating guidelines into personal policies or a code of profes-

219

sional practice that prohibit sexual relationships between organizational members and prohibit the hiring of spouses or relatives into the organization. Such guidelines may differ significantly from agency to agency. In general, a code of professional practice can reduce social and sexual closure in health and human service organizations by explicitly defining:

- The responsibility of the worker to sustain his/her physical, emotional, and social replenishment both for the benefit to themselves and to their clients.
- The values and attitudes expected in both peer and client relationships.

Changing Role Conditions that Violate Personal Life Space Any conditions in the work environment, that break down the barrier between one's professional and personal life, will work to promote the social and sexual closure of the organization. A key preventative strategy for such closure is the identification and alteration of these role conditions. Conditions that are frequently mentioned as disruptive to one's private life include excessive role demands that require overtime and taking work home, extended periods of on-call/emergency responsibilities, excessive travel demands causing limited time with family and friends, shift work that creates social isolation, extensive demands for non-work time meetings and activities, and the inability to accrue or take compensatory time.

Structuring the Social Needs of the Organizational Family Organizational group process can occur through design or the lack of it. Organizations, which appear to have decreased the most blatant and most destructive aspects of social closure, attempt to structure the relationships, identify, and process of the group. Such organizations, first of all, define roles clearly, maintain task-oriented directives on a day-to-day basis, establish professional competence and performance as the criteria for achieving status within the organization and provide managerial modeling on the type and quality of desired work relationships. In addition to the above, these organizations recognize and manage the needs of workers as social beings.

It is important to realize that people working closely together will develop close friendships and an alliance with the group as a unit, and that occasions need to be provided whereby the group and its members can celebrate their existence and their affection for each other. Rituals can be developed within the organizational structure which facilitate this celebration for the organizational family and the extended family, i.e., spouses, children, patrons, etc. These can often take the form of anniversaries of the program's existence, birthdays of staff, parties celebrating the reaching of particular program goals, going-away parties for staff who are leaving, etc. One agency studied by the author noted, after some very destructive social and sexual relationships between staff, that many of the difficulties had started when staff, due to a number of program difficulties, had stopped meeting as a group in a structured setting. It appeared to them that there was something about those occasions which provided some boundaries and models for what staff relationships should look like outside the work setting. Without such a structure, the contact between group members continued but in a much more destructive manner.

The goal is to utilize social relationships to enhance the quality of life in the organization without having such social needs supersede the achievement of program objectives. The group process of health and human service agencies can be monitored by supervisors to make sure the energy of the group has not moved from the treatment of clients to a focus on the social interactions of staff members. This monitoring process includes looking at:

- The amount of time staff spend with clients compared to the amount of time with each other.
- What percentage of unstructured staff time is spent on organizational or client issues compared to the amount of time on outside issues?
- The tenor of meetings in which the program, and in particular, clients, are discussed, (Are clients discussed in a respectful and serious manner? Do staffings reflect a serious attempt to use the combined staff expertise to better understand and improve the treatment of clients, or are staffings marked by "Ain't it Awful," "Look How Hard We Try," "Waiting for Santa Claus," or by cynicism, sick humor, and an unstated feeling that staffings are an

extended coffee break and social hour for the staff while maintaining the facade of dealing with program issues); and

- Whether supervisory time reflects a professional review of staff activities or a social review of extra-program happenings.

Shaping the Sexual Culture of the Organization It was noted in Chapter Seven that every organization has a sexual culture reflected in the language, artifacts, ethics, values, attitudes and relationships present in the organizational environment. Sexual cultures differ significantly from organization to organization, as well they should. The sexual culture of each organization needs to be congruent with its mission. The sexual culture of a clinic specializing in the treatment of sexual dysfunction or a counseling center for rape victims obviously needs to be different from the sexual culture of a job placement center. In the former examples, the sexual culture of the organization is itself an integral part of the treatment process. To illustrate how aspects of the sexual culture can be consciously shaped to inhibit the sexual closure of the organization, the section below outlines important components of the sexual culture of organization whose services may include helping clients with issues related to sexuality. The reader should review these as illustrative examples, and remember the admonition that sexual cultures must be shaped to reflect the unique needs and clientele of the organization. The following strategies were components of the sexual culture of organizations such as mental health centers, youth service agencies, family counseling programs, women's shelters, and chemical dependency programs. The purpose of these strategies was to promote healthy, non-exploitive relationships between staff and between staff and clients.

A. Permission to Address Sexuality There are clear permissions in the environment, reinforced by staff training, for both staff and clients to address problems and concerns related to sexuality. There are clearly stated values and expectations that staff will address issues of sexuality in a professional, direct and non-judgmental manner.

B. The Language of Sexuality A shared language has been developed to discuss issues of sexuality. The language contains carefully selected words that facilitate communication, are non-derogatory and non-exploitive, and do not offend the sensibilities of clients or staff.

C. Feelings Versus Behavior The culture contains permission and encouragement for staff to share feelings of sexual attraction to each other (as, for example, as an issue in supervision with group co-therapists) and to share (in supervision) feelings of sexual attraction to a client. There are, at the same time, discouragements or cautions about sexual relationships between staff and strong prohibitions against staff-client sexual relationships.

D. Staff-Client Boundary Issues The organization's code of professional practice explicitly states guidelines and standards for staff client boundary issues. The code:

- Defines a "client". Does client include family? Does client include a person that called for information but never received direct service? Does a client ever stop being a client? Is there a prohibition against a counselor having a sexual relationship with someone a month after they were terminated as a client? A year after?
- Requires that staff bring to the attention of the supervisor any pre-existing relationship with a client, e.g., relative, friend, son's teacher, etc.
- Provides supervisory action to prevent involvement in dual relationships like the above that could compromise the quality of services.
- Defines and delineates appropriate versus inappropriate social contact with clients. Under what conditions, if ever, is it appropriate to visit a client in his/her home? Is it ever appropriate to invite a client to your home? Is it appropriate to go out to lunch with a client? Are there any prohibitions or restrictions on socializing with clients?
- Sets limits that reduce the potential exploitation of clients. Is it appropriate to accept a gift from a client? A flower? A $1000 check? Can I buy a house through a client who is a realtor? Can I

accept this client's offer to return his/her portion of the real estate companies fee to me as a gesture of appreciation?

- Prohibits any form of sexual intimacy between staff and clients.

E. Sexuality and Supervision The process of clincial supervision of counseling activities is designed to provide assistance to the counselor in objectively managing the issue of sexuality to the benefit of the client and to confront the progressive violation of intimacy barriers and warning signs that often precede staff-client sexual contact. These signs include:

- The counselor's preoccupation with sexuality at the exclusion of more immediate and pain producing problems in the client's life.
- Clinical decisions by the counselor that increase or prolong contact with the client, e.g., excessively long interviews or prolonged continuation in treatment.
- Signs of increased dependency between counselor and client, e.g., increased crises, telephone calls, or letters between appointments.
- The counselor seeing the client outside office setting under questionable pretext.
- The client and counselor dressing up for their appointment.
- Observation of seductive or courting behavior between counselor and client.
- Resistance by the counselor to bring the client's case into the supervision process.
- Resistance to expanding one-to-one counseling to group, marital or family sessions when clinically appropriate.

The organization also utilizes the supervision process to confront problems that are created within the organization due to outside social or sexual relationships between staff.

F. Sexual Harassment There is a strong prohibition in the sexual culture against any form of sexual harassment.

Repetition of unwanted sexual advances, demeaning sexual humor, and the use of language that is debasing or disrespectful, is consistently confronted as inappropriate behavior.

G. Gossip Gossip and indirect communications of a judgmental and condemning nature about the outside social and sexual activities of staff are confronted as acts of personal and organizational sabotage.

When to Confront Outside Social and Sexual Relationships: The question when to confront problems due to the existence of outside social and sexual relationships has been a difficult one for many managers. After numerous mistakes in judgement, the considerable greying of hair, and at least some amount of hard earned wisdom, the author would recommend the following position. The role of the manager in this area involves three discrete functions:

1) The manager must confront any behavior of staff that violates the letter or intent of the agency's code of professional practice.
2) The manager must confront problems directly related to the role performance of individual employees.
3) The manager must confront problems that disrupt the harmony and quality of team relationships whether the source of these problems arose from staff interactions internal or external of the work setting.

Social and sexual behavior of staff, that does not impinge on any of these three areas, is none of the manager's business and to confront such behavior would be a violation of the privacy of the employee. It is crucial that managers be extremely specific in what it is he/she is confronting. Consider the following incident as an example:

Two agency counselors have developed a sexual relationship and are at a period where there is serious conflict in the relationship. One counselor wants to solidify the relationship through marriage; the other refuses to consider this as an option. This relationship breaks into the life of the agency when, after a turbulent night, the counselors come to work and refuse to talk to one another, refuse to work as co-therapists in group, which is part of the assigned role responsibilities of both, and participate in a loud shouting match within earshot of a number of agency clients.

Now, if the Code of Professional Practice of this agency, prohibits sexual relationships between staff, then the manager confronts the very existence of the relationship. If there are no such prohibitions, then the manager confronts not the relationship but the refusal to perform assigned responsibilities, the failure to utilize supervision to address conflict between co-therapists, the lack of professionalism in maintaining team relationships, and the atrocious example of problem solving and lack of emotional control demonstrated to clients. Lacking any prohibition of such relationships, what is confronted is not the relationship itself but the consequences of the relationship upon the organization and its delivery of services to clients.

It may also be important for the manager to examine and set aside his/her own personal feelings about such outside relationships. Consider the following example from the author's experience. It came to my knowledge as a manager that two of my supervisors (counselors) were involved in a sexual relationship. This created a great deal of emotional turmoil for me. First, the female counselor was extremely attractive and I had spent considerable energy managing my own sexual attraction to her in order to effectively perform my supervisory role. Secondly, the male counselor was married, and I knew and greatly respected his wife. What I found, upon self-examination, was that my desire to confront the relationship had more to do with my own feelings of envy and jealousy and my anger that the male counselor was jeopardizing his marriage than it had to do with my role responsibilities as the manager. The fact was that the relationship between the two counselors had not, at this early stage, had any impact on the performance of either counselor or the functioning of the team.

11.7 Opening Closed Systems: Some Guidelines And Cautions

How does one begin to re-open an organizational system that has gone through, and is still in the stages of extreme organizational closure described in this book? This is the question that often confronts the manager who knows something is seriously wrong with their organization but is unsure how to alter this condition. This situation may also confront the new director who inherits a closed organizational family, or the organizational consultant who has been called in to help with one of the crisis episodes in the closed organizational family. While many of the strategies outlined in this chapter to prevent the process of organizational closure can also be used as corrective strategies, there are some unique problems that must be addressed in reversing the process of organizational closure.

Good Intentioned Strategies That Create Casualties It is common to make the erroneous assumption that all problems which involve interpersonal conflict within organizations are basically communication problems that will be resolved when we get the parties talking. It is a surprise therefore, to find that bringing parties together sometimes increases rather than decreases the conflict. This may be particularly true when the closed organizational family is brought together as a whole for a "staff group" or "staff retreat". The failure in this assumption is that conflict in closed organizational families grows out of the over-connectedness and bonding between staff. Interventions in closed systems must loosen the bonds between staff and produce role differentiation - not create further intimacy.

At the point a consultant is brought in to work with a closed organizational family, most organizational members are physically and emotionally depleted. They usually are in a state of extreme vulnerability. Staff, who have been hanging on by their fingernails, may snap under the emotional intensity of a process oriented staff group. What staff need is a reprieve from the emotional stimulation of the closed system, not an intensification of that stimulation via group therapy. Process-oriented groups break down intimacy barriers and increase bonding between group members -- the exact conditions closed organizational family members do not need.

An important principle in planning interventions into closed organizational families is that there are high risks of emotional casualities with any strategy that increases intimacy between members, increases emotional stimulation, or increases new demands for adaptation by opening the system too quickly.

<u>What</u> <u>To</u> <u>Do</u> <u>With</u> <u>The</u> <u>High</u> <u>Priest</u> An important issue in opening closed systems is the question of whether such closure can be reversed without a change in leadership. The answer depends on the degree of organizational closure that has been reached at the point where there is a recognized problem. Many organizational leaders recognize fairly early in the progression of closure that there is a need to address internal problems before such problems seriously undermine the mission of the organization and the health of organizational members. Under these circumstances, the system may be able to open up under their leadership. Once, however, the late stages of closure have been reached, it is doubtful that closure can be reversed without new leadership. Many managers, including this author, at some time in their career have reached the decision after much soul searching that organizational problems had developed that were unresolveable under his/her leadership and that the best thing they could do for the organization was to leave. Unfortunately, management science has not found a commonly used way to reward such honesty by providing these managers a way out of these organizations with their self-esteem intact. The author left a leadership position of one organization feeling incompetent, confused and incapable of understanding how he had helped create, and lost control of a painful process described in this book as the progression of organizational closure. Organizational leaders who perceive neither the need nor the desire to remove themselves from the high priest position continue to escalate the closure process to the point no outside intervention is possible until a major crisis occurs. This crisis is usually precipitated by the gross deterioration in the health and performance of the high priest e.g., psychiatric illness, addiction, sexual exploitation of clients, misuse of agency funds, etc. Outside intervention is then possible through the board or a new organizational leader.

With increased sophistication in our knowledge of organizational life, it may be possible to avoid much of the above pain and turmoil. It may be possible to define predictable developmental stages in the life of an organization - each of which may require a different type of leadership style, personality and skills. Some managers may have the flexibility to adapt and effectively see an organization through all these developmental stages. Others may become specialists who will be brought in to provide leadership during one developmental stage only to leave as the next developmental stage emerges. Some managers may be selected to create and others selected to maintain. A managerial career specialty may evolve that involves nothing but starting programs, reorganizing programs and managing programs during periods of crisis. Rather than chastising such managers for their inability to stay with one organization for the long haul, they will be seen as highly competent and valued management specialists. Such a perspective could help us understand the need for a change in leadership or a change in the role and function of the leader as an organization's needs dictate movement from closure to greater openness.

Bringing Replenishment to a Depleted System   The most important initial role of any consultant (or new director) working with a closed organizational family is to provide a source of needed replenishment for organizational members. Recommendations for the consultant or new director include the following:

A. Listen   Begin by assessing the individual and collective health of the organizational family. In systems which experience high levels of emotional pain and conflict, this process can best be done through one-to-one interviews with staff. In systems experiencing less conflict, a combination of one-to-one interviews and small group interviews can be utilized. The purpose of these interviews is to collect data and to build a supportive, nurturing relationship with each organizational member. In these interviews, the manager can give each staff member an opportunity to:

● Share information about his/her personal backgrounds (I am interested in you as a person).
● Share his/her history in the organization and how they have experienced that history. (I need your help to understand our history.)
● Identify both the strengths and major problems confronting the agency (I need your help to plan our future).
● Identify both stressors and areas of insufficient support (I want to enhance your health and enjoyment of what you do).
● Provide recommendations on resolving organizational problems and future program directions (I will listen to and respect your ideas).

229

The interview process can provide an important vehicle for emotional catharsis and emotional support for organizational family members. The process can also break the pattern of secret meetings with unstated agendas that usually plague closed systems. The consultant or director can announce to all staff the purpose of the interviews, distribute a written copy of the major areas or questions that will be addressed in the interviews, and stick to the prescribed interview structure.

B. Provide Strokes (Affirmations) Through the interview process and all interactions with staff, the major goal is to replenish and restore the self-esteem of organizational members. This is provided through personal contact, listening, and providing verbal praise to individual members, organizational units, and the organizational group as a whole. All early interactions and activities should seek to reduce emotional demands and increase emotional rewards.

C. Outside Replenishment Boundary transactions can slowly be increased to provide an additional source of personal and professional strokes from outside the system. The increased presence in the organization of outside professional resources and increasing member access to outside sources of professional support can be instrumental in rebuilding the self-esteem of the organizational family.

Making Sense Out of the Pain and Chaos One of the most disturbing aspects of the late stages of organizational closure is the inability of members to comprehend what has happened to themselves and to the organizational group. Member confusion is internalized as personal craziness or angrily projected and blamed on other organizational members. The humanistic passions and values that fueled the creation of the organization have gone stale and now leave members emotionally untouched. Meaningful professional and personal relationships have been ruptured into remnants of unresolved conflict and resentment. Mutual support and loyalty has turned to fear and paranoia. Collective guilt flourishes over the organizational impasse and the scapegoating and extrusion of members from the group. The incongruence between the group ideal and the soap opera atmosphere eats away family pride and replaces it with shame and self-indictment. Such primitive emotions scream for a cognitive answer to the question: "what happened"? The second function of the outside consultant who intervenes in a closed system is to help provide members an answer to that question.

It is the task of the consultant to help organizational members find words and labels to help describe and understand the changes within themselves and within the organizational family. One of the most fulfilling aspects of the author's organizational studies has been to watch the healing that occurs when I describe to workshop participants the detailed description of the stages of organizational closure and its consequences upon individual staff. The concepts, descriptions and labels help bring order out of chaotic emotional experiences. By providing a cognitive handle on such experience, the consultant is able to relieve some of the pent-up emotional energy and initiate the first stages of healing within the organizational family.

This healing is made possible by providing a cognitive model that reduces individual guilt, relieves fears and concerns about one's sanity, decreases the need for blaming and other forms of projection, and affirms the value and integrity of individual staff and the organizational family as a unit. Messages implicit in this cognitive model include the following:

- You are not alone! Many organizations have gone through the same process with only minor variations. It is a rare service organization that doesn't go through this process at some point in its history.
- You are not crazy! The emotional turmoil you are all experiencing springs from aberrations in the structure and process of the group, not from individual psychopathology. You are bright sensitive people that inadvertently got caught up in a process that undermined your individual and collective health.
- No one is to blame! There are no villains, there are only victims. The turmoil in your organizational family grew out of a slow and subtle progression of closure which no one recognized or consciously controlled. Most closure occurs because there is a

231

period where each of us has needs that are met by such closure. We all participated in the process of closure without an awareness of its eventual consequences.

- The process is reversible! We may not be able to go back to where we were but we can move forward and regain our individual health and restore respect and harmony in our relationships with one another.

Providing Structure and Safety At this early stage in the intervention process the consultant has collected a tremendous amount of data from organizational members and has begun the process of emotionally replenishing members. Some conditions in the environment will already have begun to improve. Some improvement usually occurs from the point where there is an open acknowledgment of the problem and an announcement that an outside consultant will be brought in to provide assistance. During the early stage of intervention, many workers will already have become more positive in their approach to their work and there will usually be increased expressions of hopefulness about the future of the organization. The history of closure within the organization, however, will have most members continuing to have fear about what is going to happen. The task of the consultant/director at this stage is to provide both structure and safety.

Providing structure and safety usually involves creating a plan and process aimed at resolving organizational family problems, decreasing immediate stressors and bringing a halt to any continuing scapegoating.

A. The Long Range Intervention Plan: At an earlier stage, organizational members have begun to make sense out of the closure process and come to some understanding of how problems developed within the organizational family. The goals at this stage are to give members a clear sense of future directions and insure their involvement in the problem-solving process. Based on the data gathered in staff interviews and consultant and managerial recommendations, a plan is prepared and presented to the organizational family. This process should be characterized by the following:

- The plan and its verbal presentation should openly acknowledge the major problems confronting the agency. The first goal is to break the no-talk rule governing communications about agency problems.
- An outline of the problems and strategies should be presented in written form at the same time it is verbally presented to staff. There is something about capturing such issues on paper that brings them under our control. The goal is to make hidden agendas explicit. The new message is: agency problems will be brought out into the open, confronted directly and resolved.
- The plan will clearly articulate where we need to go. The plan says this is where the organization needs to be with this problem six months from now. The plan should include both programmatic and service issues and problems in the emotional life and relationships within the organizational family that must be resolved to meet those programmatic goals.
- The plan should outline in broad terms the process by which each problem will be addressed. This area is generally less well-defined and open to refinement and participation by staff. The basic message is: directly confronting and resolving problems is not negotiable; how we approach solving problems is negotiable.
- Organizational leaders should solicit support from organizational family members to participate in the problem solving and healing process.

B. Decreasing Immediate Stressors: By decreasing immediate stressors, organizational leaders demonstrate that the process started will result in concrete, observable changes in the work environment. These actions demonstrate evidence of good faith on the part of organizational leaders and instill hope in the change process. One of the most productive actions at this stage is to postpone non-essential projects or to renegotiate production timelines to free up emotional energy for the process of change.

C. Aborting the Process of Scapegoating: One of the most dramatic interventions, that organizational leaders can take to decrease fear and increase feelings of security and safety, is to bring to a halt the continued scapegoating of any organizational members. Such actions decrease feelings of vulnerability not only for the scapegoats, but for all organizational members. The new director of a closed system often inherits a situation where a scapegoat is on the verge of extrusion from the organization. By preventing such extrusion and restoring the functioning of the scapegoat through increased supports, the new leader provides a powerful message about how staff will and will not be treated within the organizational family.

Letting People Out Bringing In New Blood As noted early in this book, healthy organizational systems have a fairly predictable and desirable rate of staff turnover. Closed systems inhibit this normal developmental separation of some members from the organization. The new director or consultant working in a closed system will inevitably confront a backlog of individuals who, for whatever reasons, needed to leave the organization but didn't because of the emotional and financial bonds to the system and their deteriorating self-esteem.

Given the above, it is not a goal of the new director to keep all current staff within the organizational system. In fact, part of the success of a new director could be measured by his or her ability to assist members to get out of the system whose needs can no longer be met there. In this case, the directors job is to:

- Enhance the self-esteem of these workers so they feel they are marketable and have something of value to offer outside the organizational family.
- Enhance these members' boundary transactions to increase the chances that they will find a position that meets their next stage of professional development needs.
- Decrease the emotional bonds between these individuals and the organization.
- Help these members get out of the organizational family with a sense of completion, fulfillment, and emotional closure of the experience.

- Demonstrate to other organizational members both the permission and preferred process for members to leave the organizational family.

The old value system of the closed system must be changed through a perspective that views the exit of a member as a potentially healthy and desirable event. It is important to recognize that there are employees who developmentally are in a parallel role to a seventeen-year-old adolescent in a nuclear family system. For the health of the individual and the system, constructive ways must be found to facilitate his/her separation from the system.

If there is a failure to let such individuals out of the organization, they can prove very disruptive to the process of healing and redefining the organizational family. It, quite honestly, is to much to ask of them to emotionally reinvest and commit themselves to changing a system from which they need to separate. When such individuals are allowed to move out of the organizational family, space is created to bring in new members with new ideas and perspectives that can further facilitate opening up the system.

Untangling Current Relationship Agendas Perhaps one of the most difficult and painful jobs of the new director or consultant working to open a closed organizational family is the process of untangling the relationship problems that have grown out of the professional, social and sexual closure of the system and that continue to impair the ability of the team to function effectively. Suggested guidelines in this area include the following:

- Old relationship wounds between organizational family members that don't impair work performance should not be re-opened by the supervisor except at the request of the individuals involved. Given the emotional depletion of closed organizational family members, raising old agendas may increase rather than decrease conflict.
- Where relationships have deteriorated through the social and sexual closure of the organization, separate those individuals to the greatest extent possible within the organizational structure and particularly avoid placing such emotionally

conflicted individuals in a power oriented relationship, e.g., supervisor - supervisee. The goal is to remove or limit the ability of old and current non-professional emotional agendas from spilling into the process of client treatment and team functioning.

- Recognize that some emotional conflict in relationships can be so painful and so primitive as to be unresolveable in the short run e.g., counselor leaves husband (who is also a counselor at the agency) and marries her husband's supervisor. It may be necessary to assist members with such emotion and conflict-ridden relationships to separate from the organization both for their own needs and the needs of the organizational family.
- The general guideline is that any relationship problems that impair worker performance will be confronted and either resolved by participants, or at a minimum, suppressed so as not to interfere with job functioning.
- The goal in interventions into closed systems is to clean up old emotional agendas and move this aspect of supervision to the present tense-bringing relationship problems into the supervisory process as they occur.

Burying Old Ghosts Individuals who are extruded or run away or just leave the organization under conditions of extreme emotional conflict often become ghosts that continue to haunt the organizational family. Though no longer physically present, members continue to feel their presence or the events surrounding their termination. These ghosts are created by the lack of permissions, procedures and processes earlier described as essential for the effective separation of a member from the organizational family. A key factor in opening closed systems is the ability of the director or consultant to bury these old ghosts. Such burial requires that organizational family members expiate and bring to emotional closure their feelings about the lost member and the events surrounding their exit from the organization.

Some years ago, the author worked with an organization that had gone through a number of the stages of closure described in this book, to include the extrusion of several key staff members by the high priest. The most painful extrusion to the organizational family occurred to a counselor who challenged the faith system of the high priest. This counselor was fired and asked to leave the agency immediately. Years later staff described the painfully poignant picture of staff watching at the windows as the counselor slowly carried the box of his belongings to his car and drove away. Years later this event crystallized how both the extruded counselor and the high priest (who had left) would haunt this organization. The image of the counselor triggered a high level of collective guilt - as if all members had witnessed a crucifixion, and through their silence, had bloodied their hands. The image of this event would also show how the high priest would continue to haunt the organization for some time after he left. This organization came under new leadership that encouraged assertive behavior and participation by staff in decision-making. The new leader was confused by the silence and low-risk communications by staff until he realized that each time he asked staff to provide some self-criticism of the program, they were silenced by the image of the counselor carrying his belongings across the parking lot. While there was a new explicit message to staff, the deeply ingrained message within the organizational family was that those who challenged the existing belief system would be victimized.

This same story also reveals the process of burying such ghosts. By expiating their feelings about the extruded counselor and the high priest and by being supported in their new level of participation, the staff at this agency eventually would let go of the old prohibitions that ruled their professional conduct. Another event also helped bring a final catharsis to this episode. A chance encounter between the new director and the extruded counselor resulted in the counselor visiting the program for the first time since he had been fired. This visit allowed the counselor to go back and emotionally close an episode that had devastated his self-esteem, and it gave staff members an opportunity to talk with him and share their feelings about the event. The counselor ceased being a ghost and became a person and the ghost of the high priest lost some of its power.

Renegotiating Values and Beliefs Another critical intervention in opening the organizational family is the process of renegotiating organizational family norms, values and beliefs. This not only involves moving away from the inflexibility and dogma of the closed system. It also requires building in a regular process by which values and beliefs can be refined based on changes in the outside environment, changes in the needs of organizational family members and changes in the needs of clients.

The involvement of organizational family members in rethinking and redefining their treatment philosophy and approaches, and the involvement in a process of developing an agency code of professional practice, can be two key components of this reformulation of who the organizational family is. Such reformulations usually result in a broadened treatment philosophy that allows more individualized approaches to client needs, a clear articulation of ethical and client boundary issues, and a professional stance that increases professional interactions and relationships outside the system.

The On-Going Process of Opening the System At this point, most of the strategies for the prevention of professional, social, and sexual closure can also be utilized as vehicles to promote movement toward the middle of the organizational closure continuum. The only caution is to again point out to the reader that the pace of opening the extremely closed system should be carefully monitored. If the pace of increasing boundary transactions is too rapid, it will prove extremely stressful to organizational family members who may wish to again seek refuge in the closed system. The stimulation of increased boundary transactions must be offset with a commensurate level of emotional and personal support from within the organization.

The intervention process into each closed organizational family has many unique aspects. It is hoped, however, that the general guidelines set forth in this section will help other consultants and directors conceptualize and plan such interventions.

Interventions into Disengaged Organizational Families Most of this book has focused on understanding and intervening in closed organizational systems. This last chapter in particular has focused on the small health and human service agency, and its inherent tendency to move towards organizational closure. The author would be remiss, however, if this chapter on boundary management were closed without making some brief comments on interventions into disengaged organizational systems.

In Chapter Four, a continuum of three organizational types was described based on the degree of closure, measured by boundary transactions. The types included the enmeshed organizational family, the self-regulated organizational family and the disengaged organizational family. The self-regulated organizational family was postulated as the healthy model due to its flexibility to move back and forth on the closure continuum in response to changing needs. It is obvious from this model that interventions to improve the health of disengaged systems would be remarkably different from interventions for enmeshed systems. The goals of interventions in disengaged systems is, in fact, to create a greater degree of organizational closure to move the agency toward the center of the closure continuum. A detailed discussion of such strategies is beyond the scope of this book, but some general strategies that have been used in interventions with complex, bureaucratic, disengaged systems included the following:

- The development of a clear and cohesive statement of mission and purpose of the organization.
- Increased visibility and physical presence of organizational leaders inside the organizational family.
- Increased large group activities to reinforce agency identity.
- More charismatic, less formalized leadership.
- Loosening of intimacy bonds within microsystems of the organization.
- Increased boundary transactions between microsystems of the organization.
- Increased definition of organizational boundary.
- Periodic tightening of gatekeeping functions to reduce boundary transactions and increase internal cohesiveness and identity.

It is hoped that this brief list will give the reader pause the next time he/she picks up a management recipe book that assume organizations are homogenous entities that are controllable by a set of fixed management interventions. When it comes to management strategies that impact boundary transactions, it should be clear that a highly successful intervention for one organization could prove disastrous to another.

Chapter 12
Promoting Health and Productivity in the Microsystem

The purpose of this final chapter is to move away from broad organizational strategies related to boundary management and to catalogue a number of stress reducing management interventions at the microsystem level of the organization. This chapter will address the following four questions:

- What strategies are available to the manager to reduce those stressors that are most frequently experienced by workers and that produce the most severe stress-related deterioration in performance?
- What strategies are available to the manager to increase the level of personal and professional supports experienced by workers in the work environment?
- What organizational strategies can be implemented to promote the overall health of workers and reduce the individual vulnerability of workers to professional stress?
- What approaches are available to the manager to respond to employees who are experiencing a stress related deterioration in their work performance and personal health?

12.1 The Goal Of Role Homeostasis

A model for the microsystem analysis of stress was outlined in Chapter Nine and examined the level and intensity of role stressors and role supports and how such stressors and supports were filtered through the preferred defense structure of each worker. The implicit goal of this model was to organize the work environment in such a manner that each worker could achieve and sustain role homeostasis. Role homeostasis was described as a condition in which a worker could successfully perform his/her role responsibilities and do so without a stress-related debilitation of personal health and interpersonal functioning. This model identified three points of analysis and intervention for stress-related problems. The model outlines a systems strategy to:

- Assess and identify the level and intensity of role stressors and to manipulate the work environment to reduce role stress conditions;
- Assess and identify the level and intensity of role supports and to manipulate the work environment to increase role supports; and
- Assess problems in the preferred defense structure of individual workers and to intervene individually and collectively to enhance the strength and flexibility of workers' preferred defense structures.

The next sections will outline strategies to achieve the first two categories of these interventions-reducing role stressors and increasing role supports in the work environment.

12.2   Strategies To Assess Role Stress Conditions

Many managers and supervisors are instinctively aware of the existence of stress-related problems in the work environment though they often underestimate the degree and impact of such stress on the work unit. The initial step in addressing stress-related problems in the work environment is the systematic collection of data to identify both the extent and nature of role stressors in the organization This analysis can be conducted as part of a broad organizational effort that was recommended in the last chapter or may be initiated by a departmental supervisor.

Most organizations already have internal data that when carefully scrutinized can identify important aspects of the impact of stress on the organization and employees. It can be extremely useful for an organization to look at the following categories of data by worksite location, work unit, and job title or category:

- health care costs
- workmen's compensation claims
- absenteeism and tardiness
- employee turnover
- accidents

- grievances
- requests for unit transfer
- lost materials due to breakage or theft
- consumer complaints regarding services or products
- exit interview data from employees leaving the organization

Additional sources of data can come from formal employee surveys, ongoing mechanisms for employee feedback ranging from suggestion boxes to employee forums with top managers, employee health screening, and the use of special outside consultants to conduct a formal assessment of stress-related problems. The goals of this initial step are to:

- Identify the extent and nature of role stressors in the organization.
- Assess the impact of such stressors on the organization.
- Establish areas of baseline data by which future intervention strategies can be evaluated.

12.3 A Schema For Strategy Implementation

The author recommends the following seven-step process for implementing microsystem strategies to reduce role stress conditions:

1) Identify and define the stressor as clearly and completely as is possible with available data.
2) Develop a strategy with employee participation to address the stressor and identify what data will indicate if the strategy has been successful.
3) Implement the strategy on a small scale and on a time limited basis.
4) Check data to evaluate the strategy.
5) Identify any unanticipated repercussions of the strategy on other parts of the organization. (Did reducing stressors in one unit escalate stressors in another unit?)
6) Based on outcome, either fully implement strategy or consider alternative strategies to test.
7) Build in a mechanism to continue to evaluate and refine the strategy.

12.4 Manipulating The Work Environment To Reduce Role Stressors And Increase Role Supports

The following sections will outline intervention strategies to address various aspects of the thirteen role stressors discussed in Chapter Nine.

12.5 Strategies To Address Role-person Mismatch

Role-person mismatch was defined earlier as the misplacement of a worker into an unsuitable role given the worker's level of knowledge and skills, level of stress tolerance or style of stress management. Strategies to reduce problems of role-person mismatch include the following:

A. The Recruitment, Screening, Selection, and Role Placement Process Most problems of role person mismatch occur due to flaws in the process of selecting new members to add to the organizational family. A review of this process must include a recognition of the forces that contribute to errors in employee selection and role placement. The following observations are offered related to this process:

- The work overload due to the loss of a microsystem team member will create pressure to make a speedy, but not necessarily effective, hiring decision. An appropriate and short-term reduction in unit workload will serve to decrease such pressure.
- Forces at work in the applicant, from financial need to the ego-involved competition for the job, can contribute to misplacement. It is the judgment of the manager, who knows the knowledge and skill demands and stress inherent in the open position, that must determine the issue of match, not the ego-involved judgment of the applicant.
- Unvalidated assumptions about the knowledge and skills a candidate possesses contribute to role-person mismatch. Such assumptions must be tested both in the interview process and in checking professional references.

244

- Once the manager gets the first inkling during an interview that he/she has found the person for the job, the thoroughness and level of scrutiny in the interview process tends to radically decrease. It is imperative that the manager recognize this tendency and force the continued rigorous examination of the candidate. Such "first inklings" are often triggered more by the personality of the applicant than by the applicant's technical knowledge and skills.
- Interviews measure presentation of self and one's ability to articulate how to perform a job. Such interviewing skills are not necessarily synonymous with actual performance abilities. Reference checks are essential to assure that a candidate's performance skills are commensurate with his/her interview skills.
- Most job applicants are inclined to list references that will assure the prospective employer that the candidate can walk on water. Insist on supervisory references in addition to co-worker and colleagial references. Test the objectivity of references with direct questions related to the candidate's weaknesses, areas of needed skill development, types of roles the candidate would find most stressful, and problems in prior roles and how they were resolved.
- Once role misplacement has occurred, numerous forces will work to postpone correction of the problem, e.g., an inevitable "honeymoon period", the difficulty many managers have when they confront performance problems, an assumption that early performance problems are just the transition to a new role and will work themselves out, new priorities after the hiring that divert the manager's attention and decrease close observation of the new employee, the tendency of a new employee to overachieve during the role entry period, and the manager's difficulty in confronting his/her mistake in judgment in the selection and placement process.

A systems perspective on role-person mismatch dictates a formal review and refinement of the process of recruiting, screening, selecting, and placing workers. Such a perspective is imperative to avoid blaming and punishing workers for what is essentially a flaw in the structure and process through which new members are added to the organization. Many areas of private industry have refined this recruitment and selection process to an extremely sophisticated science. The small health and human service agency whose limited resources preclude the use of high priced consultants in this area, may find local volunteer resources from the private sector who can provide invaluable assistance in refining organizational procedures to reduce problems of role-person mismatch.

B. Honesty Versus Salesmanship in Position Promotion
   Objective data is crucial for the manager to determine if the role-person mismatch will meet the needs of the organization. Objective data provided to the applicant on the reality of organizational life is equally crucial in the applicant's decision whether his/her needs can be met in a relationship with the organization. Whereas the last section cautioned the manager about the over-zealous, potentially underqualified candidate who sneaks into the organization, this section cautions the manager not to attempt through salesmanship to seduce a reluctant candidate into the organization.

   A misrepresentation of conditions in the overall organization and in the position an applicant is seeking can lead to serious problems of role-person mismatch. Strategies to reduce such problems include the following:

   ● The manager/interviewer must provide an honest preview of the job role and the organization. Most managers demand a "no surprise" stance from employees who work for them. Employees joining an organization deserve nothing less from those organizational representatives involved in their hiring. If there are fiscal problems, clearly summarize to the applicant the information on this issue that is available to other organizational members at the same level. If there are serious problems of staff conflict, communicate their nature and intensity. If there are particular stressors unique to the role the applicant is seeking, communicate them clearly and completely. If the manager/interviewer has done an effective job, the new employee should enter the organization without illusions and find exactly in the work environment both the demands and rewards he/she had been led to expect.

- With many positions, it may be helpful to offer a selected candidate an opportunity to spend a half or full day at the job site before making his/her final decision to accept the position. This allows the candidate to sense how he/she feels in the physical and social environment in which he/she will be working and to assess both the skill and adaptational demands that will be placed on him/her in the role.

C. Permission for Early Exit Even in the best of circumstances, both a manager and the applicant may overestimate the applicant's ability to manage the technical and emotional demands of a position. This collective error in judgment, may be difficult to confront by both parties and, unfortunately, is usually addressed long after the traditional probation period has passed. The key to this dilemma is the ability of the supervisor to first rule out that performance problems are not due to environmental factors over which the employee has no control and to confirm the lack of success in providing training to upgrade skills and role performance. Given these circumstances, the supervisor must confront the misplacement firmly and directly and try to provide the worker with permission for an early and guilt free exit from the organization. Providing support and supervision of the supervisor going through this situation will significantly increase his/her willingness and potency in confronting one of the most stressful situations for a supervisor.

D. **Avoiding Misplacement Through Promotion** A particular
type of role-person mismatch can occur not with the new
employee, but with the lateral or upward movement of an
existing employee within the organizational structure.
Here one discovers the erroneous assumption that exemplary performance in one role can be used to predict
successful performance in a different role. The usual
scenario is to take someone who has demonstrated outstanding knowledge and skills in one role and promote
him/her into a role with different skill and adaptational
demands. This type of misplacement creates a double
loss. First, the organization has lost the individual in the
old role in which he/she made an outstanding contribution. Second, the organization has lost the full benefit of
the new position due to the employee's inability to transfer skills or master the skill demands of the new position.
Such misplacement is first countered by confronting the
internal dialogue of the manager and the administrative
dialogue surrounding the promotion process. Such
dialogue warning signals include the following:

- "He/she will be upset if he/she doesn't get the position."
- "We owe it to him/her because he/she didn't get an
  earlier position he/she interviewed for."
- "He/she has been in the department longer than
  anyone else."
- "We have to reward his/her loyalty."
- "He/she is going to become a management problem
  if he/she doesn't get the position."

All of the above indicate that a decision to change an
employee's role in the organization is about to be made
out of guilt rather than an assessment of organizational
needs and employee competence and adaptability.

Avoiding role misplacement through promotion hinges on
two additional strategies. The first involves clearly identifying knowledge, skill, and adaptation requirements for
each role in the organization so that the issue of trans-
ferability of skills from one role to another can be

objectively assessed. The second strategy is to build in career paths within the organization that:

- Allow people through professional development activities to try on new areas of knowledge and skill for personal comfort and fit e.g., a counselor attending a management workshop.
- Prepare people internally with expanded knowledge and skills for greater role options.
- Provide career and salary ladders within technical and speciality areas. In this way, employees do not have to seek out new roles, which they don't enjoy and can't perform, solely to seek greater financial rewards from the organization.
- Provide outplacement counseling for advancement discouraged employees.
- Provide paths back into specialty roles for managers and supervisors who desire such moves.

The author prefers the term "career paths" over "career ladders" because the latter term connotes an expectation that one must move upward within the organization. A career path, which may move up, down, and laterally through the organization, may better meet the needs of an employee and the organization. The concept of career path recognizes that the developmental needs of both the employer and the organization change over time and allows both to renegotiate the nature of the relationship congruent with these changing needs.

12.6   Strategies To Address Role Conflict

Problems of role conflict grow out of incongruous demands from simultaneously held roles. Role conflict can reflect:

- Incompatible role expectations within a single role communicated from one source, e.g., "John, I want this to be the best quality project we have ever done, and I want you to complete it below our budget projection." (Message to the manager of a poorly designed, under-bid project.)

- Incompatible expectations within a single role communicated from multiple sources, e.g., pressure applied on a construction foreman from management to speed the completion of a building process, and simultaneous pressure from the labor force to slow completion due to the fact they will be laid off as soon as the work is completed.

- Incompatible expectations on a particular issue generated from participation in two or more roles, e.g.,
  - 7:00 a.m. family role communication: "Sarah, its really important to John that you get home early tonight and attend his school play."
  - 9:00 a.m. work role communication: "Sarah, I know it's short notice, but tonight is the only time the board committee can meet to discuss your proposal."

Strategies to address role conflict must start with an acknowledgment that some degree of role conflict probably is inevitable both in simple and complex organizations. Completely eliminating role conflict for all members of an organization is unrealistic and impossible. Given this, the management goal becomes to reduce the incidence and intensity of those types of role conflict most detrimental to both individual and organizational health. Such strategies include the following.

A. Identifying Role Conflict at an Early Stage It is crucial that managers watch for early signs of role conflict when an organization is first created, new units are added or deleted, or when internal roles are realigned through some level of reorganization. Signs that may indicate role conflict include:

- Worker statements indicating contradictory demands.
- Supervisors competing for access to a worker's time and skills.
- Worker confusion over role priorities.

250

- Interpersoanl conflict that on the surface may appear to be personality clashes but may be problems in the organization of role expectations.
- The failure to complete key tasks because of unclear accountability to assign and monitor their completion.
- A consistent pattern of stress symptoms associated with a particular role.
- High incidence of turn-over in the role.

B. Defining Sources of Accountability Where sources of accountability are undefined or vaguely defined, a worker becomes vulnerable to multiple and potentially contradictory demands from the work environment. Role conflict emerges from the failure to define key elements of power and authority in organizational relationships or from flaws in this definition process. A major source of worker support, as will be discussed in more detail as it relates to role ambiguity, is the clear definition of how power is distributed in the organization and how each person/role in this chain of authority can affect the worker. While a worker may experience multiple demands from the environment, it is crucial that he/she have the knowledge of which demands take priority by virtue of the definition of who has ultimate authority to judge and reward or punish his/her performance. An essential strategy in reducing role conflict is the clear definition (through organizational charts, policies and procedure manuals, and job descriptions) of power and accountability within the organization.

While this premise may seem obvious and simplistic to some readers, it is the author's experience that the issue of power is a very uncomfortable one in the health and human service fields. Many managers and supervisors, particularly those that have risen from the ranks of helpers into positions of leadership, fail to define power and authority due to their own discomfort with the issue. They would prefer to manage without an explicit definition of their power to control work assignments, determine personal and monetary rewards, and to take disciplinary action including terminating a worker's membership in the organization. In such settings, it may be necessary to provide experiences in management training that address the issue of power, if these managers are to be able to implement the necessary strategies to reduce role conflict.

C. Reducing the Number of Sources of Accountability
Another strategy in reducing role conflict is to reduce the number of sources of accountability placed on the worker. A worker with two bosses will inevitably experience problems in role conflict. With rare exception, each worker should have one source of accountability which represents the most basic unit in the relationship between the worker and the organization. All expectations placed on the worker within the organization must be channeled through this relationship by an organizational value that prohibits by-passing this relationship to place demands upon the worker. A situation, for example, in which a hospital president by-passes three levels of organizational hierarchy to place a direct demand on an employee, is guaranteed to produce instant role conflict.

D. Addressing Role Integrity Problems Role integrity problems occur when there is a conflict between one's personal values and the values inherent in the work environment. Mechanisms to address this special type of role conflict include the following:

- Explicitly define organizational values so issues of value conflict are identified in the employee recruitment and selection process, not months later as a recurring issue in role performance. (See earlier discussions on the Code of Professional Practice.)
- Provide permission to raise conflict over values in the process of supervision. There are very few professions in which different ethical and value issues don't arise in the course of performing one's role responsibilities. Employees, who are particularly sensitive to such issues, need permission

and opportunities to identify and personally resolve sources of discomfort related to these areas.

- Build in opportunities for work units collectively to discuss and explore ethical and value issues inherent in service delivery. Assume that your most assertive employees may be articulating issues and areas of discomfort shared by other members in the work unit.

- Where ethical or value issues betweeen the employer and the organization become irreconcilable, either create role assignments that minimize value conflicts, or allow the employee guilt-free exit from the organization.

E. Providing Mechanisms for Resolving Incompatible Demands Given the inevitability of some levels of role conflict, it is helpful to build in mechanisms (a person and a process) for resolving role conflict when it occurs. Take, for example, the following common situation in a small organization with one secretary:

> Four staff members each bring in typing that each announces must go out that day. The total amount of typing is impossible to complete in the available time. Lacking an escape valve of some kind, the secretary, experiencing a classic case of role conflict (and role overload), must decide whose work has the highest priority.

The example of an escape valve that could be built in is an understood procedure that when this situation arises, the secretary takes all the material to the office supervisor who makes decisions on priorities, negotiates the priorities with the workers involved, or seeks additional resources to get the work completed within the desired timelines.

F. Building in Supports for Areas of Unresolvable Role Conflict A basic principle of managing stress in the microsystem is that when a role stressor is unchangeable, additional supports must be built in to sustain worker health and performance under such conditions. Consider the example of employees who by job definition must spend up to eight days a month on marketing trips out of town. Employees in such roles who have a family will inevitability experience some conflict in the expectations placed on them in their roles as spouse and parent and in the job demands that physically remove them from access to their family for a significant period of time. If the travel demands are unchangeable, what support mechanisms can be built in to offset the incompatible job role demands/family role demands placed on this worker. Examples of increased supports could include:

- Flexibility in when trips are scheduled each month to minimize disruption in important family role functions, e.g., daughter's music recital, birthdays, and wedding anniversaries, etc.
- A liberal policy on allowing spouse/family to accompany workers on business trips. This provides family members special periodic rewards related to this aspect of their family member's job responsibilities.
- A liberal policy on compensatory time during months of excessive travel that allows the worker greater access to his/her family when he/she is not traveling.

The failure to provide such supports in this type of obvious role conflict can potentially undermine the health of the worker and the worker's ability to sustain personal and intimate relationships outside the work setting.

12.7   Strategies To Address Role Ambiguity

Role ambiguity is a stressful role condition that reflects an organization's failure to define role expectations adequately. Role ambiguity may be present as a result of inadequate planning or task orientation in an organizational unit or it emerges from rapid change or turnover in a unit that has the effect of constantly disrupting and altering role expectations. Strategies to address role ambiguity include the following:

A. <u>Defining</u> <u>Role</u> <u>Expectations</u> The first task to reduce role ambiguity is clearly defining the role expectations of each member of the microsystem. This definition is communicated verbally and in writing. The written component usually includes an overall job description that clearly and thoroughly defines the activities and outcomes to which the worker will be held accountable. Wherever possible, measurable outcomes should be attached to each activity area to communicate to the worker the standard of acceptable performance by which his/her activity will be measured. A second component of this initial strategy is to communicate those general standards, e.g., attendance, to which all employees will be held accountable. These general standards are often defined in agency personnel policies or in an agency code of professional practice.

B. <u>Defining</u> <u>Task</u> <u>Priorities</u> A second strategy to address role ambiguity is to define for workers a framework or a process by which priorities are set on their role responsibilities. This area communicates to the worker the different value placed on his/her various responsibilities by the organization. Such definitions, outlined in broad terms and in the day-to-day supervision process, assist the worker to make decisions when time constraints allow the worker to complete only one of numerous potential role activities.

C. <u>Defining</u> <u>Preferred</u> <u>Methods</u> <u>of</u> <u>Task</u> <u>Completion</u> This area of role planning clarifies whether the worker will be held accountable for outcomes only or both the process and outcome of role activity.

The first type of accountability says:

"You are responsible for generating $75,000 in sales per quarter. How and where you generate such sales is up to you."

The second type of accountability says:

"You are responsible for generating $75,000 in sales per quarter. The sales must come from only the counties listed on this sheet. Here is a pamphlet that I will go over that outlines the standards we will expect you to follow in marketing our products and services."

The first example held the worker responsible for only the results of his/her activity. The second example held the worker accountable for not only what they were to do, but how they were to do it. From the standpoint of reducing role ambiguity, either method is preferred as long as the organization's choice is explicitly defined to the worker.

D. Defining the Accountability Structure The third strategy to address role ambiguity defines, in addition to what the worker is accountable for, also to whom the worker is accountable. Defining who the boss is for each worker is an integral strategy to reduce both role conflict and role ambiguity.

E. Defining Organizational Rewards and Punishments The final strategy to be discussed, which relates to role ambiguity, is the clear definition of rewards and punishments that will accompany successful or unsuccessful role performance. The earlier noted strategies established a framework by which rewards and punishments can be rationally organized by management and anticipated by workers. A more detailed discussion of rewards and punishments is incorporated in the next section which addresses problems of inadequate role feedback.

12.8 Strategies To Address Inadequate Role Feedback

This section will explore supervisory strategies that provide workers with feedback on: 1) the adequacy of role performance, 2) methods of improving role performance, and 3) the adequacy of adjustment to the work milieu.

A. Utilizing Basic Principles of Reinforcement It is imperative that management systems incorporate the growing body of knowledge from the behavioral sciences that reveals the forces that shape and sustain human behavior. A few such basic principles are listed below that will be utilized to guide later discussions:

- When a behavior is followed by a reward (reinforcement), the probabilities increase that the behavior will be repeated.
- The time between the desired behavior and the reward should be as small as possible for maximum reinforcing effect.
- When a behavior is followed by punishment, the probabilities decrease that the behavior will be repeated.
- When a behavior is followed by no response from the environment, the effect is the same as punishment-decreased probability of the behavior being repeated.
- The most powerful schedule of rewards capable of sustaining behavior is a schedule of intermittent rather than fixed reinforcement.

B. Worker Performance Standards and Consequences The purpose of defining performance standards is to increase the probabilities that a worker will illicit some desired behavior that can be rewarded and sustained over time. When organizationally set standards are inconsistent with the systems of reward and punishment at the microsystem level, performance problems will decrease the ability of the organization to achieve its mission and goals. The first task of building effective systems of feedback is thus to establish clear standards for behavioral performance and then assure that the mechanisms of reinforcement (rewards) in the organization are distributed based on the effective execution of these behaviors.

C. A Critique of Personnel Evaluation Systems Many organizations rely heavily on the annual personnel evaluation as the primary mechanism of feedback on employee performance. A critique of such reliance based on the above stated principles is illustrative. The following

257

observations are offered on the annual performance appraisal meeting between a worker and his/her supervisor in the health and human service setting.

1. The Subjectivity and Vagueness of Feedback - Health and human service agencies often utilize annual appraisal formats that contain no objective performance criteria and, in fact, may utilize vague categories of evaluation that bear little relationship to the day-to-day activities of the worker. About the only category that can be objectively assessed in such systems is the worker's attendance. Consider, for example, a supervisor of a small counseling agency who meets with a counselor in an annual performance appraisal meeting and jointly reviews a form in which the supervisor has evaluated the counselor on a five point scale for the following categories: knowledge, quantity of work, quality of work, team relationships, dependability, initiative, and overall work performance. If we were to examine the annual evaluations of the six agency counselors, would we be able to identify the objective criteria by which each was scored in the team relationship category? Would the worker who scored three on the knowledge category know the body of knowledge he/she needed to acquire to move to a four rating? In general, such vaguely constructed systems provide little data that the worker can utilize to alter his/her performance. One goal of increasing effective feedback to workers may thus become revamping the personnel evaluation system to include measurable, behavioral-based performance objectives. Compare the difference between the nebulous value of three on the knowledge category with annual performance objectives in this area that stated the counselor would:

- Enroll in a master's level counseling program and complete at least three courses during the evaluation period.
- Apply and pass the exam to become a state certified alcoholism counselor.
- Attend two outside workshops to enhance his/her skills in family counseling.

These latter examples are all concrete, measurable, and within the counselor's control to achieve.

2. The Timing of Feedback - The annual performance appraisal process, lacking other on-going mechanisms of feedback, has almost no power to reinforce and sustain high levels of work performance. To assume that a two hour interview telling a worker what a great job they have done will sustain that workers performance for the more than 1700 hours they will be on the job before their next performance appraisal is exceptionally grandiose. The only value of an annual performance review is to summarize other on-going mechanisms of feedback that have already provided the worker data on his/her performance and to refine the major standards and objectives which these other feedback mechanisms will address during the coming year.

3. The Reliance on Money as a Reinforcer - Most personal evaluation systems rely heavily on the annual merit salary increase as the primary reward and concrete evidence of feedback on worker performance. The following observations are offered on such reliance:

- In practice, merit increases have little to do with the performance of an employee. Such increases are so automatic in most agencies that they simply confirm that an employee has remained in the organization another 365 days. Since the merit increase is not tied to identifiable behavior, it has little use as a feedback mechanism for exemplary performance.
- Money that is provided through an annual merit increase, is a very short-lived reward in the experience of the worker. Within a few months the worker's lifestyle will absorb the additional dollars and will provide neither tangible material rewards for his performance, nor will it be experienced as an on-going source of professional affirmation beyond the receipt of the first check in which the increase appears.

- Providing money as a reward on a fixed schedule and fixed amount once a year further decreases the effectiveness of money as a reinforcer. Agencies, with the resources to utilize money as a major reinforcer, should tie the distribution of money to performance objectives (commission systems). Agencies can also distribute additional monetary rewards based on key milestones or outstanding performance contributions (bonus systems), the latter provided on an intermittent rather than fixed schedule of reinforcement.

- In stroke deprived systems, the distribution of financial rewards can become extremely competitive and conflictual. Lacking other sources of affirmation, money becomes a symbolic issue through which staff struggle for status, personal affirmation, and recognition in such systems. By building in multiple sources of feedback, money loses this symbolic function, and its power as primary reinforcer.

- Until such time as health and human service workers are provided performance objectives and monetary incentives similar to those used in companies such as Amway and Mary Kay Cosmetics, more effective and sustainable mechanisms of feedback and reward must be built into these service systems. The next section will catalogue such mechanisms.

D. Building in Mechanisms for Strokes and Feedback: Feedback consists of a regular flow of data to each worker that identifies acceptable performance, identifies deviation from acceptable performance for purposes of self-correction and acknowledges exemplary performance. This section will review how to build in feedback that reinforces acceptable and exemplary role performance.

1. Factors that Inhibit Stroking Behavior - Few supervisors and managers appreciate the awesome power they command. Such power is usually thought of in terms of control, decision-making, and the more punitive authority

to invoke disciplinary action over those they supervise. The power referred to here is a very different kind of power and involves the ability of the supervisor to recognize and acknowledge human competence, to affirm value and worth, to express personal appreciation, to express affection and affiliation, and to validate and bolster the esteem of each worker under his/her direction. The most neglected human need in the workplace is the need for personal appreciation and affirmation. The availability of such rewards in day-to-day role performance far outstrips money and other perks in its ability to promote and sustain worker health and productivity. Unfortunately, there are numerous obstacles that inhibit the effective use of this power by supervisors. Some of these inhibiting factors include the following:

- The high level of stress built into many supervisory roles leaves the supervisor hopelessly overextended and emotionally depleted. Under such conditions the supervisor has little emotional energy available for affirming others. Strategies to address supervisory stress thus became crucial to enhance the availability of strokes to workers in the microsystem.
- Maintaining a high level of strokes in the microsystem requires the time and physical presence of the supervisor. Supervisors who experience role overload, particularly with an excess of tasks that pull them out of interaction with workers, lose both the time and access to workers to sustain such rewards.
- A supervisor, by virtue of personality, may find such stroking behavior awkward and unnatural, if not impossible. A major element in supervisory screening needs to be the search for individuals with natural skills in the identification, observation, and affirmation of competence. A desirable element in supervisory temperament is the person whose own needs are met by encouraging and acknowledging success in others.
- Managerial "self-talk" can decrease one's implementation of stroking behavior. Self-talk is the internal

dialogue that mediates external behavior. This dialogue dictates what we should and shouldn't do, can and can't do and formulates our assumptions about the needs and motivations of those around us. Unvalidated self-talk can decrease stroking behavior through such internal dialogue as:

- "They know they're doing a good job; they don't need me to tell them all the time."
- "Why should I acknowledge them; nobody ever acknowledges me."
- "She's so competent and confident she doesn't really need me."
- "I won't say anything, because I don't think she respects my judgment."
- "I'm not going to compliment him. Every time I talk to him, he has a new bitch about something."

Effective management training reprograms such self-talk and frees the supervisor to become more potent in his/her interactions in the work unit.

- A final factor that inhibits supervisory stroking behavior is skill deficiency. Acknowledging and affirming others is a skill that must be learned and refined. Human relations training can be utilized with managers to develop and refine these skills to a highly sophisticated level.

2. Mechanisms to Provide Strokes and Positive Feedback
A major goal of supervision is to build into the work unit a large number and variety of rewards that can be utilized to reinforce and sustain behaviors that promote individual and organizational health. To the creative supervisor, the list and variation of such rewards could be limitless. The following list catalogues some of the most common forms of supervisory stroking behavior:

- Verbal praise - one-on-one.
- Verbal praise of an employee in the presence of peers.

262

- Verbal praise of an employee in the presence of managers outside the unit.
- Verbal praise of teams or sub-units.
- Verbal praise of work unit.
- Letters of commendation to individual employees/copy to personnel file and agency.
- Letters of commendation to teams or unit as a whole.
- Expressions of interest in the worker.
- Soliciting ideas and technical advice from workers.
- Listening to workers.
- Shared laughter.
- Time-out periods, "You've worked late two days this week and we're finally caught up. Why don't you get out of here early today and go home and play with your kids. I really appreciate the extra effort this week."
- Access to career-path opportunities.
- Favored work assignments.
- Allocation of status symbols, e.g., titles, favored office space, etc.
- Physical stroke -- hand shakes, the literal pat on the back, hugs (where such rituals are comfortable and appropriate).
- Salary bonuses for outstanding contributions.
- Time and presence of manager in supportive affirming interactions.

3. Matching the Right Mechanism to the Right Worker - The supervisor can be most effective in his/her stroking behavior by starting with the premise that types of stroking behavior need to be uniquely matched with each worker based on the worker's needs and value system. Whereas access to career path opportunities may be a major reward for one worker, for another it may be more of a stressor than a stroke. Types of stroking behavior utilized with a worker also may need to change over time in response to the changing needs and values of the worker.

4. **Feedback and the Disciplinary Process** - Feedback --
the provision of data to self-correct or affirm the
performance behaviors of a worker -- is obviously an essential component of extinguishing undesirable behavior
and enhancing worker productivity. In fact, systems that
build in high levels of appropriately communicated feedback and high levels of strokes for role mastery, make
little use of traditional forms of disciplinary punishment.
These systems share a number of common characteristics
related to their feedback process.

- Behaviorably defined standards of worker performance are established as the baseline to which
  feedback is directed.
- There are consistent rewards for performance
  within or that exceeds the defined standard.
- Worker behavior that deviates from the norm is
  first analyzed via a system perspective:

  - Does the worker know the standard of perfor-
    mance? (Provide direction)
  - Does the worker have the knowledge and skills to
    perform the task? (Provide training)
  - Are there environmental conditions that preclude
    effective performance? (Reduce role stressors,
    e.g., role overload, inadequate equipment, etc.)
  - Are additional supports needed for effective role
    performance? (Increase supervisory supports)
  - Are behavioral/health problems interfering with
    performance? (Refer to company employee assis-
    tance program)
  - Is non-performance being inadvertently
    rewarded? (Change the reward system)

- Self-correcting feedback is directed at behavior
  when it first moves beyond acceptable limits, not
  when it has become chronic and reached extreme
  limits.
- Performance behavior that moves back into acceptable limits is immediately reinforced.

5. __Principles of Effective Feedback__ - An important skill of the supervisor is the ability to provide feedback that is honest and direct, yet protects the self-esteem of the worker. The purpose of feedback is to enhance collaboration, not increase worker defensiveness and create a conflict in the supervisory relationship. The following statements describe feedback principles related to unacceptable performances that facilitate this purpose.

- It is descriptive rather than judgmental. Useful feedback focuses on behavior (what the person did); it does not focus on the nature of someone's character (what the person is).
- It is specific rather than general. Talking to someone about his/her behavior with a particular client in a specific situation is more effective than discussing the person's "attitude problem".
- It protects the self-esteem of the recipient. A nursing supervisor who observes that a nurse could expand his/her patient care skills by experimenting with more physical contact and "silent time" with patients, is more effective than communicating that the nurse "talks too much" and is "too dominating".
- It is directed toward behavior that the worker can do something about.
- It is well timed. Feedback is most useful when provided as soon as possible following the behavior of concern. Timing also depends on the worker's readiness to hear and understand the feedback.
- It is checked to ensure that the worker has accurately understood the communication.
- The worker is given opportunity to check the accuracy of the feedback with others in the work unit.
- Feedback is best received when given out of concern, interest, and respect for the worker.

12.9   Strategies To Address Role Overload

Role overload is one of the most common stresses identified by workers in health and human service systems. This is particularly true today in areas where budget cuts and cost containment have left a smaller number of personnel to complete the work of the organization. The following discussion highlights system intervention to reduce the role overload of workers.

A. Reducing the Over-extension of the Organization The over-extension of individual workers is often a reflection of the over-extension of the organization. In systems perspective this occurs when input (the level of fiscal, human, and material resources) is incongruent with output (the service and production goal set by the organization). The major intervention under such circumstances is not to teach workers better stress management skills, but to clearly and realistically determine what the agency can and cannot accomplish with their existing resources. Areas of over commitment must be honestly confronted and cut back. The range of services may need to be curtailed. It is more advantageous for both the organization and its workers to offer five adequately staffed services, than to provide ten services of low quality due to insufficient resources.

B. Controlling the Pace of Organizational Change Controlling the pace of organizational change to reduce adaptational demands placed on workers has been a constant theme throughout this book. The strategies, noted earlier to control and regulate such change, are particularly relevant to the problem of role overload. Role overload often occurs when unexpected and uncontrolled change escalates the expectation in the quality and quantity of worker production to excessive and unrealistic levels.

C. Job Restructuring In some organizations the overall agency scope of work may be realistic, but the distribution of such work into roles is imbalanced. By reorganizing and redistributing task assignments, managers can reduce the stress (and the conflict, resentment, and guilt) that occurs when some workers bear too much responsibility while others are bearing too little responsibility.

D. <u>Managing Periods of Excessive Demand</u> Some organizations will have predictable seasons or cycles of excessive demands while others will encounter various milestones or crises that produce excessive demands on workers. While role overload is probably inevitable during these periods, when the use of additional, temporary resources is not possible, such periods can be managed to reduce wear and tear on workers. The following suggestions are offered on the management of such periods:

- Openly acknowledge the excessive demands in group settings and one-to-one interaction with workers.
- Try to set a time frame on the period of excessive demands. (Most workers can manage periods of increased demand, if they know when demands will return to normal.)
- Help workers clarify task priorities during periods of high demand.
- Present the period of excessive demand as a challenge to the team and fully utilize internal group supports.
- Provide time out periods for the group to assess its progress and receive acknowledgment and encouragement from leaders.
- Increase the personal presence, visibility, and stroking behavior of the manager.
- When the period of excessive demands ends, reduce expectations for a short period to allow workers to replenish themselves.
- Provide rewards for both individual and collective achievement through the period of high demand.

E. <u>Confronting Over-Production</u> Some problems of role overload emerge, not from the work environment, but from the personality or current needs of an individual worker. Such situations may reflect:

- The personality type of a worker who is chronically and compulsively involved in an effort to achieve more and more in less and less time.

267

- The worker who is overcompensating for fears about quality of his/her work by spending an excessive number of hours on the job.
- The worker using the work environment as an escape from an unhappy marriage or his/her inability to establish outside intimate relationships and nurturing activities.

This situation poses a dilemma for the supervisor because such workers may be some of the most productive in the organization. The supervisor may, in fact, have come to rely on such individuals to pick up extra tasks or handle emergency assignments because of their dependability. What is needed by the supervisor is a long term perspective on such over-production. Such chronic over-extension inevitably takes its physical and emotional toll on the worker. In the health and human services, such over-production also denies the worker sources of outside replenishment that is essential for the worker to sustain the quality of his/her helping relationships. The supervisor must have the perspective that over-production may produce short term benefits to the organization but may result in the eventual loss of the worker to stress-related disabilities. The following story poignantly illustrates this point:

Bryan, a Type A Personality, began working as a unit coordinator in a community mental health center shortly following his divorce. It was as if Bryan divorced his wife and married his job. There were no limits to the amount of time and emotional energy he was willing to devote to the agency. For six years, Bryan invested 12-14 hour days at the agency and was always willing to volunteer for extra duties, particularly filling in for other staff for on-call emergency work. Bryan's competence, enthusiasm, and warm interpersonal style made him one of the most respected and appreciated staff in the agency and in the community. During his sixth year at the agency and while only in his early forties, Bryan died of a massive heart attack. This was a particularly painful loss to this organization, not only because of everyone's affection for Bryan, but also because of the undertone of guilt that somehow the agency and its members had contributed to Bryan's death. There is no question that Bryan brought to the organization, in terms of his own individual vulnerability, an almost pathological compulsion for over-production. The collective guilt emanated not from what Bryan brought to the organization by way of personality, but the fact that the agency had used and rewarded Bryan's over-production rather than confront it.

There is a level of over-production that must be confronted by the supervisor as directly and consistently as he/she would confront under-production at the other end of the continuum. The following are suggested:

- Establish limits on the number of hours workers can spend on the worksite.
- Discourage workers from coming to the worksite on their days off.
- Where compensatory time systems are used:
  – require prior approval by supervisor for compensatory time (this allows for close monitoring of over-production).
  – set limits on the amount of compensatory time that can be accumulated.
  – require that compensatory time be taken as hours off within a specified time from its accumulation.
- Avoid a system that pays for vacation days not taken. Such systems reward overproduction and the failure of the worker to use time-out periods effectively.
- For managers, make rewards contingent upon effective delegation.
- Confront signs of overproduction, e.g., excessive hours on job, failure to take breaks, chronic pattern of working through lunches, coming to work sick, and volunteering for extra duties that could appropriately be done by others.
- Include self-care goals in annual performance reviews, e.g., participating in manager's health and exercise programs.
- Reward behaviors that indicate increased limit setting.

12.10 Strategies To Address Role Underload And Role Deprivation

Role underload and role deprivation are stressors that lie on the other end of the continuum from role overload. These stressors produce excessive demands for adaptation from too little rather than too much stimulation in the work environment. Whether these conditions result from the poor organization and distribution of organizational tasks or the conscious retirement of a worker on the job, it is extremely difficult for workers to sustain their self-esteem under such conditions. Strategies to address these stressors generally fall into two broad categories: job revitalization and the creation of positive alternatives outside the organization.

A. Job Revitalization One of the most rewarding activities of a supervisor can be the resurrection of an employee deemed professionally dead, and the revitalization of a role that has lost its value to the organization. Management interventions designed to achieve these ends include the following:

- Role revitalization activities seek to recapture skills and resources that are being ineffectively utilized by the organization. Where such loss is occurring, one option is to increase the complexity and range of role activities by redefining the job position. Flexibility is built into the role expansion such that the unique talents of the person occupying the position can be fully tapped by the organization.
- Exploring creative career path alternatives within the organization is a second option for persons who may have been retired on the job. If an individual's knowledge and skill levels preclude further upward advancement, both lateral and downward placement in the organization should be considered. Although the latter process of demotion is rarely considered, the placement lower in the hierarchy into a role of significant responsibility and stimulation may meet more of the individual worker's needs than occupying the currently higher position which offers no meaningful responsibilities or rewards.

270

- Some workers in the preretirement category may have been shuffled into meaningless roles due to the short time they have left with the organization. By enriching such roles (through special projects, etc.), the organization not only mobilizes the knowledge and experience of these individuals, but also allows such individuals some highly meaningful projects to culminate and bring their professional career to closure.
- Career counseling and a reinvestment in worker training are often combined with both of the above options to support the return of the worker to greater productivity.

B. Managing Disappointment/Rekindling Involvement The above suggestions reflect systems interventions but do not address how the supervisor manages the human being that has occupied the empty role for an extended period of time. The following observation and suggestions are offered:

- Assess the forces that blocked the career advancement and productivity of the employee. Was it a function of knowledge and skill deficiency? Were there problems of role-person mismatch? Were there personality conflicts with the individual's earlier supervisors? Were there personal or health problems that contributed to the loss of functioning or advancement?
- Assess how the worker has responded to the loss of previous or hoped for status and responsibilities. Most advancement discouraged employees go through initial stages of anger, bitterness, and resentment toward the organization and its leaders and eventually move to a stage of emotional resignation and detachment from the organization. What feelings along this continuum must be managed to reactivate the employee's passion and involvement in the organization?
- Recognize the forces in the individual that will resist change. You are asking an advancement

discouraged employee to reinvest emotional energy in the organization, to rekindle visions of professional accomplishment, and to re-assert his/her ego into the life of the organization. While the encapsulation of a worker into a responsibility and status-empty role may undermine the worker's self-esteem, the invisibility that comes with such a role, while painful, does afford a level of safety. The worker may have been enticed from this shelter before to experience punishment rather than rewards from the organization. Expect resistance.

- Explore systems interventions with the worker over time which allow the worker an opportunity to build trust and to test the supervisory relationship. Escalate affirming and stroking behaviors in interactions with the employee.
- Phase in the systems intervention slowly. The worker has been existing under conditions of stimulus deprivation for some time. Allow an opportunity for the worker's preferred defense structure to adapt to the increased stimulation and demands. Increase rewards commensurate with increased role activity.
- Expect periodic regression. The employee will periodically lose confidence in himself/herself and the process, and regress back to the defenses used during role deprivation. Such behavior does not indicate that the intervention has failed, only that the worker needs increased supports to continue the process.
- Recognize that a change in supervisory relationships may provoke a crisis in confidence in the worker who has been given a rebirth within the organization. The worker may attribute their renewed life in the organization solely to the presence of the supervisor, and not to their own internal power and capabilities. This crisis is often inevitable, as the supervisor who is sophisticated enough to effectively utilize job revitalization strategies will, in all likelihood, be upwardly mobile within the organization. The ability of the

supervisor to talk through this change with the employee, support the new supervisor in building a relationship with the employee, and maintain periodic contact with the employee through the transition, will help minimize this crisis.

C. Creating Positive Alternatives Outside the Organization
There are some situations in which it is in the best interest of both the worker and the organization to terminate the relationship. A worker may candidly report to a supervisor that he/she has learned all he/she can at the agency and needs to find a new, more stimulating job but feels unable to do so due to current salary level or inability to relocate. Some larger organizations provide a formal service called outplacement counseling that addresses both this situation and the needs created by employee reductions in the organization. Outplacement counseling provides assistance to find positive job alternatives for such employees outside the organization. In smaller organizations, this outplacement counseling function may be taken on by the employee's supervisor. The strategies, which were enumerated in Chapter 11 which related to providing permission and assistance for employees to get out of the organization guilt-free, are applicable here.

12.11 Strategies To Address Role Safety Hazards

Role safety hazards reflect workers' apprehension regarding the potential for physical or psychological harm in the performance of their roles. Interventions to address role safety hazards include the following:

A. Analyzing Employee Health Care Data: Analyzing employee health care data is an important mechanism to identify role safety hazards in the workplace, particularly when such data can be analyzed by worksites, by job title, by sex, and by length of employment. This data analysis is important in industrial settings where such data can reveal key areas of risk for industrial accidents. This data can dictate improved equipment or performance procedures and reveal risks for industrial disease from exposure to toxic substances that may not as yet be defined as toxic. Health care data analysis is equally important in non-industrial worksites to include settings where threats to safety may be more psychological than physical.

B. Implementing Risk Management Programs Many organizations have effectively utilized a formal risk management committee to reduce safety hazards for employees, and to service recipients and visitors who enter the worksite. Through orientation and training programs and improved procedures, for example, many hospital risk management committees have been able to reduce puncture wounds from hypodermic needles, injuries from lifting and transferring patients, and injuries to patients from falls. The risk management committee can be an extremely effective tool in identifying and reducing role safety hazards. The reader is encouraged to explore a growing body of literature which deals with risk management in numerous occupational settings.

C. Responding to Worker Issues of Role Safety While effective, risk management programs tend to focus primarily on issues related to regulatory and licensing bodies and liability risks as defined by the insurance industry. Though important, these issues may differ significantly from role safety concerns identified by employees. Employee's feedback should be utilized to identify and address role safety hazards experienced by workers. The major role safety hazard for an eleven-to-seven shift hospital nurse may not be tied to the nursing unit, but to an isolated and poorly lit parking lot through which he/she must enter the hospital at night.

D. Addressing Threats to Psychological Safety It is helpful if the manager or committee who reviews role safety hazards includes threats to psychological safety in their overall assessment and intervention process. One aspect of this issue in human service organizations is that workers operate with a very inexact science to make judgments with potentially life and death consequences. Consider the following possibilities:

- An alcoholism counselor writes a report that a client has successfully completed an educational and counseling program following the client's arrest for driving under the influence of alcohol. The report, which further states that the client cooperated fully with the program and is unlikely to repeat the offense, assists the client in retaining or reobtaining his/her drivers license. A month later, a mother and child are killed in a head-on collision with the intoxicated client.

- A counselor intervenes, as the on-call crisis worker, at a mental health center where a woman is making vague threats of suicide. After two hours of talking, the woman seems composed, more hopeful about the future, and has agreed to come in and see the counselor at the center the following morning. In the judgment of the counselor, the woman is not at high risk of suicide and not in need of immediate hospitalization. The woman is found dead the next morning from an overdose of aspirin and sleeping pills.

- A probation officer conducts a presentence investigation of a man convicted of assault and battery on his wife. The presentencing report recommended probation rather than jail, based on the following facts. It was the client's first criminal offense. The husband and wife had reconciled and agreed to go for marriage counseling. The man demonstrated remorse over the incident. Jail would burden the wife and children with financial hardship and jeopardize the husband's job of twelve years. The recommendations were accepted and the man was given probation. Two months later the wife was shot and killed by the husband in a violent argument amidst accusations of the wife's infidelity.

While such incidents are fortunately rare in the professional lives of most human service workers, the level of psychological vulnerability for these workers is great in any situation in which they must make decisions alone that can result in such profound repercussions. A key intervention to reduce such vulnerability is to implement a policy (usually a component of the Code of Professional Practice) that requires all clinical situations involving potential physical harm to the client, potential harm to others, and any other general threat to public safety, to be immediately brought into the process of supervision. Such policies assure that the full expertise and clinical judgment of the agency has been utilized to address the situation, and also, to prevent the awesome responsibility of such decisions from resting on the shoulders of one worker.

A broad spectrum of threats to psychological safety that very greatly by occupational settings can be identified and addressed through interventions that parallel the one described above.

12.12 Strategies To Address Role Insecurity

Role insecurity is the degree of uncertainty a worker experiences in relationship to his/her future role in the organization. Role insecurity may be an individual concern alleviated through feedback strategies that were identified earlier in this chapter, or it may be a collective concern of workers that permeates an entire organization. Given the macrosystem issues that have currently sparked layoffs and company closings in industries as diverse as steel plants and hospitals, this section will focus on the collective aspect of role insecurity.

A. Worker Access to Information Workers should have access to a consistent flow of accurate information about the financial status of the organization and the implications of this status to their future role in the organization. This information serves multiple purposes to include:

- Avoiding the sense of personal violation workers feel when they learn of such financial information

outside the organization, and they have been told nothing by organizational leaders.
- Providing a reality base on which workers can base effective responses and avoid the excessive emotional wear and tear that can result from unfounded fear, apprehension, and rumor.
- Involving workers as equal partners in a financial crisis.
- Utilizing workers as resources to generate cost containment activities and to develop broad strategies of crisis resolution.

B. Providing Rumor Control The fear and apprehension generated within organizations which go through rapid change or periods of financial crisis, generates a constant flow of unvalidated information and conjecture. All of this gossip serves as a powerful destabalizing force within the organization. All complex organizations inevitably generate elaborate and sometimes very sophisticated informal networks of intelligence gathering and dissemination. Many persons who hold no formal power in the organization, such as a housekeeper or an elevator operator, yield considerable influence and status based on their reputation for extracting reliable information from this network. The following story illustrates how this intelligence network operates:

At a time of the year the organization usually informed employees whether there would be a cost-of-living increase, and if so, what the percentage increase would be, the president and his three assistants had made the final decision on the annual increase in consultation with the board. These meetings were conducted with the utmost secrecy and even department directors were only told that an announcement would be forthcoming. Imagine the surprise of the president and assistants when department directors began complaining that their employees already knew what the cost-of-living increase was, that the increase was coming in a one-time lump sum check and the date the check would be mailed. The organization's intelligence network had pieced together the following:

1. The Administration had ordered a large number of envelopes from supply which roughly approximated the number of employees in the organization. (Implication? A letter would be sent to the home of all employees.)

2. A housekeeper found a torn-up carbon in the president's secretary's waste basket. Most pieces were too small to read, but the corner with the "Dear Employee" and the date of June 22 was legible. (Implication? The letter to all employees would be mailed June 22.)

3. The two employees in data processing that processed checks were told they might have to work late on the 20th for a special project. (Implication? A check will accompany the letter to each employee.)

4. An assistant administrator told one department head the percentage increase of the cost-of-living and swore him to secrecy. He, in turn, told one person and swore him to secrecy, etc.

The informal intelligence gathering network had obtained and disseminated within seven days what was supposed to be a closely guarded corporate secret. Imagine the intensity of the intelligence gathering process amid rumors that there might be a lay off.

Since information on so primitive an issue can rarely be contained, the only feasible approach is to provide clear, straightforward information through formal communication channels in a timely fashion. This maintains the credibility and power of the formal communication channels and decreases the power of the informal rumor network. During such times of uncertainty, every meeting with employees, no matter what its agenda, should function as a mechanism of rumor control.

C. The Management of Employee Reductions There are a number of principles and guidelines that can make needed lay offs less painful for the employees involved and less disruptive to the overall organization. While some of the following suggestions may seem obvious and simplistic to the reader from a large, complex organization, the material may be helpful to those from small health and human service agencies who have never had to address the issue of employee layoffs.

- Develop a layoff policy before it is needed. The key component of this policy, as it relates to role insecurity, is the clarity with which the layoff decision-making process is defined. Will layoff decisions be made by seniority or some other criteria? Are there any policy differences between salaried and hourly employees? If seniority is the primary criteria, how is it defined, e.g., by worksite, department, total employee pool, etc. Having such policies allows each worker to make a realistic determination as to the level of vulnerability he/she faces in the event of an employee reduction.
- Involve employees at early stages and successive stages of the financial crisis. Workers can be either active partners with managers in crisis resolution, or passive an impotent bystanders and victims of managerial decisions. Provide workers with the cost-cutting goals to see if they can identify alternatives to employee reductions. In many organizations, workers have come up with concrete, practical alternatives that prevented the loss of employees.
- If a layoff decision is made, avoid false or unfounded promises about the length of layoff. If the layoff appears to be permanent, communicate this status so that the workers can plan for their futures accordingly.
- When a layoff occurs, examine what supports can be extended to the affected employees. Can a representative of the unemployment office be deployed at the worksite to facilitate worker access to unemployment benefits? Can access to services from the Employee Assistance Program, such as budget counseling, be extended for workers on layoff status? Can workers still be acknowledged

by organizational leaders for their contributions? Can outplacement counseling services be utilized to help connect some affected employees with jobs in other organizations? Can opportunities be provided for workers not affected to talk about the layoff in order to minimize survivor guilt?

12.13   Strategies To Address Worker Isolation

There are a number of problems related to role connectedness that can be highly stressful for workers. These problems range from the overconnectedness and excessive bonding between workers earlier described in the enmeshed organizational family to the extreme isolation of a worker from other members of the organization. Such isolation is usually a consequence of role definitions that entail high levels of boundary transactions and minimal dependency on other members for effective role performance. The sales representative, the outreach worker, or staff working in a remote satellite office, may also experience high levels of stress, but without access to the same level of supervisory supports available to other organizational members. While such isolation often increases the vulnerability of staff, there are exceptions in which such isolation may be a buffer to excessive stress. There may be such a high level of stress and turmoil within the primary worksite that the detached worker is actually afforded greater immunity to the effects of such conflict by virtue of his or her isolation. Excluding such exceptions, the supervisor is encouraged to build in special mechanisms of support for the most isolated roles within the organization. The following mechanisms may prove helpful:

- Build a higher frequency of supervisory contacts for the isolated worker under the assumption that the worker lacks many of the peer supports available to other workers in the organization. The supervisor may not be one of many sources of support and acknowledgment for such workers, but the sole source of support.
- Create opportunities for the isolated worker to participate in group activities of the organization. Worker inclusion and reinforcement of peer relationship development can be facilitated by such

interventions as scheduling the worker to be at the primary worksite for staff meetings, in-service training, and other group activities. The worker's travel and assignment schedule should be manipulated to assure that they are included in major events within the organizational family.

- Visit the worker in the field. Identify and help the worker manage the stressors of his or her role that may differ radically from the stressors experienced by other workers in the organization.
- Build in time-out periods from field assignments that allow the worker to spend some concentrated time to periodically re-establish his/her sense of identity within and belonging to the organizational family.

12.14 The Supervisor And Microsystem Health

There is probably no more abused, nor more important species in the American workforce than the mid-level manager/supervisor. The importance of this role must be fully articulated before closing the discussion on microsystem strategies for reducing role stressors and increasing role supports. All of the strategies outlined in the last two chapters hinge on the health, knowledge, and skills of the front line supervisor. The best thing a company can do for its employees is to provide them fair, competent, and nurturing supervisors. If the supervisor, however, is to support, he/she must in turn be supported.

There is a rapidly growing technology that enables a company to humanize the work environment and promote worker health while simultaneously enhancing the production goals of the organization. It is perhaps the ultimate sin of our economic system that such technology lies dormant on bookshelves while both organizations and individual workers self-destruct. It is not enough that new management technologies fire the vision of organizational leaders. Such technology must be transfused, through support and training, into the most basic unit of the organization -- the relationship between a supervisor and a worker.

12.15 Strengthening The Preferred Defense Structure Through Health Promotion

The third component of the microsystem model for addressing stress is, in addition to reducing role stressors and increasing role supports, the implementation of company-wide and work unit programs to support the physical and emotional health of workers. These programs, often described within the rubic of wellness or health promotion, are designed to promote lifestyles that enhance the overall well-being of the worker and, by so doing, reduce the worker's vulnerability to disease, illness, and injury.

Many companies have made substantial commitments to employee health promotion activities. In the area in which the author lives, (Decatur, Illinois), the Archer Daniels Midland Company purchased a vacated public high school to create the ADM Lakeview Recreational Center -- a facility through which ADM's health promotion activities are coordinated. Made available to the companies local 1500 employees and their families, the facility hosts an extensive variety of recreational activities including company basketball and volleyball leagues, weightlifting, aerobic classes, jogging clubs, and walking clubs, with a wide variety of additional activities on the drawing board for future implementation. The company's formal health promotion program includes health screenings, monitoring and follow-up, in addition to a regular contingent of health promotion classes on lifestyle issues ranging from smoking cessation to weight loss to stress management. Companies like ADM are part of a growing movement within American business and industry committed to integrating health promotion as an integral component of the corporate culture, to enhancing worker productivity through improved health and to halting the drain of company resources due to escalating health care benefit costs. Most of the companies known to the author, who have implemented health promotion programs, have quickly concluded that such programs are both a good idea and good business. A somewhat ironic twist to this trend is the fact that health and human service agencies, while marketing health promotion programs to business and industry, have lagged behind in implementing such programs for their own employees.

A detailed outline of health promotion programs will not be presented here as there are excellent existing resources in this area available to the reader. The review of health promotion programs in 17 different companies by Rebecca Parkinson and Associates (1982) is recommended as an excellent starting point. The reports of Brennan (1982), Fielding (1982) and Kristein (1982) are also excellent starting points for the reader interested in the impact and cost effectiveness of such programs.

Given the systems perspective on worker stress outlined in this book, it should be clear that health promotion programs can and should be an essential component in the overall strategy to address in the stress workplace.

12.16 Responding To Casualties

Even in the healthiest organizations, situations may occur in which an employee experiences a deterioration in performance related to his/her experience of stress in the work environment. Companies with comprehensive programs to address stress-related problems build in mechanisms to identify such worker problems and intervene to enhance the worker's return to health and productivity. The most important of these mechanisms is the establishment of a formal employee assistance program within the company.

Employee Assistance Programs (EAP's) are confidential assessment, short term counseling and referral services available to employees on a voluntary or supervisory referral basis. EAP's often serve as a resource for the resolution of problems experienced by employees long before such problems impact job performance. When problems do affect job performance, the EAP is then an important resource for the Supervisor. With the existence of a formal Employee Assistance Program, the supervisor can focus on job performance and avoid the usual unsuccessful attempt to combine the roles of authority figure and amateur psychiatrist.

Employee Assistance Programs have historically focused on personal problems experienced in a worker's personal life that progressively impaired role performance on the job. Employee assistance counselors have focused most of their energy addressing such employee problems as alcoholism and other forms of chemical dependency, behavioral and emotional disturbances, marital and family problems, and financial problems. While such efforts provide a highly needed and valued service to both employees and the organization, Employee Assistance Programs have only recently reached a level of sophistication to address directly those stress-related problems which originate not from experiences outside but within the organization. This latter stage of development places the EAP counselor in a position to respond to the stress related impairment of the worker, and also creates the sometimes unenviable role of communicating to organizational leaders the existence of debilitating working conditions within the organization. The only alternative to this employee advocate role is to provide emotional support to workers and then send them back to the same unchanged conditions that contributed to their impairment in the first place.

Employee Assistance Programs are an essential component to responding to victims of excessive personal and professional stress. The fact remains, however, that a large number of organizations have not yet implemented such a program. In these organizations, the responsibility to assess and rectify performance problems remains with the supervisor regardless of the origin of such problems. In the absence of a formal EAP, the following suggestions are offered to the supervisor who is confronted with a stress-related deterioration in employee performance:

A. Confronting Early Warning Signs The burnout experience is a progressive loss of functioning characterized by a continuum of symptoms ranging from moderate to severe in their consequences. The disintegration of a staff person's emotional and physical health usually occurs over time with identifiable early signs which indicate the deterioration of stress management abilities. The most crucial intervention by the supervisor in the burnout process is to acknowledge, express concern for, and confront early signs of stress-related problems. By bringing such concerns into the supervisory process, the supervisor has an opportunity to halt the deterioration in both performance and health.

B. Assessing the Problem Lacking the resources of an Employee Assistance Program, the supervisor must communicate with the employee to assess the nature of performance problems. Where such problems spring from personal problems unrelated to the work environment, the supervisor can recommend that the employee seek outside professional assistance and sustain the focus of supervision on work performance. It is not the supervisor's role to offer advice or to counsel an employee about such problems. Where performance problems originate from stress in the work environment, the supervisor can take appropriate steps to reduce role stress conditions and increase supports for the worker. If these latter interventions fail, the problem was probably not related to the work environment (such as the employee who suffers from alcoholism), and the recommendation to seek outside help is again warranted.

C. **An Assessment Model for the Health and Human Service Setting** Staff who work in health and human service agencies have three areas of distinct needs that must be met for optimum performance and emotional health. (1) Each staff person has personal needs that must be met outside of and totally separate from the program. (2) Each staff member has needs that must be met in his/her professional peer relationships. (3) Each staff person has needs that must be met in his/her relationships with clients. Stress-related problems often occur when all three of these need areas are not met. A decrease in both personal and professional functioning often occurs when an employee's needs are met in one of these areas at the exclusion of the other two. By reviewing the employee's status in these three need areas, problems of imbalance can be identified and corrected. It should be emphasized that this assessment and problem identification process is done by not looking at the personality of the staff person, but looking at the break-down of supports between the staff and the work system. The problem is defined as interactional, not intrapsychic. This assessment is to identify ways the system can be manipulated to reduce stressors and produce nourishment for the staff person. It is not a diagnostic interview to enlist the staff person into "treatment" with the supervisor.

D. <u>Helping the Employee Identify and Label Burnout</u> The supervisor can be an important resource to the staff person who experiences burnout from prolonged contact with the high stress work environment. The supervisor can be particularly helpful in giving the employees some words they can use to describe what is happening to them. Many persons, who suffer from the high-stress work environment, have not identified this as the source of their stress and have simply believed they are going crazy. Identifying and labeling work-related stress can, in and of itself, free up energy for employees to begin to remobilize their personal resources.

E. <u>Communication About Burnout to Employees</u> Express communications to staff regarding burnout in pronouns of inclusion, e.g., "<u>we</u> often find <u>our</u>selves..."; "It is a common experience for those of <u>us</u> in the field to...," etc. Pronouns of inclusion emphasize a process endemic to the work environment and tend to decrease the self-labeling of the staff person, e.g., "I'm crazy; everyone else is O.K.".

Utilize self-disclosure and provide normative information about the burnout process to reinforce effectively the following messages:

- Burnout, in varying degrees, is something that nearly everyone experiences who works intensively with troubled people (<u>you are not alone</u>!).
- One can recognize and abort the burnout process before it produces serious consequences (<u>you can take control</u>!).
- One can make clear decisions and take actions that produce the nourishment necessary to re-energizie and re-establish the balance in one's work and personal life (<u>you can regain potency</u>!).

F. <u>Providing Structure</u> and <u>Mobilizing Resources</u>: The primary role of the supervisor in addressing burnout is to identify and label the source of the problem, to assist the employee in mobilizing resources to speed their replenishment and to manipulate the level and intensity of role stressors and supports to enhance the worker's return to health and productivity.

12.17   A Personal Note In Closing

It is only proper that this book should conclude by examining how to respond effectively to the victims of excessive work-related stress, for it was precisely the concern over such casualties that compelled the studies upon which the book is based. In the process of conducting those early studies, I had the very disquieting experience of listening for many hours to human service workers who became burnout victims in the midst of the incestuous dynamics described in this book. I interviewed workers whose health self-destructed from sheer physical exhaustion, workers whose marriages are now only memories, workers who fell victim to the self-medicating effects of alcohol and drugs, and workers in psychiatric settings who fell victim to the very symptoms they had been trained to treat in their clients. Nearly all of these individuals either left or were extruded from their work settings under conditions of extreme emotional pain. Many continue to struggle years later for emotional closure on the work experience and some rational understanding of what happened to them in the organization. At the time of their exit, most of these individuals received less respect, less concern and less support than would have been extended to any client seeking services in the agency in which they worked. Such individuals often became the pariahs and untouchables of our field and those of us who remain continue in our blindness or arrogance to see ourselves as immune, believing that what happened to them could not happen to us. If there is any message that collectively emerges from the voices of burnout workers, it is that we are all potential victims. Today's respected clinician may be tomorrow's untouchable.

To those readers who may have been victimized by the group process and role conditions described in this book, I hope at least some part of your review of this material has been healing. To those readers who haven't experienced much of what I've written, I hope the material will trigger warning bells that will prevent you from becoming a casualty of organizational processes you can neither understand nor control.

It has been ten years since the studies that would culminate in this book began. I conclude this milestone in my work more hopeful and more encouraged than ever before by the growing movement and developing technology to humanize the workplace. I conclude this book with the continuing belief that we will address the issue of burnout when we begin to define it as a breakdown in the relationship between the organization and the worker and stop defining it based solely on the personalities of our casualties.

Bibliography

ACKERMAN, N. W.   Treating the Troubled Family. New York: Basic Books, Inc., 1966.

ALLEN, H. J.   "Aspects of "Burnout Among Medical Social Workers." Archives of the Foundation of Thanatology. 7(2):156, 1978.

ALLPORT, G.   "The Open System in Personality Theory," Personality and Social Encounter, (Boston: The Beacon Press, 1960).

AMES, R., ROSENWALD, R. J., SNELL, J. E., LEE, R. E.   "The Runaway Girl: A Reaction to Family Stress," American Journal of Orthopsychiatry, Volume XXIV, July 1954, pp. 762-767.

BATESON G.   Naven (Stanford, California: Stanford University Press, 1967).

BENSON, H.   The Relaxation Response. New York: Morrow, 1975.

BERMAN, E.   "Some Thoughts on Sexuality and Supervision," Voices, Fall, 1976.

BOWEN, M.   "Societal Regression as Viewed Through Family Systems Theory," prepared for the Nathan Ackerman Memorial Conference, February, 1974.

BOWEN, M.   "The Family as the Unit of Study and Treatment," American Journal of Orthopsychiatry 31: 40-60, 1960.

BOWEN, M.   "The Use of Family Theory in clincial Practice," Comprehensive Psychiatry, Volume 7: 345-374, 1966.

BRENNAN, A. J.J.   "Health Promotion: What's in it for Business and Industry?" Health Education Quarterly, Vol. 9, Special Supplement, Fall, 1982.

BROWN, B. Stress and the Art of Biofeedback. New York: Bantam Books, Inc., 1977.

CARRINGTON, P. Freedom in Meditation. New York: Anchor, Doubleday, 1977.

CARROLL, J.F.X. "Staff Burnout as a Form of Ecological Dysfunction", Contemporary Drug Problems, 1980, 8,207-225.

CARROLL, J.F.X, AND WHITE, W.L. "Understanding Burnout: Integrating Individual and Environmental Factors Within an Ecological Framework" Proceedings First National Conference on Burnout, Philadelphia, PA, 1981.

CHAMBERLAIN, C. S. "Anomie, Burn-out, and the Wyatt Earp Syndrome." Law and Order. 26(3):20-21, 52, 1978.

CLARK, C.C. "Burnout: Assessment and Intervention. Journal of Nursing Administration. 10(9): 39-44, 1980.

CLARK, J. V. "A Healthy Organization" in "The Planning of Change by W. G. Bennis, K. D. Benne and R. Chin, New York: Holt, Rinehart and Winston, Inc., pp. 282-297.

COOPER, K. H. The Aerobics Way. New York: Bantam Books, 1977.

CRISWELL, G.E. "Feelings of Tiredness and Fatigue Among Psychotherapist/Dead Tired and Bone Weary". Voices. 15(2): 49-53, 1979.

DALEY, M. R. "Burn-Out" Smoldering Problem in Protective Services." Social Work. September, 1979. p. 375.

DUBRIN, A.J. et. al. "Teacher Burn-Out: How to Cope When Your World Goes Black." Instructor, January, 1979. pp. 56-62.

ELLISON, R. The Invisible Man, New York: Signet Books, 1947.

ELSTEIN, A.S. "Organizational and Psychological Problems in Developing Community Mental Health Services: A case Study." Social Science and Medicine, Vol. 6, 1972. pp. 545-559.

EMERY, F.E. AND TRIST, E.L. "Social-Technical Systems" Organizational Systems: General Systems Approaches to Complex Organizations. F. Baker, (Ed.) Homewood, Illinois: Richard D. Irwin, Inc. 1973.

ETZIONI, A. A Comparative Analysis of Complex Organizations, New York: Free Press of Glencoe, 1961.

FIELDING, J. E. "Effectiveness of Employee Health Improvement Programs," Journal of Occupational Medicine, Vol. 24, No. 11, Nov. 1982.

FRANCES, V. AND FRANCES, A. "The Incest Taboo and Family Structure," Family Process, Vol. 15, Number 2, June, 1976. pp. 235-244.

FREUDENBERGER, H.J. "Burn-Out: Occupational Hazard of the Child Care Worker." Child Care Quarterly. 1977. 6(2), 90-99.

FREUDENBERGER, H. J. AND ROBBINS, A. "The Hazards of Being a Psychoanalyst." The Psychoanalytic Review. Vol. 66, No. 2. Summer 1979.

FREUDENBERGER, H.J. The Staff Burn-Out Syndrome, Washington, D.C.: Drug Abuse Council, Inc., 1975.

FRIEL, M., TEHAN, C.B. "Counteracting Burn-Out for the Hospice Care-giver." Cancer Nursing. 3(4): 285-93, 1980.

GARTE, S.H. and ROSENBLUM, M.L. "Lighting Fires in Burned-out Counselors." Personnel and Guidance Journal. 57(3): 158-160, 1978.

GINSBURG, S.G. "The Problem of the Burned Out Executive." Personnel Journal. 53(8): 598-600, 1979.

HALEY, J. Strategies of Psychotherapy, New York: Green and Stratton, 1963.

HARRISON, W. D. "Role Strain and Burnout in Child-Protective Service Workers." Social Service Review, March, 1980.

HAYNES, W. D. Stress Related Disorders in Policemen.San Francisco: R&E Research Associates, Inc., 1978.

HEMINGWAY, P. The Transcendental Meditation Primer. New York: Dell Publishing Co., Inc., 1975.

HENDRICKSON, B. "Teacher Burnout" How to Recognize It; What to Do About It." Learning. Vol. 7 (5); 37-39. January 1979.

HESS, R. AND HANDEL, G. Family Worlds: A Psychological Approach to Family Life. Chicago: University of Chicago Press, 1959.

HOFFMAN, L. "Enmeshment and the Too Richly Cross-Joined System," Family Process, Vol. 14, Number 4, pp. 457-468, December, 1976.

HOLMES, T.H. AND RAHE, R.H. "The Social Re-Adjustment Rating Scale." Psychosomatic Research. 11: 213-218, 1967.

JACOBSEN, E. Modern Treatment of Tense Patients. Springfield, IL Charles C. Thomas, 1970.

JACOBSEN, E. Progressive Relaxation. Chicago: University of Chicago Press, 1929.

KAHN, L., WOLFE, D., QUINN, R., AND SNOEK, I. Organizational Stress: Studies in Role Conflict and Ambiguity. New York: John Wiley & Sons, Inc., 1964.

KALES, J. D., MARTIN, E. D., SOLDATORS, C. R. "Emotional Problems of Physicians and their Families." Pennsylvania Medicine. 81(12) 14-16, 1978.

KERR, M.E. "Bridge Over Troubled Waters: A Work Systems Experience," presented at the Georgetown University Symposium on Family Psychotherapy, November, 1973.

KNAUERT, A.P., DAVIDSON, S.V. "Maintaining the Sanity of Alcoholism Counselors". Family and Community Health. 2(2): 65-70, 1979.

KRAMER, M. AND SCHMALENBERG, C. E. "Dreams and Reality: Where Do They Meet?: Journal of Nursing Administration. Vol. 6., No. 5, 1976, pp. 35-43.

KRAMER, M. Reality Shock: Why Nurses Leave Nursing. St. Louis: Mosby, 1974.

KRISTEIN, M. M. "The Economics of Health Promotion at the Worksite," Health Education Quarterly, Vol. 9, Special Supplement, Fall 1982.

LARSON, C. C., GILBERTSON, D.L., AND POWELL, J.A. "Therapist Burn-Out: Perspectives on a Critical Issue." Social Casework. November 1978. p. 563.

LENHART, R.C. "Sounding Boards: Faculty Burnout-and Some Reasons Why." Nursing Outlook. 28(7) 424-5, 1980.

LEVI, L. Preventing Work Stress. Reading, Mass.: Addison-Wesley Publishing Company, 1981.

LEVINSON, D.J. The Seasons Of A Man's Life, New York: Knopf, 1977.

LIDZ, T., FLECK S. AND CORNELISON, A. Schizophrenia and the Family, New York: International Universities Press, 1965.

LIDZ, T., CORNELISON, A.R., FLECK, S., AND TERRY, D. "The Interfamilial Environment of Schizophrenic Patients". American Journal of Psychiatry. 114: 241-248, 1957.

LUSTING, N., DRESSER, J., SPELLMAN, S., AND MURRAY, T. "Incest," Archives of General Psychiatry, Vol. 4, pp. 31-40, 1966.

MCGREGOR, D.M. "The Human Side of Enterprise" in Readings in Managerial Psychology (edited by Leavitt, H. J. and Pondy, L. R.) The University of Chicago Press, Chicago, 1973.

MCLEAN, ALAN A. Work Stress. Reading, Mass: Addison-Wesley, 1979.

MADDISON, D. "Stress on the Doctor and His Family." Med Journal, August 31, 1974. 2(9) : pp. 315-8.

MANBER, M.N. "Being a Doctor May Be Hazardous to Your Health." Medical World News. August 20, 1979. 20(17): 68-70, 74-75, 77-78.

MARSHALL, R.E., KASMAN, C. "Burnout in the Neonatal Intensive Care Unit." Pediatrics. 65(6): 1161-5, 1980.

MASLACH, C., JACKSON, S.E. "Burned-Out Cops and their Families. Psychology Today. 12(12): 58-62, 1979.

MASLACH, AND JACKSON, S.E. "Lawyer Burn-Out." Barrister. Spring 1978. 5(2), 8, 52-54.

MASLACH, C., PINES, A. "The Burn-Out Syndrome in the Day Care Setting." Child Care Quarterly, 1977. 6(2) 127-137.

MATTINGLY, M. A. "Symposium: Stress and Burn-out in Child Care." Child Care Quarterly. 6(2): 88-89. 1977.

MAWARDI, B. H. "Satisfactions, Dissatisfactions, and Causes of Stress in Medical Practice." Journal of the American Medical Association. 1483-1486, 1979.

MENDEL, W.M. "Staff Burn-out: Diagnosis, Treatment, and Prevention." New Directions for Mental Health Systems. 1979, 2, 75-83.

MENUCHIN, S. et.al. Families of the Slums, New York: Basic Books, 1967.

MINARD, S. "Family Systems Model in Organizational Consultation: Vignettes of Consultation to a Day Care Center," Family Process, Vol. 15, November 3, (Septebmer, 1976) 313-320.

MITCHELL, D., MITCHELL, CATHY AND OFSHE, R. The Light on Synanon. USA: Wideview Books, 1980.

MITCHELL, M. D. "Consultant Burn-Out." The 1977 Annual Handbook for Group Facilitators. LaJolla, California: University Associates, Inc. 1977.

NELSON, J.G. "Burnout - Business's Most Costly Expense." Personnel Administrator. 25(8): 1980: 81-87.

OLSON, D., SPRENKLE, D., AND RUSSEN, C. "Circumplex Model of Marital and Family Systems: 1. Cohesion and Adaptability Dimensions, Family Types, and Clinical Applications" Family Process, Vol. 16, No. 1, April, 1979. 3-28.

PARKINSON, R. AND ASSOCIATES. Managing Health Promotion in the Workplace: Guidelines for Implementation and Evaluation. Palo Alto, California: Mayfield Publishing Company, 1982.

PELLETIER, K.R. Mind as Healer, Mind as Slayer: A Holistic Approach to Preventing Stress Disorders, New York: Dell, 1977.

PETER, L. The Peter Principal, New York: Morrow, 1969.

REED, M.F. "Stress in Live-In Child Care." Child Care Quarterly. 1977. 6(2), 114-120.

REED, S. "What You Can Do to Prevent Teacher Burnout." National Elementary Principal. Vol. 58 Number 3. March 1979. 67-70.

REISS, D. "Varieties of Consensual Experience. I. A Theory for Relating Family Interaction to Individual Thinking," Family Process. 10: 1971. 1-27.

REISS, D. "Varieties of Consensual Experience II. Dimensions of a Family's Experience of its Environment," Family Process. 10: 28-35, 1971.

SCHAFFER, H.R. "The Too Cohesive Family: A Form of Group Pathology," International Journal of Social Psychology. 10: 266-275, 1964.

SEIDERMAN, S. "Combatting Staff Burn-Out." Day Care and Early Education, Vol. 4. 1977, 6-9.

SEYLE, H. Stess Without Distress. New York: Signet. 1974.

SEYLE, H. The Stress of Life. New York, Toronto, London: McGraw-Hill Book Co., Inc., 1956.

SHEEHY, G. Passages. New York: E.P. Dutton, 1976.

SHOSTAK, A. Blue-Collar Stress. Reading, Mass.: Addison-Wesley Publishing Company, 1980.

SHUBIN, S. "Burn-Out: The Professional Hazard You Face in Nursing." Nursing. 78,8(7) July 1978. 22-27.

SCHULTZ, J. and LUTHE W. Autogenic Training: A Pycho-Physiological Approach in Psychotherapy. New York: Grune and Stratton, 1959.

SMITH, M. When I Say No, I Feel Guilty. New York: Bantam Books, 1975.

SPECK, R. V. AND ATTNEAVE, C. L. Family Networks, New York: Pantheon Books, 1973.

STIERLIN, H. Separating Parents and Adolescents. New York: Quadrangle, 1974.

STORLIE, F. "Burn-out: The Elaboration of a Concept." The American Journal of Nursing. XIX, No. 12 (1979), 2108-2111.

STOTLAND, E. AND KOBLER, A. The End of Hope: A Social Clinical Study of Suicide, New York: Free Press of Glencoe, 1964.

STOTLAND, E. AND KOBLER, A. Life and Death of a Mental Hospital. Seattle: University of Washington Press, 1965.

TAUERWIER, G. "Decruitment: A Solution for Burned-out Executives." International Management. 33(4): 44-47, 1978.

TERREBERRY, S. "Evolution of Organizational Environments" Organizational Systems: General Systems Approaches to Complex Organizations. F. Baker (Ed.) Homewood, Ill: Richard D. Ilwin, Inc., 1973.

"The Burn-Out Syndrome" in Training Manual for Human Service Workers in Major Disasters. National Institute on Mental Health, DHEW. Publication Number (ADM) 79-538, 1979.

TOFFLER, A. Future Shock. New York: Bantam, 1970.

TRIST, E.L. "On Socio-Technical Systems," in The Planning of Change by Warren G. Bennis, K.D. Benne and R. Chin, New York: Holt, Rinehart, and Winston, Inc., 282-297.

VACHON, M.L.S. "Enforced Proximity to Stress in the Client Environment." Canadian Nurse 72(9), 1976, 40-43.

VACHON, M.L.S. "Motivation and Stress Experienced by Staff Working with the Terminally Ill." in Davidson, G. ed. The Hospice, Washington Hemisphere Publishing Corporaton, 1978. 113-122.

VALLE, S. "Burn-Out: Occupational Hazard for Counselors." Alcohol Health and Research World. 3(3), Spring, 1979. 10-14.

VAN AUKEN, S. "Youth Counselor Burnout." Personnel and Guidance Journal. 58(2): 143, 1979.

VASH, C. L. The Burnt-Out Administrator. New York: Springer Publishing Company, 1980.

VENINGA, R. "Administration Burnout--Causes and Cures." Hospital Progess. 60(2): 45-52, 1979.

WALLACE, J. "Tactical and Strategic Use of the Preferred Defense Structure of the Recovering Alcoholic" New York: National Council on Alcoholism, 1974.

WARMATH, C.F. AND SHELTON, J.L. "The Ultimate Disappointment: The Burned-Out Counselor." Personnel and Guidance Journal. December 1976. 172-175.

WEINBERG, S. K. Incest Behavior. Syracuse, New Jersey: Citadel Press, 1955.

WEISKOPF, P.E. "Burnout among Teachers of Exceptional Children. Exceptional Children. 47(1): 18-23, 1980.

WHITE, W. L. A Systems Response to Staff Burn-Out. Rockville, MD: HCS, Inc. 1978.

WHITE, W.L. "Healing Ourselves: Taking Care of the Treatment Family." Focus on Alcohol and Drug Issues, Vol. 6, Number 4, July/August, 1983. 4-31.

WHITE, W. L. Incest in the Organizational Family: The Unspoken Issue in Staff and Program Burn-Out. Rockville, MD: HCS, Inc., 1979.

WHITE, W.L. "Managing Personal and Organizational Stress in the Care of the Dying" in Hospice Education Program for Nurses. U.S. Department of Health and Human Services, Health Resources Administration, Hyattsville, Maryland, 1981.

WHITE, W. L.   Relapse as a Phenomenon of Staff Burn-Out Among Recovering Substance Abusers. Rockville, Md: HCS, Inc. 1979.

WHITE, W.L.   "The Organizational Context of Staff Burn-out" in D.J. Ottenberg & E.E. Maden (Eds.) Proceedings of the 12th Annual Eagleville Conference: Ethical Issues in Substance Abuse Treatment. Eagleville, PA: Eagleville Hospital and Rehabilitation Center, 1980.

WYNNE, L. et al., "Pseudo Mutality in the Family Relations of Schizophrenics." Psychiatry. 21: 205-222, 1958.

YABLONSKY, L. Synanon: The Tunnel Back. Baltimore, MD: Penquin Books, 1967.

ZWEBEN J. E. AND DEITCH D. A.   "The Emergence of Prima Donnahood in Prominent Psychotherapists." Voices Spring, 1976, 75-81.

Glossary

BOUNDARY - the invisible circle which encloses a system, separates it from its environment, and distinguishes members from non-members.

BOUNDARY MANAGEMENT - the conscious manipulation of the frequency and intensity of boundary transactions as a management tool to control the pace of change and the level of adaptational demands placed on workers.

BOUNDARY PERMEABILITY - the degree of resistance or difficulty in making boundary transactions.

BOUNDARY TRANSACTIONS - the reciprocal flow of people and ideas across the boundary of the organization.

BURNOUT (PROFESSIONAL) - a deterioration in one's personal and interpersonal performance that is directly related to continued contact with high-stress work environments.

BURNOUT (ORGANIZATIONAL) - a stage of stagnation and demise that occurs when tasks essential to the survival of the organization fail to be adequately completed due to the stress-related deterioration in performance of a large number of organizational members.

BURNOUT (AUTHORITARIAN - MORAL APPROACH) - the denial of the existence of burnout and the definition of stress-related behaviors as problems of a worker's character, values and motivation to work.

BURNOUT (CLINICAL APPROACH) - the definition of burnout as a problem of individual psychopathology.

BURNOUT (COGNITIVE APPROACH) - the definition of burnout as emerging from an individual's irrational and unrealistic beliefs and expectations about one's self and one's profession.

BURNOUT (ENVIRONMENTAL APPROACH) - the definition of burnout as a problem of unhealthy physical and social conditions in the work environment.

BURNOUT (SYSTEMS APPROACH) - the definition of burnout as the multiply caused breakdown in the relationship between the individual worker and the organization.

BURNOUT (TRAINING APPROACH) - the definition of burnout as a problem of skill deficiency, to include the lack of both technical knowledge and skills and stress management skills.

CAREER LADDERS - a planned sequence of vertical promotions within an organization or within one's professional field.

CAREER PATHS - a planned sequence of role positions that, while enhancing professional development, may involve upward, downward or lateral movements within an organization or within one's professional field.

CLOSURE - the progressive reduction in organizational boundary transactions that creates a loss of outside replenishment and increased intimacy between organizational members.

CODE OF PROFESSIONAL PRACTICE - the explicit definition of the ethics, values, and relationship boundaries that will guide workers in conducting the business of the organization.

DECOMPRESSION ROUTINES - rituals that signal to ourselves and others that one part of our life (work) is ending and another part is beginning (personal life).

DISENGAGED ORGANIZATIONAL FAMILY - an organizational family that is characterized by high boundary permeability. The lack of a clear sense of agency mission, which results in ambiguous role definitions and minimal connectedness between organizational members, produces high rates of professional burnout.

DOUBLE BIND COMMUNICATIONS - contradictory verbal messages communicated over time to workers by organizational leaders and supervisors with an accompanying prohibition against seeking clarifications about the incompatible messages.

ECOLOGY (ORGANIZATIONAL) - the study of the relationships and inter-relationships between workers and their organizational environment.

ECOSYSTEM - the multiple layers of environment that encompass a professional role, to include:

a) the basic work unit (microsystem);
b) the total organization (mesosystem);
c) the family, neighborhood, cities, etc. (exosystem);
d) broad political, economic, social forces in the culture and world at large (macrosystem).

ENMESHED ORGANIZATIONAL FAMILY - a rigidly closed organizational family that is characterized by low boundary permeability. The inability of staff to make transactions outside the enmeshed organizational family for support and replenishment produces high rates of burnout.

EXOSYSTEM - the outside environment within which an organization must exist.

EXTRUSION - the manipulation (e.g. firing) of a worker out of the organizational family (often through a scapegoating process).
GLOSSARY

FEEDBACK - the transmission of self-correcting and self-affirming information to workers on the process and outcome of their professional performance.

GATEKEEPERS - those persons who control through the regulation of the physical and social environment, who, when, where, and under what conditions organizational boundary transactions can occur.

GENERAL ADAPTATION SYNDROME - Hans Selye's concept of the body's automatic three stage response to any demand for adaptation (1. alarm reaction 2. resistance 3. exhaustion)

GHOST (ORGANIZATIONAL) - the loss of an individual whose emotional significance was so great or whose exit was so painful that organizational members continue to operate as if the person was still in the organization.

HEALTH PROMOTION - organizational strategies and programs that promote healthy lifestyles and enhance the overall wellness and quality of life of employees.

JOB RESTRUCTURING - the reorganization and redefinition of task responsibilities within a job position.

MACROSYSTEM - political, economic, and social changes in the world and culture at large that affect the organization and alter the basic relationship between people and work.

MESOSYSTEM - the entire organization including all of its organizational units and employees.

MICROSYSTEM - the smallest organizational unit surrounding a worker.

ONTOLOGY (ISSUES OF) - personal factors that influence one's vulnerability to stress in the work setting.

ORGANIZATIONAL FAMILY - the conceptualization of an organizational group as a family system; those persons identified as organizational members and any other persons, who by virtue of frequent interaction or influence on internal decision-making, constitute the organizational group.

ORGANIZATIONAL FAMILY (EXTENDED) - the professional, social and intimate relationships of organizational members that serve collectively to both buffer and link the organizational family and outside world.

ORGANIZATIONAL INCEST - a stage in the life of an organization marked by workers increasingly meeting their personal, professional, social and sexual needs inside the boundary of the organizational family.

OUTPLACEMENT COUNSELING - a formal program provided by an organization to facilitate the hiring of workers by other organizations, such as in the case of the advancement discouraged manager.

PREFERRED (PERSONAL) DEFENSE STRUCTURE - each individual's preferred pattern of thinking, feeling, and behaving when confronted with high demands for adaptation.

PROFESSIONAL CLOSURE - low boundary permeability that forces organizational members to meet most, if not all, of their professional needs within the organizational family.

PROFESSIONAL STRESS - the demand for adaptational change experienced in the performance of one's professional role.

PROJECTION - attributing one's own feelings, desires, fears, motivations, etc., to others, as in a guilty worker projecting blame on others for his/her mistakes.

REPLENISHMENT NETWORK - the number and intensity of nurturing and affirming relationships and activities available to a worker.

RISK MANAGEMENT - a formal program designed to assess and reduce a worker's risks of injury, illness, and disease in the performance of his/her roles.

ROLE AMBIGUITY - inadequate knowledge of: 1) role expectations 2) task priorities, 3) methods for task completion; 4) accountability structure, and 5) rewards and punishments.

ROLE BOUNDARY MANAGEMENT - the ability of the worker to maintain a distinct separation of his/her personal life and work life.

ROLE BOUNDARY MISPLACEMENT - the misplacement of staff with skills in interior organizational positions into boundary positions.

ROLE BREAKDOWN - the failure of an individual's stress defense system that results in decreased role performance and decreased physical and emotional health.

ROLE CONFLICT - incongruous demands and expectations from two or more simultaneously held roles.

ROLE CONNECTEDNESS PROBLEMS - one's degree of isolation or overconnectedness to other members of the organization.

ROLE DEPRIVATION - the sudden or gradual removal of all significant responsibilities from an individual--forced retirement on the job.

ROLE FEEDBACK - the availability of regular information on 1) adequacy of role performance, 2) methods of improving performance, and 3) adequacy of adjustment to work milieu.

ROLE HOMEOSTASIS - the relative balance between role stressors and role supports that allows workers to adequately perform their roles with no stress-related disruption of their physical or emotional health.

ROLE INSECURITY - the degree of uncertainty experienced in relationship to one's future role in the organization.

ROLE INTEGRITY CONFLICTS - conflict between one's personal values and values inherent in the work milieu.

ROLE OVERLOAD - excessive and unrealistic expectations regarding quality of work to be completed within a given time frame.

ROLE/PERSON MISMATCH the incongruency between: 1) an individual's knowledge and skill level and the skills required to perform tasks of a given role, 2) an individual's level of stress tolerance and the level of stress endemic to a particular role, and 3) an individual's style of stress management and the methods of stress management officially and informally sanctioned within an organization.

ROLE REVITALIZATION - the restructuring of a job role to increase its level of professional stimulation and its importance to the organization.

ROLE SAFETY HAZARDS - the degree to which one experiences apprehension about potential physical or psychological harm in the performance of one's professional role.

ROLE STRESSOR - conditions within the work environment that decrease one's ability to perform organizational tasks and threaten and decrease one's self-esteem.

ROLE SUPPORTS - conditions within the work environment that increase one's ability to perform organizational tasks and increase one's self-esteem.

ROLE TERMINATION PROBLEMS - failure to provide permissions, procedures, and processes to allow members guilt-free exit from the organization.

SCAPEGOATING - a style of avoiding the emotional pain and conflict within the organizational family by diverting family attention to the problem employee.

SELF-REGULATED ORGANIZATIONAL FAMILY - an organizational family that regulates the degree of organizational closure based on both internal and external feedback. Boundary permeability fluctuates depending on staff needs for outside support and replenishment and on staff needs for organizational closure during periods of transition and crisis. This organizational model produces the lowest incidence of burnout of the three organizational family types.

SELF-TALK - the internal dialogue that enhances or inhibits acting on certain feelings or thoughts.

SEXUAL CLOSURE - low boundary permeability of an organization that forces an increasing number of workers to meet their sexual needs within the organizational family.

SEXUAL CULTURE - the ethics and values related to sexuality in an organization that are expressed through language, artifacts, attitudes, roles and the spoken and unspoken rules governing relationships between organizational members.

SOCIAL CLOSURE - low boundary permeability that forces organizational members to meet most, if not all, of their social needs within the organizational family.

STRESS - the demand upon the human body for an adaptational change.

STRESS RESPONSE - the generalized and specialized reactions or adaptations of an individual to stress.

STRESSORS - those situations, conditions or agents that produce stress.

STROKES (STROKING BEHAVIOR) - personal rewards and affirmations of one's value, e.g., verbal praise or salary bonuses for exemplary performance.

TRIANGLING - a pattern of communication between two people in which significant messages to each other are communicated through a third party.

TYPE A PERSONALITY - Personality style marked by the compulsive drive to achieve more and more in less and less time.

Index